Tricks

of the Podcasting

Masters

Robert Walch and Mur Lafferty

800 East 96th Street, Indianapolis, Indiana 46240 USA

Tricks of the Podcasting Masters

Copyright © 2006 by Que Publishing

International Standard Book Number: 0-7897-3574-1

Library of Congress Catalog Card Number: 2006922249

Printed in the United States of America

First Printing: June 2006

09   08   07   06   4   3   2   1

Trademarks

Warning and Disclaimer

Bulk Sales

Que Publishing offers excellent discounts on this book when ordered in quantity for bulk purchases or special sales. For more information, please contact

U.S. Corporate and Government Sales

1-800-382-3419

corpsales@pearsontechgroup.com

For sales outside of the U.S., please contact

International Sales

international@pearsoned.com

ASSOCIATE PUBLISHER
Greg Wiegand

ACQUISITIONS EDITOR
Todd Green
Michelle Newcomb

DEVELOPMENT EDITOR
Todd Brakke

MANAGING EDITOR
Gina Kanouse

PROJECT EDITORS
Kristy Hart
Dan Knott

COPY EDITOR
Bart Reed

INDEXER
Brad Herriman

PROOFREADER
Debbie Williams

TECHNICAL EDITOR
Craig Patchett

PUBLISHING COORDINATOR
Sharry Lee Gregory

BOOK DESIGNER
Anne Jones

PAGE LAYOUT
Nonie Ratcliff

Contents at a Glance

Table of Contents

Foreword

FDR used his fireside chats to comfort the nation at a time of great turmoil because he understood the power of the spoken word, especially when it could easily be distributed to the masses. For too long that power has only been available to a very select few. But no longer. Back in March 2005, my wife, Elizabeth, introduced me to a technology that she felt could help revolutionize the distribution of the spoken word. As usual, she was right; podcasting allows virtually anyone to project his or her voice over the Internet because it's so inexpensive, simple, and intuitive. And the great thing about podcasting is that we are just scratching the surface of its astounding potential.

I began podcasting with Elizabeth because we wanted to talk to more people about the importance of fighting poverty through our One America Committee website (http://oneamericacommittee.com/). Before Hurricane Katrina struck the Gulf Coast in late 2005, most major media outlets hardly covered the issue of poverty. And although there was some discussion of the issue immediately after the storm, the media quickly lost interest, and poverty returned to the back of most people's minds. With podcasting, however, Elizabeth and I were able to bring thousands of listeners right into our home to let them know what they could do to help.

The opportunity to produce a podcast is available to everyone—you don't even need a computer. But it helps to have some advice. Several books on the market can help you set up your own podcast, but *Tricks of the Podcasting Masters* is different. This book does not discuss only technical matters like plugging microphone A into mixer B; it seeks to give you the knowledge, skills, and outlook you need to make your podcasts more appealing. Podcasting is not a science; it's an art. *Tricks of the Podcasting Masters* teaches the art of podcasting, and it does so in a voice that is original and engaging. In choosing this book, you've made a wise choice.

I've worked with both Rob and Mur on my One America Committee podcasts, and in that time they have shown me that they're professionals who know exactly what they're doing. Both of them started podcasting back in December of 2004 when podcasting was not even four months old. Since then they've learned what works and what doesn't. In this book, Rob and Mur share not only their wisdom, which is immense, but also the wisdom of some top podcasting experts—skilled podcasters who have proven that they can build and hold a large audience.

Podcasting literally gives people an opportunity to have their voice heard. Whereas blogs and websites allow people to communicate in written form, podcasts allow people to hear not just the message, but also the tone and the passion of the podcaster. The emotions conveyed in the spoken word make it a powerful medium—something that radio outlets have known since the days of FDR. In the age of the fax machine and the Internet, the spoken word had taken a back seat to text. No longer. Now that people are rediscovering the power of the spoken word through podcasting, anyone who has a message can easily get it to thousands of people.

There is a quote you may have heard: "With great power, comes great responsibility." I hope that you will use this tremendous power responsibly so that you can be a cause of positive change. One day I hope to hear your voice, strong and purposeful and rich with ideas for a better world. One day I hope to hear your voice as the voice of a leader. With the help of this book, and with determination and focus, that day could come soon.

—Senator John Edwards

About the Authors

Rob Walch graduated from the University of Dayton in 1988 with an Engineering degree, and then received his MBA from the University of Connecticut in 2004. He has held positions of design engineer, chief engineer, product manager, director of business development, and VP of sales and marketing all in the electronics industry. In late 2004, Rob launched podcast411.com, the first website/podcast combination dedicated to teaching people how to podcast. On April 1st of 2005, he left his position as VP of sales and marketing to become a full-time podcaster. He now consults for many different companies and individuals, including Senator John Edwards and the One America Committee. In addition, he also speaks about podcasting, with presentations at the Podcaster Con at UNC, the Newspaper Association of America Marketing Conference, the Apple Store in Kansas City, and many other appearances. He lives in Overland Park, Kansas with his wife, son, and dogs.

Mur Lafferty graduated from the University of North Carolina in 1995 with a degree in English, which helped her greatly in her chosen career as a grumpy barista. She then served time as an administrative assistant, a web developer, a webmaster, and then a web marketing manager before falling off the technology mountain and landing in the land of the laid off. She began to pursue a career as a freelance writer, and has contributed to over 15 role-playing books and four magazines. In 2004, she began podcasting as an outlet to release her essays in a show called Geek Fu Action Grip. In mid 2005, she started a new podcast focused toward frustrated fiction writers (a group in which she squarely sits) called I Should Be Writing. Her podcasting efforts have spread to include running the podcasting rig for other podcasters, including Senator John Edwards and Elizabeth Edwards, and speaking at Duke and UNC. Podcasting and writing aside, she is a stay-at-home mom to a 3-year-old daughter. She lives in Durham with her husband, daughter, and dog. She feels here is a safe place to admit that she is not a cat person.

Dedication

From Rob:

To Karyn, my love and the mother to our son, whom you carried inside you while this book was being written. Thanks for waiting until the book was done before giving birth.

From Mur:

To Jim for support, love and many eldritch games of Arkham Horror, and to Fiona for the many naps so Mommy could write.

Acknowledgments

From Rob:

Thanks to Mur for putting up with my overuse of capitalization and other writing issues that just had to be so painful for her to review. To Scott R.—you have become a great friend and someone I truly respect. Likewise Paul K. Your advice, friendship, and contributions to this book and my podcast setup are greatly appreciated. Todd Green, thank you so much for taking this from an idea to a reality, and to the rest of the Que team, especially Todd Brakke and Michelle Newcomb. Your support has been greatly appreciated. To Craig Patchett, without whom the podcasting world and this book would be quite a bit different. To all my past guests, thank you for sharing your advice with those starting out. And to J.C., your leadership motivated me more than anything else to switch careers.

From Mur:

I would like to thank the many people who made this book possible—firstly, Rob who included me on this project, and secondly the wonderful people at Que, especially editors Todd Green, Todd Brakke, and Michelle Newcomb. We definitely could not have done this without all of the podcasters who helped us along the way, including but not limited to: Andy Affleck, Evo Terra, Michael R. Mennenga, Scott Sigler, Tee Morris, Mark Jeffrey, Summer Brooks, Jason Adams, Patrick McLean, Steve Eley, Derek Colanduno, Swoopy, James Patrick Kelly, Marc Gunn, Russell Holliman, Michael A. Stackpole, Paul S. Jenkins—and if I've forgotten anyone, then it's Rob's fault.

We both would like to thank our listeners; your feedback has been the fuel that feeds our shows.

Finally, a very special thanks to Senator John and Elizabeth Edwards, not just for being a part of this book and supporting us, but more so for being a part of the podcasting community.

We Want to Hear from You!

As the reader of this book, *you* are our most important critic and commentator. We value your opinion and want to know what we're doing right, what we could do better, what areas you'd like to see us publish in, and any other words of wisdom you're willing to pass our way.

As an associate publisher for Que Publishing, I welcome your comments. You can email or write me directly to let me know what you did or didn't like about this book—as well as what we can do to make our books better.

Please note that I cannot help you with technical problems related to the topic of this book. We do have a User Services group, however, where I will forward specific technical questions related to the book.

When you write, please be sure to include this book's title and author as well as your name, email address, and phone number. I will carefully review your comments and share them with the author and editors who worked on the book.

Email: feedback@quepublishing.com

Mail: Greg Wiegand
           Associate Publisher
           Que Publishing
           800 East 96th Street
           Indianapolis, IN 46240 USA

Reader Services

Visit our website and register this book at www.quepublishing.com/register for convenient access to any updates, downloads, or errata that might be available for this book.

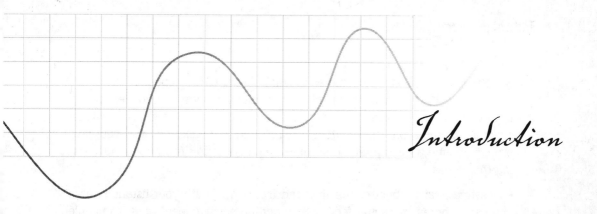

Introduction

> "*Podcasting is not just about delivering audio or video content over the Internet—it is about delivering audio or video content over the Internet in a manner that is convenient for the audience.*"
>
> **—Rob, podCast411**

At the beginning of 2004, the term podcast did not even exist; by December of 2005, the New Oxford American Dictionary had declared the term podcast the word of the year. Podcasting created a whole new industry, with companies such as Libsyn, Odeo, Podshow, and Podtrac popping up. Podcasting also created new media stars such as Dawn and Drew, Wichita Rutherford, Madge Weinstein, and many, many others. In Chapter 1, "A Brief History of Podcasting," we will look at the rapid growth of podcasting to help you better understand this phenomenon.

Yes, podcasting has become the "hottest" new technology on the Internet. However, podcasting is so much more than a technology; it truly is an art form, and those who have the most popular podcasts figured that out early on. Throughout this book, we will be sharing advice from some of the biggest names in podcasting (including, of course, our own opinions). We will list some popular podcasts as examples of what we are talking about in the different sections. We recommend you check out the shows we mention, especially if they are similar to what you are doing. If you do not see a show that is an exact match for what you are doing, you should feel lucky because you have probably found a good niche. If nothing else, podcasting is all about addressing the niches.

Podcasting is also about connecting and interacting with your listeners. As a podcaster, there is no better feeling then getting positive feedback from people who enjoy the work you put into it (see Figure I.1). What follows is some feedback sent to the RaiderCast, which they were kind enough to share with us.

"Greetings from one of the hardest places in Iraq. I won't say where that is, so you'll just have to take my word for it. A group of us just want to take the time and opportunity and show some love for the Raiders. We tried to take the coolest shot out here we could find. Hope this works. The four individuals—Cpt. Smith, Command Sergeant Major Rodriguez, Spc. Claude, and Staff Sergeant Henderson (holding football)—are all from four different locations and met for the first time when deployed here. As soon as we found out we were all Raiders fans, it was a wrap. Why is it Raiders fans always travel in packs, no matter where they go? Is there a force stronger than the nation? I also wanted to thank each of you for the various podcasts that you have done. Podcasts are just awesome, hands down. It's just a great way to stay in touch with the team. I appreciate all that you do to keep Raiders fans in touch with everything. The season is dismal, but hey we'll make the best out of it. Thanks again from all of us. Keep the podcasts coming. Feel free to post these pics. Will send more soon. Feel free to give us a shout out here in Iraq on the podcasts! Thanks again."

Staff Sergeant Kevin Henderson

If you have already been signed by XM or Sirius, then this book is probably not for you. But for anyone else who is podcasting—or is thinking of podcasting—we feel this book contains a boatload of helpful information that can speed you on your way, regardless of the type of podcast you produce. For the beginning pod-caster, we cover topics ranging from picking your title, selecting your subject matter, and setting your schedule, and then move on to more advanced topics such as covering the different methods for conducting an interview. For those already experienced in podcasting, we talk about issues with the Recording Industry Association of America (RIAA) and how they control music, where to get podsafe music, how to better interact with your audience, how to promote your podcast inside and outside of the podcasting community, and how to generate revenue from your podcast.

FIGURE I.1

Picture of RaiderCast podcast listeners from Iraq. (Image courtesy of TheRaiderCast.com.)

Whether you are trying to educate, entertain, motivate, or persuade, as a podcaster you will have the opportunity to touch the lives of people not just around the corner but also half way around the world. With podcasting, there are no rules—none from the government and definitely none from other podcasters. No matter what you say or don't say, you will never have your podcast canceled. It will go on as long as you want to continue doing it. There are, however, suggestions and advice gathered from hundreds of podcasters that we share with you throughout this book. We feel these suggestions will help improve the content of your podcast, improve your ability to attract new listeners, and, if you desire, generate some revenue from your podcast.

Our podcasting information doesn't end with the book, however. Please join the discussion of the constantly changing world of podcasting at the Tricks of the Podcasting Masters forum http://totpm.forumup.org. Contributing in the discussion will allow you to have some input on future versions of this book. You can learn more about ForumUp in Chapter 12, "You're Nothing Without Your Audience."

LAYING YOUR FOUNDATION

A BRIEF HISTORY OF PODCASTING

I loved it [podcasting]. I was watching Doc Searls and what he was doing in terms of writing about it, and then I talked to Adam (Curry) pretty early on and I wanted to write something just to get something in the magazine as soon as possible, because I just had a sense that this was pretty amazing. There were a lot of different things that were coming together.

—Heather Green, *Business Week*

odcasts, or *audioblogs* as they were first called, started as a collaborative effort between Dave Winer and Adam Curry. Back in 2001 the two talked about a better way to deliver audio and video via the Internet and felt that a new XML format called Really Simple Syndication (RSS) was the key. Dave Winer introduced the RSS enclosure tag into the RSS 2.0 specification. But it was not until mid–September 2004 when Adam Curry made public his iPodder software to automatically download and transfer MP3 files to an iPod that podcasting really took off. We won't bore you with *all* the details on the history of podcasting, and we cannot begin to mention all the different people in addition to Adam and Dave who contributed to the podcasting phenomenon.

Three key factors came together in the Fall of 2004 that helped podcasting take off. First, quite a bit of media attention was cast toward blogs and their effect on the presidential election in the United States. Popular bloggers Dave Winer (Scripting News at www.scripting.com) and Doc Searls (Doc Searls Weblog at http://doc.weblogs.com/) in particular helped bring media attention to podcasts by constantly mentioning them on their respective blogs. Second, Adam Curry and his celebrity status helped raise the interest of the media. Call it morbid curiosity, but many in the media just could not believe that this VJ from MTV with the "great hair" could actually be a really talented techno-geek, and they had to find out more. Third, Apple's iPod was making big news, and anything that was even remotely related to the iPod

> **NOTE** This section represents only a brief glimpse at the history of podcasting. If you're interested in exploring every nook and cranny of how podcasting has evolved, check out the Wikipedia entry for *Podcasting* at http://en.wikipedia.org/wiki/Podcast.
>
> For more on RSS and syndication, check out the Wikipedia entry at http://en.wikipedia.org/wiki/RSS_%28protocol%29

was grabbing the media's attention. This made the term *podcasting* automatically memorable (some people do not like it, but never underestimate the power of a good brand name). With all of these factors coming together in the Fall of 2004, the media had something they wanted to report on.

One of the first "big media" mentions of podcasting was in *Business Week* by Heather Green on October 25, 2004: "Get ready for the next Wave—Podcasting." A year later Heather, when asked what about podcasting amazed her the most, said:

> *"I have never seen anything become adopted as quickly as this has become, and equally I have never seen big companies jumping in as quickly as they have. Like Clear Channel or Infinity or all of these other media companies. And so really just the rate of adoption from people who understand the power of this and who love the idea of what it unleashes in terms of people's voices on a grassroots level to the mass media jumping in has been just incredible for me."*

—Heather Green, *Business Week*

What was just a few handfuls of "audiobloggers" on Labor Day of 2004 turned into a group of a few hundred "podcasters" by New Year's Eve of 2004. In the beginning, a Google search for the term "podcast" would have given you less than 30 results. Early in 2005, multiple waves of press articles were written about podcasting and podcasters. At the same time these articles appeared, a premier online directory of podcasts, called Podcast Alley, emerged with a voting system and top-10 list that soon became the *de facto* standard to find new podcasts. By the end of May 2005, a search in Google for "podcast" yielded over 10 million results. Additionally, the number of people podcasting had grown from hundreds to multiple thousands, with a listener base estimated to be in the 150,000 to 200,000 range. In less than nine months, podcasting had grown from a distribution method into a full-fledged community movement.

In Late May 2004, Adam Curry was asked how would he define what a podcast was.

"I would have defined it differently half a year ago, until I really started to look at what is happening and why people are listening and how they are listening....

"Six months ago I would have said it is a show that is distributed through an RSS feed. But that's really not the case.... What is going on, based on my statistics on the downloads, is that 15% to 20% of my listeners are subscribed to the RSS feed and the rest are clicking on my website to download....

"It really dawned on me people are really in love with the content and not the RSS feed. They are just listening because they like it. It is just a form of online audio, or maybe you want to call it radio—that does not really matter to me—which is something that has been going on the Internet for a long, long time. What really made it happen is that we have MP3 players and we have iPods. That is what really gave people a disconnect from the network: you download it, take it with you, and listen when it is convenient for you. It is audio programming distributed on the Internet usually consumed on a portable player."

—Adam Curry, Daily Source Code

On May 22, 2005, Steve Jobs announced at the *Wall Street Journal*'s "D: All Things Digital" conference that Apple would start to support podcasts within iTunes sometime in the next 60 days. Less than 40 days later, iTunes v4.9 was released, not only with built-in support for subscribing to podcasts, but also with a top-100 list. This release has been both a blessing and a curse for independent podcasters, and we will talk about that more later in this chapter.

When Yahoo! launched podcasts.yahoo.com in early October 2005, there were an estimated 15,000 podcasters, and a search in Google for "podcast" yielded over 58 million results. That's 3,866 results for each podcaster. To get an idea of the significance of that number, compare it to blogs, of which there were over 70 million at that time, and a Google search on the term generated 403 million results. That's less than six results per each blogger. Why mention these stats? It shows that although there has been a tremendous amount of hype surrounding podcasting, by comparing it to blogging, we see there are far fewer people who are actually doing podcasts than would be expected. That's important because there's an opportunity for new podcasters to build their audience, and this book is built to help you do just that.

Independent Podcaster Resources

This book is for anyone who is producing a podcast already or is planning on using one of the podcast-creation services (Odeo, AudioBlogs.com, Podblaze) to create one. This book is not intended to teach you how to create an RSS feed or how to hook up your recording equipment. Although we will discuss some technical issues, the main focus of this book is on improving the content of your podcast, promoting your podcast, and, if you desire, monetizing that podcast. Our advice is based on conversations with many of the "Masters of Podcasting" as well as our own trials and errors. If you are looking for technical help on creating an RSS feed or other technical issues regarding podcasting, you can find plenty of good tutorials on the Net. Start by going to http://www.podcast411.com/page5.html for a list of some of the best free tutorials on podcasting. If you are looking for a book focused on the technical issues with podcasting, such as Que's *Absolute Beginner's Guide to Podcasting*, shown in Figure 1.1, we suggest the following:

  Absolute Beginner's Guide to Podcasting

  Publisher: Que Publishing

  Page Count: 240 pages

  Authors: George Colombo and Curtis Franklin

  Authors' podcast: Ultimate Podcasting

  Podcasting for Dummies

  Publisher: Wiley

  Page Count: 340 pages

  Authors: Tee Morris and Evo Terra

  Authors' podcasts: Morevi: The Podcast and The Survivor's Guide to Writing Fantasy, The Dragon Page

Here are some additional books on podcasting for beginners:

  Podcasting Solutions

  Publisher: Apress

Page Count: 240 pages

Authors: Michael Geoghegan and Dan Klass

Authors' Podcasts: Reel Reviews, Disneyland Resort Podcast; The Bitterest Pill, Old Wave Radio

- *Secrets of Podcasting*

Publisher: Peachpit Press

Page Count: 212 pages

Author: Bart Farkas

Author's Podcasts: Unknown

FIGURE 1.1

Que's Absolute Beginner's Guide to Podcasting provides a detailed introduction to the world of podcasting.

This is by no means a complete list of all the books on podcasting—there are many others. With all these other books on podcasting, you may be wondering why you will need this one. The short answer is, where the other books are great at getting you up and running, this is the first one to concentrate on the content and promotion of your podcast. The vast majority of podcasters have fewer than 250 subscribers. According to Feedburner, over 42,000 podcasts are published using its service, but less than 40 of those podcasts have more than 1,500 subscribers. Less than 80 have more than 750 subscribers.

The reason for this lack of subscribers comes down to two issues: content and promotion. You need good ideas on improving both if you want to grow your listener base, and that is what this book is here to help you with.

iTunes Enters the Playing Field

When iTunes version 4.9 was released in late June of 2005, it included support for subscribing to podcasts. It was widely reported that in the first two days after its release, users had already activated 1 million subscriptions to podcasts. Granted, although subscriptions do not equal subscribers (many users were subscribing to multiple podcasts), it's still a significant number that went far beyond the general consensus that only about 200,000 to 250,000 people had ever subscribed to a podcast (and honestly, that number is probably high). By the end of 2005, the various published surveys and reports indicated that anywhere from 1 million people on the low side to about 5 million people on the high side had subscribed to at least one podcast. Even if you go in the middle of that range, it is still a greater than 10 times increase in subscribers since the release of iTunes v4.9.

On the Pro Side

The community accepts that iTunes (see Figure 1.2) has been both a blessing and a curse for the independent podcaster. For the most part, we feel it has been a good thing for podcasting. Don't worry, though. We haven't sold out to the Man just yet, and in the next section we'll talk about the ways the iTunes whirlwind has been a detriment to podcasters. But even given that, iTunes has undeniably done its share of good too.

Public Awareness and Apple's Media PR Juggernaut

If a tree falls in the woods and no one hears it, did it really happen? Or more to the point, if a podcaster rants into a microphone and no one is subscribed, was the podcast really funny? What Apple has done more than anything else is help spread the word about podcasting. No company in the world does a better job at PR than Apple...period. Steve Jobs has mentioned podcasting in all his major keynote speeches since June of 2005, and that means each time the press is also reminded about podcasting.

A true story: At a major media company a friend had been trying to wave the podcasting flag since January of 2005, but was not getting any uptake. He sent around links to different podcasts, directories, and news articles on podcasting, but he could not get anyone to take notice. Then, right after the launch of iTunes v4.9 in June, a vice president in that company sent around an email to all employees talking about this great new thing called podcasting. He talked about how many downloads Apple's "New Music" podcast was getting per week and said to contact him with any questions and that there was "more to come."

FIGURE 1.2

The main iTunes podcasting page.

Like many niche technologies, people do not take notice until a major company like Apple gets behind it. And it was not until after Apple was fully behind podcasting that many people started taking it seriously—or for that matter had even heard about it.

Ease of Subscribing

Before iTunes v4.9, if someone wanted to subscribe to a podcast, they needed to go and download a third-party software application such as iPodder Lemon (now Juice), iPodderX (now Transistr), or Doppler (still Doppler) and install it on their computer. Then they needed to find the RSS feed (a term with which many users are still unfamiliar) of the podcast they wanted to subscribe to and then figure out how to actually subscribe to it using the particulars of the program they downloaded. For many "flashing 12's," this was either way over their heads or just too much work.With the release of iTunes v4.9, whose user base is over 100 million, listeners could easily find and subscribe to shows from within iTunes itself. Naturally, this greatly increased the potential listener base. Additionally, with iTunes, you as a podcaster can put a link on your site that allows potential subscribers to just click it and then iTunes opens right up to the page for your podcast. With just one more click, the person is subscribed to your show. No copy and pasting, and no adding strange software on to their computers. This ease of use more than anything has made iTunes a plus for all podcasters.

> **NOTE**
>
> A "flashing 12" is a person with no technical inclinations. The name comes from the fact that when you walk into their house, their VCR is flashing 12:00, because they can't figure out how to program it.

Centralized "Must Be On" List

There are over 100 different podcast directories, but none is as important to a podcaster as iTunes. One thing that Apple has done by being the first major company to support podcasts is to create a directory everyone wants to be in. This is good for listeners because it gives them one place to go to find most of the podcasts available.

Enhanced Podcasts

Although enhanced podcasts are not for everyone, podcasts such as The MommyCast and The K9Cast have done a good job integrating enhanced podcast features into their shows to help improve the listener experience. Enhanced podcasting makes sense for many educational and commercial reasons. However, there's the issue that not all MP3 players can handle this format (AAC), although it is supported by all the iPods (75% to 80% of the market) and is an open standard. Hopefully, more MP3 manufacturers will add support for AAC in the future.

> **NOTE**
>
> Enhanced podcasts are specially encoded audio files with additional data inside them, such as images, chapter marks, and URLs. These items are time-coded to appear at a specific point during playback. If you are talking about building a model airplane, you can time-code the pictures to change as you progress through the project. If you have a long show, you can include chapter breaks so people can jump directly to different sections of your show. And if you want to include links to websites or advertisers you mentioned during the show, you can include those. Unfortunately, as of March 2006, you still need a Mac to create an enhanced podcast.

On the Con Side

So, given everything iTunes has done for podcasting, you might wonder how anyone could malign it. The sad truth is that anyone who says iTunes and its support of podcasting has been nothing but a blessing for podcasters obviously has their paycheck signed by Steve Jobs. For the rest of us, and most specifically independent podcasters and those looking for independent podcasts, iTunes (since the release of v4.9) has brought with it lots of angst and frustration. Some of the major sources of frustration are listed here, and if you have been podcasting or looking for podcasts for any amount of time, you probably have a few others to add. (We're not even going to get into the whole issue of iTunes-specific RSS tags and the lousy job Apple did in letting people know about those tags.)

No Easy Way to Contact Apple

One of the most frustrating things for many podcasters has been trying to get their podcasts listed on iTunes. Some have been trying since June of 2005, when v4.9 launched. The problem comes with the inability to get any real feedback to and from Apple—what we call the infamous "iTunes black hole." The problem is that the main way to interact with Apple with regards to podcasting is through an email robot at the following address:

http://www.apple.com/support/itunes/musicstore/podcast/

Currently, if you enter your feed into iTunes and there's any issue with the feed, you will get a message back stating you need to fix the feed. Then after you fix it and you go to resubmit, iTunes comes back and states that the feed is already in there—hence the "black hole." The feed does not show up in iTunes for you to click "Submit a concern," yet it says the feed is in there. There are

Helpful Resources

If you are an independent podcaster, you need to make sure you validate your feed on all the feed validators before you submit it. Feed validators look at the code that makes up your RSS and catches any bugs or glitches. The best ones tell you what's actually wrong with the code when they find an error. Taking the time to do this is more palatable than having your feed fail and you sitting in the dark, wondering why no one is subscribing. You can locate these validators at http://rss.scripting.com/ and http://feedvalidator.org/.

You also need to look at the tutorial Apple put out at http://phobos.apple.com/static/iTunesRSS.html.

More importantly, look at the feeds from about 5 to 10 podcasts that are already in iTunes before submitting yours. Compare their RSS (especially the iTunes-specific tags) to yours; if there's any issue with your feed, you are going to be lost in the iTunes black hole.

One additional place to try and get help for iTunes issues is at http://discussions.apple.com.

From there, choose Producing Podcasts from under Pro Digital Production. Here, you will find other people with similar issues, and oftentimes one of them may be able to help. Apple does monitor this discussion forum and will help out with some of the questions reports of podcasters waiting three and four months with no resolution on getting their podcast entered.

Interface Issues when Searching

When it comes to scanning for new podcasts, iTunes is not the best directory, or even in the top 50%. The layout of the directory with the different lists has some real issues. iTunes breaks its directory down into genre lists, with 21 broad categories to choose from, ranging from Arts & Entertainment to Travel. If podcasters choose to do so (and many spammers do), they can change the name of their podcast to "- *Show Name* -". The lists are sorted alphanumerically, which means a hyphen (-) or other special characters can move your show up to the top of the lists (see Figure 1.3). If you go through all the different lists, you will see these spammers at the top. But in some ways you can't fault the podcasters for trying to move up in the lists. Apple needs to address this issue, because it makes the directory look second or third rate. One suggestion has been to just kick anyone out of the directory that does this, and eventually we think Apple will have no choice but to do just that. So be warned if you are or plan on using this technique.

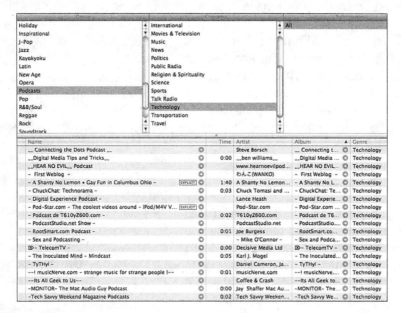

FIGURE 1.3

Alphanumeric directory list from iTunes showing spamming.

Confusing Top-100 List

There are many different reports on what Apple's iTunes Top-100 list is based on. Adam Curry stated Apple told him it was based on new subscriptions over the past 24 hours. However, some industrious souls were able to take advantage of problems Apple was having with subscriptions to use scripts to spam new subscriptions for a few different podcasts to test out some theories. What they found was that the Top-100 list was based on new subscriptions over a period of four to five days, with a weighted average toward the more recent days. What is uncertain is if there's any weight bias based on the total number of subscribers.

Apple has yet to come out and say this is exactly what the Top-100 list is based on, but one thing is for sure: If you are a featured podcast, you will get more new subscribers, and Apple heavily biases the number of featured podcasts toward big media companies and not toward independent podcasters, who make up the majority of podcasts in the iTunes directory.

Now some would say never blame on malice what can easily be explained by lack of resources. In other words, it is very likely that the people at Apple making this decision are picking only those they have heard of, and do not have the time to look into the different independent podcasts available. So when CNN releases a podcast, in their mind it is a safe choice, rather than, say, looking into what The M Show (www.themshow.com) is all about.

Heavy Big Media Bias

Only about 15 to 20 of the Top-100 podcasts on iTunes are now independent podcasts, compared to over 70 when it first launched. And only two to three independent podcasts are now regularly in the top 20. It would be great if Apple would decide to focus a little more on the independent podcasters again, the ones who grew podcasting as a grassroots movement. Unfortunately, it appears Apple is happy to play on AstroTurf. If Apple would take just a few hours a week looking for some of the better independent podcasts and then showcase them on the front page of iTunes, it would go a long way toward helping promote the indies. For this we suggest the folks at Apple take a look at what Yahoo! is doing. Over half of the shows that Yahoo! features each week come from indie podcasters.

The bottom line isn't that Apple is evil. Far from it. Apple is a great company, and with all its other products it has set the bar very high. We're just trying to hold them to those same standards. We do believe in time Apple will work out most of these issues, and clearly we believe the sooner that happens the better.

Alternatives to iTunes

In the wake of iTunes changing the face of podcasting came two other players on the scene: Odeo, a relatively new service, and the veteran Internet network Yahoo!

Odeo had a name powering it—one of its creators was Evan Williams, co-founder of the popular weblog tool and website Blogger. At first, it was merely another directory, another place to go to find a podcast, but soon it became more. Now Odeo allows you to listen to podcasts on the site and through its downloadable player, as well as sync the podcasts directly to your MP3 player. Although it's unlikely that Odeo will ever make iTunes obsolete, it does serve as an alternative for people who enjoy the system. And considering how popular it is becoming, it seems many people do. Unlike iTunes, however, Odeo also offers creation tools and hosting services, aiming to become a one-stop hub for podcasters and listeners alike (see Figure 1.4). At first, many people felt this was overly ambitious, and several podcasters didn't believe Odeo's creation tools would work for direct recording on its site as promised. But Odeo's "Flash recorder," although not having the flexibility of Audacity or Garageband, does produce a clean sound and automatically saves recordings to MP3 files. The only downside is that users must use a separate ID3 program to add that vital information (more on ID3 tags later).

FIGURE 1.4

Odeo allows you to podcast directly from its site.

Yahoo!, a long-standing hub for Internet users, got into the podcasting game in the Fall of 2005. Like Odeo, it offers several services to both listeners and podcasters alike, serving as a directory and a tool to subscribe, download, and sync with an MP3 player.

For podcasters, Yahoo! offers one of the most comprehensive tutorials online for beginners, including tips on finding a subject to cover, what equipment you need, the basics of recording, how to find a hosting provider, and how to find podcast directories to market your show.

Yahoo!'s other main offering to existing podcasters (or, as we saw earlier, "indie" podcasters) is the simple gift of its huge customer base. Just as Apple introduced millions of its iTunes users to podcasting, Yahoo! also let another massive Internet community know about podcasting—not only what it was, but also what they could do with it. By bringing more listeners into the mix, Yahoo! allowed many podcasters to see their subscriber numbers spike again, as well as the total number of podcasts. Sometimes we get so entrenched in our little podcasting communities that we forget it's still in its infancy, and the rest of the world has yet to discover it. The larger companies have been instrumental in spreading the word about podcasting (they did better than we did, truth be told).

Although these directories seem to be similar, they each strive to have at least one feature that sets them apart. Odeo attempts to be a one-stop podcasting hub for listeners and podcasters alike, providing tools for listening and creating. Yahoo! brings its entire community to the party, giving the existing podcasters more listeners and enticing new podcasters to join. Although it may be difficult to keep up with them all, they're each worth watching.

Beyond Odeo and Yahoo, there are of course programs that focus only on being an RSS aggregator, or in popular terms, "podcatcher." Table 1.1 provides details on a few.

Table1.1   Popular Podcatchers

Name	URL	Cost
Juice	http://juicereceiver.sourceforge.net/index.php	Free
Transistr	http://transistr.com/	$24.95
Doppler	http://www.dopplerradio.net/	Free

iPodderX (now Transistr), developed by August Trometer and Ray Slakinski, was one of the first aggregators and was quickly followed by iPodder Lemon (now Juice). Transistr boasts more features than Juice, but then you have to pay to use it. Still, thousands of listeners are so pleased with Transistr that they wouldn't go to a free program if you paid them.

David Versus Goliath?

In the beginning, podcasting was just the independent podcasters—a person, a mic, and a computer, with the whole Internet available to listen. Okay, well, the whole Internet didn't listen. But a small focused niche did—mostly other podcasters. We listened to each other and promoted each other. When there were a couple of hundred podcasters, we were small, unknown, and close-knit. We were podcasters, a tiny group, but still a group. We would proudly proclaim that to others just so we could explain to them what podcasting was, because we knew they hadn't heard of it. We'd either get the response, "Oh, uh, that's one of those Internet things, right?" or "Cool! How do you do it?" and thus another podcaster was born.

We knew it wouldn't last. While businesses were just getting into blogs in 2004, podcasts were still outside the radar. Apple sat quietly in the corner, the dormant volcano. We watched it warily, wondering when it was going to erupt. Would it rain lava down on our heads? Or would it create a magnificent new island paradise? We continued to podcast, knowing the day would come—the day we were no longer the only kids in the sandbox. We just didn't know when.

When iTunes v4.9 launched in June of 2005 with support for podcasting, it brought millions of new listeners with it (once the kerfuffle of "How do I get my podcast listed in iTunes?" died down). One unexpected result of the launch was that the majority of podcasters suddenly found themselves wearing a new badge, one they hadn't coined: the indie podcaster. We no longer saw the usual suspects at the top of the podcast heap: Suddenly there was a Disney podcast, and a *Queer Eye for the Straight Guy* podcast. It had taken 10 or so months, but the big businesses had finally decided to try podcasting out for themselves, and many podcasters—now "indie" podcasters—wondered what this would do to their subscriber numbers, not to mention their ranking on the various Top-50 sites.

It took a while for the average listener to catch on, but many of the big media podcasts were nothing but repackaged content. Strip existing content of the ads and convert the audio to MP3, and you've got a podcast! Fans of *Queer Eye* realized they were just hearing the tips from the end of the show again. Some networks claimed to have podcasts about shows, but just had someone rehashing the plots of the shows on the podcast, which was of little interest to some people. Most, however, were so entranced by the newness of the technology that they eagerly downloaded the content again, and the repackaged shows became popular.

Some corporations got it right. NPR now podcasts many of its more popular shows, and PBS and the Discovery Channel also have podcasts. Some popular television programs have podcasts that add to their content instead of rehashing: *Battlestar Galactica* (http://scifi.com/battlestar/downloads/podcast/) has DVD-like producer commentary that goes along with the newest episodes, requiring you to listen to the podcast as you watch the episode. The official *Lost* podcast (http://abc.go.com/primetime/lost/podcasts.html) has interviews with the cast, stories about filming, and discussions of the latest episodes by executive producers.

The key point that big media needs to understand is that podcasting is an offshoot of the brand they are trying to sell. At first it may not make them any money. It was this reason that businesses moved so slowly into websites back in 1995: Where was the money? Now if businesses don't have a website, many assume they're too far behind the times to do business with. Whether it makes them money or not, they need a site as part of their marketing plan—and they may need to eventually view podcasting the same way. One thing is for sure: Podcasting is catching on with corporations faster than blogging did. In the meantime, what happens to indie podcasting?

Indie podcasting will never die, the same way personal home pages and everyday blogs haven't died, even though corporations have their own pages and blogs. The people who do it, the individuals, do it because they love it. Unlike the corporations, we don't do it to make money, we don't do it to establish or imprint a brand. We find our passion and talk about it, and other people with that passion flock to us. Knitters have their own podcast, as do fans of Celtic music. Gaming geeks (both computer and board) have many podcasts to listen to, and fans of political debate also have content to access.

Several pundits like to turn big media versus indie podcasts into a competition. David versus Goliath is a favorite metaphor, but we don't think it fits in this scenario. Although many popular podcasts saw their rankings fall on some of the sites when corporate podcasts came onto the scene (the independent podcasters in the top 20 in iTunes are few), we don't know any indie podcasters who have quit because of the emergence of the corporations. Even if their ranking has dropped, few podcasters have seen their listener numbers drop since the corporations got into podcasting. If your fans love your show, they're unlikely to dump you just because their favorite TV show also has a podcast. Just like choosing among TV programs, people have room for more than one podcast in their lives.

So, now that you've got your crash course in podcasting history, let's go on to personalities. Before you dream of a subscriber base in the tens of thousands, you might want to see how some people actually achieved those numbers.

Chapter 2

WHAT THE PROS ARE DOING

"Podcasting grants me the terrifying freedom to make something as well as I know how. There's no excuses. No editors, no production executives, no advertisers, no English teachers telling me what I can and can't do. It's just my voice and my words and a microphone. If it sucks there's no one else to blame. And that's terrifying. But there's also no one to hold me back. And that's liberating. I CAN GET IT OUT THERE."

—Patrick McLean, The Seanachai

One of the first questions a new podcaster asks (right after, How can I make money?) is, What makes a podcast popular? It's a topic that can seem nebulous—either you've "got it" or you don't. But the podcasters who have thousands of listeners must be doing something right, and many of them use the same techniques, even if their podcast topics are as different as Bill Cosby and Andrew Dice Clay.

In this chapter, we study the most popular podcasts and their recipes for success. Don't copy them; the world does not need another Dawn and Drew clone. However, if you study what they do right and apply it to your own idea, then odds are good you'll grab the listeners.

Popular Podcasts

We all have our favorite podcasts, but there are a handful that have stayed at the top of the heap for months on end, proving that they have widespread appeal and staying power. Perhaps there is no better proof that podcasting spans the gulf of interests in that the biggest podcasts show a wide variety of interests, from sex to religious searching to fiction to technology. The top 20 of any podcast directory will likely show a wide variety of shows, from the G-rated to the X-rated, from the detailed and informative to the wacky and fun.

The following 15 podcasts are not the top podcasts of all time, but they commonly reside at the top of any podcast list. We'll discuss briefly what they do and the qualities of these podcasts that make them so popular.

G-Rated Podcasts

It will probably come as no surprise to you that G-rated podcasts have no swearing, violent content, or sexual situations, and most consider them to be safe to listen to around any member of the family.

Catholic Insider

http://www.catholicinsider.com/scripts/index.php
Frequency: Weekdays

Catholic Insider is one of the most popular "Godcasts," very likely due to the charismatic host: Father Roderick Vonhögen, Catholic priest of the Archdiocese of Utrecht, The Netherlands. Breaking the traditional view most people have of priests, Father Roderick is dedicated to his many podcasts, quite knowledgeable about the technology around podcasting, and offers a spiritual look at the world that is less preachy and more celebratory. People of many faiths other than Catholicism listen to Father Roderick.

In his podcast, he covers everything from the Church itself to his own views on pop culture, such as *Star Wars* and *Harry Potter*, to religious news (see Figure 2.1). He shows a passion for podcasting that goes above and beyond most people's. It is this passion that makes Catholic Insider so entertaining; he loves what he is doing, both podcasting and within the Church, and it comes through and ropes in his 4,000–6,000 worldwide listeners.

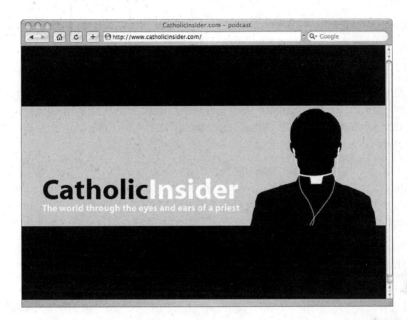

FIGURE 2.1

The Catholic Insider: It's hip, cutting-edge and Catholic.

Free Talk Live

http://www.freetalklive.com/
Frequency: Daily

A popular political talk radio show, Free Talk Live bills itself as a show where the listeners are free to talk about anything. A show that appeals greatly to Libertarians, it separates itself from the norm of the conservative/liberal argumentative talk shows by welcoming any and all opinions.

The show has become a favorite with podcast listeners for many of the same reasons it has been successful on the radio: It appeals to the Libertarian audience, which has been growing a great deal in past years, as well as the lack of screaming talking heads when a heated discussion ensues. The website is welcoming with an active forum community.

Inside Mac Radio

http://www.osxfaq.com/radio/
Frequency: Daily except Sunday

Inside Mac Radio is another radio-come-podcast. This already-popular San Francisco radio program got a worldwide audience with podcasting. Macintosh computers have had a rabid following for decades, and those fans are downloading the Inside Mac Radio show at a frightening pace.

Inside Mac Radio has daily updates with news from the Mac community, including things people are doing, Apple news, and of course how-to's on gadgets and the Mac OS. The podcast is hosted from the OSX FAQ home page, a page that lists news, events, and a forum for Mac help and discussion. The podcast is a logical extension of that.

Inside Mac Radio is an obvious example of people taking an established audience and giving them more of what they love: discussion on all things Apple. It is a one-stop podcast for Mac fans, with tips, advice, and entertainment.

Media Artist Secrets

http://www.fmstudio.com/blog/
Frequency: Weekly

Media Artist Secrets is a podcast that proves you don't have to have an hour-long podcast to be informative and popular. Host Franklin McMahon produces a podcast of 10–15 minutes, with the simple desire to push creative people further in their business. Whereas most creative-focused podcasts aim to help people with their creativity, McMahon's focuses on the business side.

What really makes his podcast work is the fact that his advice is broad enough to appeal to any creative person—writers, photographers, graphic designers, and so on—and it's yet detailed enough to be quite useful to any person trying to make a business from their creativity. McMahon is friendly and energetic, with his can-do attitude winning him the Podcast and Portable Media Expo's Best Business Podcast award for 2005.

Pottercast

http://www.the-leaky-cauldron.org/pottercast/
Frequency: Weekly

This is the podcast for the very successful website dedicated to the *Harry Potter* books and movies. Hosted at the Leaky Cauldron (http://www.the-leaky-cauldron.org/), the

Pottercast is the place for news, interviews, discussion on the books and movies, and on-the-scene reporting when new movies and books come out.

Pottercast is one of the few podcasts with a community of people behind it instead of just one or two people. Gathering a group of people to work on a topic that millions of people worldwide are passionate about is just one recipe for a good podcast. Like some of the other top podcasts, Pottercast took an existing fan base (those of the Leaky Cauldron website) and turned them on to a podcast—their podcast, as a matter of fact. With thousands of *Harry Potter* fans eagerly awaiting the next movie and book, Pottercast effortlessly takes those fans and gives them what they want: a weekly dose of Potter discussion. The podcast reads emails and plays audio clips of the fans' comments, which often spark lively discussions among the hosts.

This Week in Tech

http://thisweekintech.com/
Frequency: Weekly

Fans of Leo Laporte mourned the day his television show *The Screen Savers* was cancelled, and they flocked when he began podcasting. Another podcast that shot to the top of the popularity dog pile once launched, This Week In Tech gives Leo his soapbox again to discuss tech news.

Leo often has co-hosts, which change on occasion. His guests bring their own flavor to the show, giving information and news from their own area of expertise. The show, affectionately called "TWiT," allows Leo Laporte fans to continue hearing from him.

PG-Rated Podcasts

The PG-rated podcasts are still clean enough to be on mainstream radio, and their language is usually clean enough for kids. Their topics tend to stray into more adult territory, approaching sexual or violent topics without hesitation, but with little more detail than prime time television.

Diggnation

http://revision3.com/diggnation
Frequency: Weekly

Diggnation is the podcast that accompanies the popular website, Digg.com, a technology news site. Readers of the site vote on the most popular stories, and the stories with the most votes get the headlines on the front page. Diggnation does a weekly rundown of the most popular stories, with its hosts, Kevin Rose and Alex Albrecht, adding their own opinions.

Diggnation shows what can happen when a popular website attempts to branch out into podcasting (see Figure 2.2). If done correctly, it can add a great deal to the content of the site, bringing in more listeners and readers. They also have an established listener base right there in their daily visitors to the site. An already-captive audience is gold to a podcaster.

FIGURE 2.2

Diggnation allows those obsessed with "digging" another outlet for cool news stories.

Escape Pod

http://www.escapepod.org/
Frequency: Weekly

While several people have toyed with the prospect of podcasting their fiction, only one podcast started out legally recording others' fiction: Escape Pod. The first paying market for fiction writers in podcasting, Escape Pod purchases sci-fi stories and then has people other than the author narrate them. Steve Eley, the editor of Escape Pod, uses a clever cross-marketing tool in that he asks podcasters to read for him, attracting those podcasters' listeners to his podcast.

Steve manages to remain a paying market for stories solely on donations. He reminds all his listeners at the end of every show that he pays his authors for their fine stories and that he is able to do this as long as the listeners support the site. After six months of podcasting, Escape Pod was in the black, still comfortably purchasing stories. Steve makes Escape Pod work by being the first (and possibly only) podcast to do what it does, encourages other podcasters to help, and manages to gather some excellent fiction.

> **CAUTION**
> While listening to the Escape Pod podcast is typically a PG experience, its subject matter and style can range anywhere from G to X.

[Note: Escape Pod's stories vary greatly in content, so we've placed them in the PG category in hopes that you'll listen for each show's individual rating before listening in front of your kids or at work.]

The Signal

http://signal.serenityfirefly.com/
Frequency: Weekly or more frequently

The Signal charged onto the scene in the Summer and Fall of 2005, carrying a large crew of writers, newshounds, and voice talent and banking on the hungry fans of the cancelled cult-hit TV show *Firefly*. Originally designed to be a short-term fan-driven viral marketing tool for the movie *Serenity*, it proved so popular that the crew had to plan a second season to keep the fans happy.

The Signal works because it has a large crew, so no one person is stuck doing a ton of work. With the group working at it, the hour-long podcast is filled with relevant, intelligent, and informative material that complements the show instead of rehashes plotlines. The Signal includes essays on the characters, the plotlines, translations of the Chinese phrases used in the show, and interviews with the cast. It has even had celebrity contributions with renowned fantasy author Tracy Hickman sending in essays about the sci-fi world of *Firefly*. The Signal proves that podcasting does not have to be a solitary, or even a two-person effort.

Skepticality

http://www.skepticality.com/index.php
Frequency: Weekly

Tired of pseudoscience and annoyed about the fact that important science was not making it onto news organizations' current events radar, friends Derek and Swoopy created Skepticality, the science podcast with a snarky angle. They interview scientists and debunk myths, popular thinking, and pseudoscience.

A wildly popular podcast, Skepticality appeals to science-minded geeks and skeptics alike, and is one of the few podcasts to have gained a large following outside the podcast community through its marketing to scientists and skeptics via mailing lists (see Figure 2.3). The obvious chemistry as two old friends works well on the show, and the intelligent banter keeps listeners tuned in to each installment.

FIGURE 2.3

Derek and Swoopy aren't afraid to ask the tough questions on Skepticality.

Michael and Evo's Slice of SciFi

http://www.sliceofscifi.com/
Frequency: Weekly

Michael R. Mennenga and Evo Terra are hosts of the popular science fiction literature-focused podcast and radio show Dragon Page: Cover to Cover and the science fiction/beer podcast Dragon Page: Wingin' It. But they figured they didn't have enough to do, so they made a podcast dedicated to science fiction in television and movies. It was this podcast that became their overnight success.

They launched it in conjunction with Trek United, the organization dedicated to saving *Star Trek Enterprise* from cancellation. Thus, they had a wide audience of Trek fans to lure to their podcast. Currently their team of newshounds focuses on all science fiction on television and the big screen. They are also known for conducting enthralling interviews with the stars of those shows and movies. In part because of the dependable cult following that goes with quality SF programming (a following the Nielsen ratings seem none too familiar with), Slice of SciFi has a large audience.

R-Rated Podcasts

Getting into the "definitely not kid-safe or work-safe" areas, the R-rated podcasts say pretty much whatever they like in terms of swear words, including, but not limited to, the dreaded "f-bomb." They do stay clear of graphic sexual description, however.

Daily Source Code

http://curry.com/
Frequency: Weekdays

This is the big one, the most common "first listened to" podcast. Adam Curry has kept his show consistent since show #1, with news, promos for other podcasts, music (both pod-safe—legal to play on podcasts—and not, until November 2005 when he went completely pod-safe), and insights into his life. It's still the place most podcasters—and listeners—go for news and promos. Most podcasters consider having a promo played on DSC as the brass ring of podcast promotion, and many create promos simply for Adam to hear.

Adam's strengths reside in consistency as well as his unique position in the podcast community with his connections to Podshow. When Adam reports news, you can bet it's likely breaking news that can have the entire podcast community buzzing. His easy and likable attitude makes him a favorite of many listeners.

Earthcore and Ancestor

http://www.scottsigler.net/
Frequency: Weekly

Earthcore and *Ancestor* are novels by Scott Sigler. He had some trouble getting *Earthcore* published through conventional methods, so he decided to serialize it in a podcast. Although self-publishing is a hit-or-miss venture in most cases, Sigler made podcasting work. Marketing it as the first podcast-only novel (the first podcasted novel was Tee Morris's reading of his and Lisa Lee's novel, *MOREVI: The Chronicles of Rafe and Askana)*, he began releasing it weekly and received a huge following.

Sigler received as many as 10,000 listeners to his book, caught the notice of small publisher Dragon Moon Press, which did a print run of the book, and became a favorite of many other podcasters, including Dawn and Drew. Sigler was a marketing wizard with the podcast, making sure everyone in the podcasting world knew about it. He got the word out early, and continued pushing the novel throughout the lifespan of the book. He started podcasting his second book, *Ancestor*, in late 2005 and boasts around 7,000 listeners. Although the podcast of *Earthcore* is over, the files are still available for download, and the book remains on many podcasting Top-20 lists. *Earthcore* is the poster child for not being too shy to market your podcast. Remember, no one else will do it for you.

X-Rated Podcasts

What can we say? The X-rated shows hold nothing back. Nothing. Trust us. Nothing is taboo for these podcasts, and they *will* push the boundaries with so much glee that it's hard not to enjoy the ride. (That is, as long as you're not easily offended. Or your kids aren't around. Or parents. Or priest. Well, you get the drift.)

The Dawn and Drew Show!

http://dawnanddrew.podshow.com/
Rating: X
Frequency: Weekdays

Another podcast veteran duo, Dawn and Drew, was the first couple-cast, breaking the ground for the many to follow. Every day they place their welcome mat out for anyone to peek inside their marriage, and that's an unadulterated view, including intimate details such as arguments, sex, and Dawn's time of the month.

Their appeal is clear: They hold nothing back. It's like watching your neighbors through their window as they live their lives, and they're welcoming you to do so! It's voyeurism without the guilt. Many of Dawn and Drew's listeners say they see the couple as their best friends, and they have a large worldwide reach of fans that crave their raunchy, unabashed look at the world.

Keith and the Girl

http://www.keithandthegirl.com/
Rating: X
Frequency: Weekdays

Part couple-cast, part comedy show, Keith and his girlfriend, Chemda, bring their brash New York podcast to the aggregator each day (See Figure 2.4), giving their uncensored opinions of Hooters waitresses, lesbians, and, well, anything that comes to mind. More "in your face" than Dawn and Drew, they came onto the scene in March of 2005 and have been incredibly popular ever since.

Keith and the Girl have a talent for brashly stating what a lot of people think, but don't feel comfortable expressing. The draw of podcasting for several people is the lack of rules, and this podcast pushes the envelope. Enjoying the lack of the FCC regulations, Keith and the Girl daily tell the world their opinions on everything.

FIGURE 2.4

Keith and Chemda's cute site. Don't be fooled.

Podfading

Just like with any good blog or TV or radio show, popular podcasts come and go. *Podfading* is a term that Scott Fletcher from Podcheck Review coined to describe a discontinued podcast (see Figure 2.5).

One of the earliest examples of a well-known podfader is My Pods' Forecast. In this unique and quirky show, the host would use his testicles ("pods") to predict the future through his patented method "the cup, the lift, the drop," where depending on which "pod" was in front of the other after the drop, he would get a yes or no answer. The host, who was from the U.K., predicted such things as the lottery, the stock market, and the Golden Globes. On his last show he used his pods to determine whether he should change the baby's nappy (diaper) or should he leave it for his wife to change. The answer was "leave it for the wife," and he was never heard from again.

FIGURE 2.5

Although fans may miss it, you can't deny the faded Reality Bitchslap Radio went out in style.

Conversations with Podfaders

Even the most popular podcast can fade for any number of reasons. In this section we talk to some of the more prominent podfaders that have exited the realm of podcasting. In the next section, we tie together the lessons learned from these and other podfaders.

Catlas from the Catlas Podhead Podcast

This was a tech podcast released twice a week in which the host would talk about interesting software and websites. The shows were typically about 20 minutes in length, and the listener would almost always take away a few nuggets of valuable information.

TotPM: *Why did you decide to stop podcasting?*

Catlas: *I guess I just burned out. I took on too much too fast, and it became work instead of fun. I have recently taken up bicycle riding with a local cycle club, and we ride about 100 miles a week. I have also been triathlon training. I am a huge outdoor fan, and when summer rolls around I do not spend much time inside on the PC. I guess I never realized how much computer fun is a winter sport for me.*

I had told my subscribers I was taking the summer off and would return in September, but now (September 3rd, 2005) it looks like I will be cycle training until November, and I didn't want to keep putting my podcast off so I just decided to end it. It was sad for me, but in order for me to prepare properly for a cast, it takes about 5 to 8 hours of research and preparation to create one, and right now I don't have those 10 to 16 extra hours a week.

TotPM: *Are you looking at podcasting again in the future?*

Catlas: *Maybe I will start one again in the future, but for now, since I have not done one all summer, I felt like I had lost most of my subscribers. If I do ever podcast again, I will only commit to one cast a week. Two was too much for me.*

TotPM: *Are you still listening to podcasts?*

Catlas: *No, when I quit podcasting, I also quit listening to other podcasts. I mostly listened to other podcasts to stay abreast of the movement. So when I quit, it all went.*

Kevin from Next Gen Games

This was a tech podcast released twice a week that focused on video games. The host covered news and reviews of different video games with a heavy slant on the European video game market.

TotPM: *Why did you decide to stop podcasting?*

Kevin: *Sadly moving out here to Tampa from the U.K., along with college, meant I have not had time to podcast. I was also getting frustrated with my audio quality and unsure if I should [have] continued with it.*

TotPM: Are you looking at podcasting again in the future?

Kevin: Podcasting is one of the areas I am constantly looking at to innovate in. I have a desire to podcast personally but do not feel happy with my production level or consistency. There are other areas I am looking at, such as directories and community.

TotPM: Are you still listening to podcasts?

Kevin: Yes I am listening to podcasts daily, though some weeks less than others.

Landon from Landon Explains It All

This was a progressive Christian podcast released twice a week. Landon played some podsafe music but mostly focused on issues in the news from a progressive Christian perspective.

TotPM: Why did you decide to stop podcasting?

Landon: I stopped doing my podcast for a couple of different reasons. One, life got too crazy. Even though the medium has a reputation for being somewhat spontaneous and off the cuff, it takes a lot of work to do a good show. I would count myself in the group that wants to make sure that if I am going to put out some sort of product, it needs to be worthwhile to the folks that might download it. That means that I needed to spend a lot of time prepping my show, getting talking points down, and making sure that everything flowed together. I wanted music that was good and under the radar, so I had to spend time searching for it.

Then there was the actual recording of the show and the post-production that I needed to do to ensure that I didn't sound foolish. All told I probably spent 5 to 6 hours on each 40 minute show, and, when you try to do two shows a week, that basically amounts to a part-time job.

The second reason is that I kind of ran out of things to say. I was never a fan of folks that sat down with their microphone and just rambled for 30 to 40 minutes—I found it pointless and annoying. If I was *going to take the time to record, and if someone was going to take the time to download and listen, then I wanted to make sure that what I was giving them was worthwhile. I started out trying to give people a taste of progressive Christianity, and when I ran out of time and stuff to say, I quit.*

TotPM: Are you looking at podcasting again in the future?

Landon: I think about starting up again a lot, but my life is so hectic that I usually dismiss the urge. I'm blogging regularly (www.landonville.com) as part of a spiritual practice, but that takes nowhere near the time that podcasting does, and so I'm more likely to stick with that.

TotPM: Are you still listening to podcasts?

Landon: Yes, I try to keep my ear to the ground on what Christians are doing with podcasting.

Brian from She Said, He Said

She Said, He Said was a couple cast released about once a week. They presented general chit-chat about life from the perspective of a husband and wife.

TotPM: Why did you decide to stop podcasting?

Brian: Short answer: life got in the way.

Long answer: Jen started volunteering with the Red Cross about two months before Katrina hit. When Katrina hit, she started devoting more and more time to the Red Cross, which left less and less time for podcasting. Podcasting was also taking more and more time to do—even though we never had a script or planned much. We had to find a time when our daughter was asleep and we were both in the "podcasting mood," and then it took maybe an hour or so to record a 30-minute show, then I had all the post-production, file conversions, tagging, uploading, etc., etc. It ended up taking way too long, and with precious few hours of free time together we decided podcasting just wasn't what we wanted to do.

We met a lot of great people through podcasting, many of whom we are still in contact with. That's probably the best thing we got out of it—well, that and doing something together that brought us closer. I had a blast doing it with my wife—how many other husbands in the world can say they tried podcasting with their wife and enjoyed it?

TotPM: *Are you looking at podcasting again in the future?*

Brian: *No. It was fun while it lasted, but we have other things to occupy our free time now. Podcasting was a phase for me—I'm a geek and have done many programming projects in my free time (http://pipasoft. com), and I collect coin-op arcade games (http://thebrokenjoystick.com). I consider podcasting a phase I went through. I tried it, it was fun, and I moved on. I launched Candy Addict (http://candyaddict.com) a few months after we stopped podcasting and that is taking up my late-night free time now.*

TotPM: *Are you still listening to podcasts?*

Brian: *I am, but way fewer than I did at the peak. I was listening to about 20 or so podcasts. Now I am an avid fan of podcast audiobooks (podiobooks) and have three or four of those going at any one time. I only regularly listen to two other non-audiobook podcasts: The Sitter Downers and Jimmy Jett.*

How to Avoid Burnout

When it comes to avoiding podfading, it is important to understand the reasons why people podfade. Based on our conversations with those just listed and many other podcasters, we've come up with five of the most common reasons for a podcast to podfade.

Lack of Time

By far the number-one reason for podfadivitis is a lack of time. Many podcasters talk about sleep deprivation and being up until 3:00 a.m. or later working on their show. There is only so long you can physically and mentally keep up such a hectic schedule before you burn out. It is very important for you to sit down and work out a schedule for doing your show. The next time you start doing a show, get out the stop watch and time how long it takes from prep work through recording through postproduction and posting of the show. Then plan your week/day accordingly.

What is very interesting is that many podcasters also talked about doing too many shows in a week. One thing to remember is moderation. If you feel like the show has become an anchor on your life, try reducing the number of shows you do. For example, if you are doing a daily show, drop back to Monday, Wednesday, Friday. Just make sure you communicate the change to your listeners. If you are not passionate about your show, it will come through to the listeners and they will move on.

Lack of Interest

This is the response we heard most from those who started podcasting just to podcast. After a while, they realized this was a lot of work and it just was not as exciting as when they started. The best way to avoid this is not to do a podcast unless it is about a subject that really interests you. If you love collecting all things related to Pug dogs and talking about that collection, then you have a subject you are likely not going to lose interest in. If you find yourself now lacking interest in your show but not wanting to give up on podcasting, reinvent the show. Nothing is stopping you from changing the focus of the show. That is the beauty of podcasting—you own the show. Granted, you may lose all your listeners, but chances are if you are losing interest in your show, most of your former listeners are probably losing interest too. Of course, you will want to change your podcast's name if the change no longer fits the current title. After all, you do not want a show called PugCast to be about collecting Persian rugs. In this case, we would recommend you start up the new show and then on the old show do a final farewell telling your old listeners that the show is being podfaded and giving them information about the new show. You will be surprised by how many people will follow you over to the new show even if they previously had no interest in the new subject.

Lack of Material

Some subjects are so niche that it is hard to find material to talk about. If you have picked a subject for which you feel it is hard to fill a show with quality material, you can do a couple of things. First, reduce the length of your show. There is nothing stating how long your show should be, and you are not locked into the length of previous shows. A 10-minute show that is packed full of information and is quick and snappy is far more enjoyable than a 30-minute show with only 11 minutes of material. Think about Episode 1 of *Star Wars*—15 minutes of great information stretched out over 2 hours. Don't let your show suffer from Episode 1 disease.

The other thing you can do is invite guests who have knowledge in your subject matter. No one says you have to do it all yourself. Having a guest or two will help break up a show and often add additional insight you may have been lacking. Plus, guests often bring exposure to listeners/fans of that guest whom you might not have had access to otherwise.

Lack of Listeners

A lot of podcasters use the service Feedburner to track the number of subscribers they have for their podcast, only to find the answer is, "not many" (see Figure 2.6).

FIGURE 2.6

Subscriber numbers for a podcast (sometimes the truth hurts).

This is the one that causes the most frustration with podcasters, and very often the frustration isn't warranted. We talked to people who had 75 listeners and were happy with their listener base. We talked to others who had 750 and were very frustrated with the count. The fact is, as of December 2005, more than 90% of all podcasts, based on stats from Feedburner, had less than 250 listeners. This is a hard thing to avoid at first. Unless you are a celebrity such as Wil Wheaton, you are not going to come out of the gate with 2,000 listeners. The best way to avoid a lack of listeners is to give listeners something they feel they need to listen to and then market the heck out of your show. That is what this book is about. So keep on reading.

Lack of Funds

One thing early podcasters who were popular faced was high bandwidth bills. Many of these podcasters paid for their own webspace to host their podcasts, and the more traffic you have the more you're likely to pay to maintain that space. Since that time, services such as Libsyn (www.libsyn.com) and Podlot (www.podlot.com) have come along, offering unlimited bandwidth for a very reasonable cost. But beyond bandwidth there are other costs to look out for.

Bazooka Joe of the Small World podcast interviews all types of people for his show. On one interview he made a call to the U.K. over POTS (plain old telephone system) and

> **NOTE**
>
> VoIP stands for *Voice over Internet Protocol.* You may also hear it referred to as *Internet telephony* or *digital phone* (from your local cable company). Without getting too techie, VoIP is basically a way of digitally making a phone call over the Internet, as compared to the analog method using the plain old phone system we grew up with. For more information, visit http://en.wikipedia.org/wiki/Voip.

he racked up a $63 phone call. Joe does a daily show, and it doesn't take Will Hunting to do the math. The best solution to this particular problem is to look to Skype (www. skype.com) and other VoIP (Voice over IP) services.

Then there is the cost for equipment. It is very easy to go out and spend multiple thousands of dollars if you try to get the very best of everything, but that doesn't mean you should. Look at Dawn and Drew, clearly one of the most popular podcasts. They did their show with a $20 Logitech microphone for the first nine-plus months. Here is the best way to avoid the issue of lack of funds:

- Spend in moderation for equipment purchases.
- Use Skype or another VoIP service if you need to make long-distance calls.
- Look for a low-cost unlimited-bandwidth provider for hosting your podcast's MP3 files.

We will talk more about how to generate revenue for your podcast later in Part III of this book. Remember, podcasting is supposed to be fun, and if you are not having fun, then chances are you may wind up in the "Conversations with Podfaders" section of this chapter in later editions.

Chapter 3

PODCAST GENRES

"Do your research. Know what you're talking about.
Act professionally. Find your niche."

Paul Tevis, Have Games, Will Travel

Most podcasts don't fit into any pigeonhole. Michael and Evo's Wingin' It fits under science fiction and comedy, while you can consider The Dawn and Drew Show! to be an audioblog, a couple cast, comedy, and sex/adult. Still, when you consider the kinds of podcasts that exist, most podcasts have one dominant category they fall into.

Does your podcast have to fit neatly into one of these categories? Not really. This is not a bookstore where if the publisher can't figure out where to put your book, you're not going to get shelf space. Podcasts that find themselves unclassifiable, and yet still entertaining, will get listeners. In fact, word of mouth by other podcasters continues to be the best way to get listeners.

Still, the categories help out when it comes to placing your show in podcast directories, most of which allow you to put your show in more than one category or subcategory.

In this chapter, we have listed the most popular categories, with some examples of successful podcasts in each, things to think about in each genre, and what makes these particular genres work. If you're thinking of doing a religious podcast, or "Godcast," you'll want to check out the others in the genre to see what they're doing. You'll want inspiration, but you won't want to copy them directly. And you have less chance of copying the popular podcasts accidentally if you hear what they're doing.

Audioblogs

By far the most popular podcast type, the audioblog, is what attracts most new podcasters. If you search the descriptions of podcasts, most of them contain "talk about whatever is on my mind" or "my thoughts while I sit on my hour-long commute." Like written blogs, audioblogs reflect the personality of the host, discussing either her life or her view on current events.

Most podcasts could fall under the audioblog moniker by default. If an individual person talks about things she enjoys, you can argue that the show is a blog. Dan Klass's The Bitterest Pill (www.thebitterestpill.com) is an audioblog that he uses to tell stories of his life as a stay-at-home dad and actor (see Figure 3.1). However, his stories are so well told and entertaining, the show is often considered a comedy podcast.

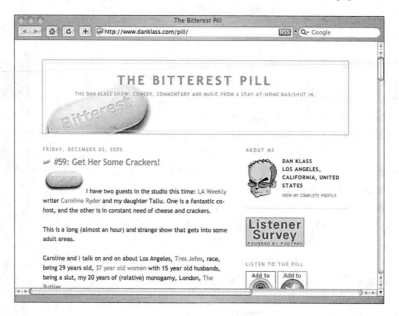

FIGURE 3.1

The homepage for The Bitterest Pill audioblog.

Table 3.1 summarizes a few examples of good audioblogs. Following that, we take a deeper look at what makes each of them worth a subscription.

Table 3.1   Noteworthy Audioblogs

Host(s)	Podcast	Website URL
Robert Keeme	KeemeCast	www.keeme.com
Corby	Twisted Pickle	www.thetwistedpickle.com
Dan Klass	The Bitterest Pill	www.thebitterestpill.com

KeemeCast

Robert Keeme hosts this podcast from his home in Arizona, which he shares with OS1, OS2, and OS3 (his three daughters, OS stands for Offspring). They are often guests on his show, along with his good friend the Abbott. The show is released two to three times a week and has a length that varies from 10 minutes to 1 hour per episode. KeemeCast is R-rated.

"I do it like I live my life. I am a stream-of-conscious person. I'll be talking to you and I'll start on one thing and we will end up a million miles away in 2 to 3 minutes. People call me crazy; I say I am eccentric. I tell a story about something that has happened in my past, same thing I do with my blog."

—**Keeme, KeemeCast**

Twisted Pickle

Corby ninjacasts from his home in Omaha. What is ninjacasting? Well, Corby has not informed his wife that he is podcasting. Yup, this has "train wreck" written all over it. So tune in to see if this is the episode where his wife finds out and kicks him out of the house. He releases new shows about four to six times a month, with a length that varies from 20 minutes to 1 hour. This show is R-rated.

"Every show seems to be a little bit different. I honestly do not know what I am going to talk about until probably the day of. Since I am ninjacasting, I have to take the opportunity to record something when it comes. So depending on the notes I have jotted down for that particular day that develops into the show. And I do really talk about a wide range of strange topics. Most of it is things that I have done or experiences I have had, or strange things that I have seen. But every

now and then I will go into an individual story that will take up the major meat of that particular podcast. So when you tune in, you are really not sure what you are going to get, but you can pretty much be sure that it is going to be a bit off the wall, kind of strange, sometimes a bit vulgar, but all around it is a good laugh."

—Corby, Twisted Pickle

The Bitterest Pill

This show is hosted by Los Angeles stay-at-home dad/comedian/actor Dan Klass. Dan is one of the icons of podcasting, and his show is one of the favorites among other podcasters. The Bitterest Pill is released between one and four times a month, with a typical length of 25 to 30 minutes per episode. This show is G-rated.

Dan is a master storyteller, weaving his domestic stories effortlessly with his tales of acting auditions. Occasionally he features guests on his show, ranging from his toddler daughter who is refusing to nap to other podcasters. Whatever he's talking about turns interesting with his sardonic and entertaining tone. Called the "Stay-At-Home Father of Podcasting" by Tony Khan of WGBH, Klass's show is a perfect example of how to turn your everyday life into something immensely entertaining.

Keys to Successful Audioblogs

There are several keys to making a successful audioblog podcast. The first is simply determining what stories will appeal to your listeners. Do you commonly tell stories about your life that have your friends laughing at your wit or riveted at the tension you built, or are they nodding politely while checking their watch, or perhaps even actively trying to walk away? Gauge your audience in real life and see. Your presentation is also important here; a knack for storytelling can make the most boring story interesting. You will also want to keep track of whom you're talking about: Are your parents going to listen to this? What about your boss? If you think you're anonymous, will they be able to recognize you?

Then again, if you're choosing to be anonymous, like some podcasters prefer, you can say whatever you like and hope that the people close to you, professionally or personally, aren't digitally savvy, don't listen to your podcast, and aren't terribly bright. Anonymous podcasters have freedom granted by anonymity, but they do not get the bonus of having their name known in the podcast community (or local or national media). You must weigh the plusses and minuses and decide for yourself.

Audioblogging is much like regular blogging: Have something to talk about, make sure your grammar and spelling are good (or, in the podcasting sense, make sure your audio quality is good), don't say anything that would devastate your life if your boss, mother, or spouse would hear it, and attempt to be engaging at best or entertaining at least.

Comedy Casts—Shock Jocks, Skits, Standup...

When it comes to shock jocks, Bibb and Yaz were the first ones to take full advantage of the freedoms of podcasting. Although the things Yaz says may make Bibb wince, they would definitely cause the program director at any radio station to go into cardiac arrest for fear of the FCC fines that would follow. But at the end of their show, Bibb and Yaz are not making calls to their lawyers—they don't even have lawyers, they just post the show and get ready for the next one.

There has never been a platform for shock jocks more inviting than that of podcasting. Forget Sirius or XM, because anyone there still needs to answer to the board of directors. Although Howard Stern might think he is getting unlimited freedom to do whatever he wants, we all know there are some strings attached to that $500-million check. Now some would say the world does not need shows like Bibb and Yaz or Distorted View Daily, where even George Carlin would be shocked, but to dismiss them entirely is to miss the point.

The endgame is that there are just as many good podcasts that are extremely funny and are G- or PG-rated as there are those that are R- or X-rated. Which you prefer to listen to or model your podcast after is purely a matter of personal taste. In this section, we give a good mix of all (see Table 3.2). What is nice to know is that if you have the desire to do a comedy show, no matter what rating your tongue is, you have a place to express yourself with podcasting.

Table 3.2 Popular Comedy Podcasts

Host(s)	Podcast	Website URL
Tim Henson	Distorted View Daily	www.distortedview.com
Bibb and Yaz	The Bibb and Yaz Podcast	www.bibbsrevenge.com
Jesse Thorn	The Sound of Young America	www.splangy.com
Scott Fletcher	Podcheck Review	www.podcheck.com
Clinton Alvord	Comedy4Cast	www.comedy4cast.com

Distorted View Daily

Tim Henson started this show back in 1997 as a streaming audio show. It has evolved over that time into what it is today: one of the funniest and twisted shows on the Net. If you listen to this show, at some point you are going to say, "Oh, that is just wrong." The show is released each weekday, and the typical length of an episode is 15 minutes. The show is X-rated.

"Everyday on Distorted View, I scour the Web for the most bizarre and twisted stories in the news. I then present them to you, complete with my own unique (read: crass, vulgar, childish, and inappropriate) commentary. You'll also hear comedy sketches, weird and unusual erotic stories, and prank calls. The show's content is not for the fainthearted. Its appeal lies in its irreverence and disregard for political correctness."

—Tim Henson, Distorted View Daily

The Bibb and Yaz Podcast

Bibb and Yaz host the first shock-jock podcast. This show makes infamous New York shock jocks Opie and Anthony look tame. They release one show a week, with a typical length running from 2 to 3 hours per episode. This show is X-rated.

"Our podcast is the uncensored rantings of two Jersey guys who live a stone's throw away from the urban jungle. While most people might not understand the humor in our points of view or even the terminology we might use, in our minds it all makes complete sense. New listeners may find that we come across as harsh or extreme, but after a few listens people realize we just like to poke fun at the things and ideas that make people feel most uncomfortable. The show also acts as an open forum to attack society's ills and things that most people are afraid to talk about in public, but readily talk about behind closed doors: religion, sexual preference, race, and disabilities."

—Gary Bibb, The Bibb and Yaz Podcast

The Sound of Young America

This show is hosted by Jesse "America's Radio Sweetheart" Thorn and Jordan Morris. Jesse is one of the hardest working self-promoters in podcasting. You can learn a lot about self-promotion by looking at what Jesse is doing with his podcast. This show is released once a week and is typically 1 hour in length. The show is PG-rated.

 "In some ways the format changes from week to week, but it usually ends up being something like this: We have an introductory segment, a little bit of banter, show preview, then I do a little bit of an intro, maybe 5 minutes of talking. Sometimes I tell a story of something that has happened to me recently. Once in a while we have a contest for the people that listen in on the radio. I then do one segment that is sometimes an interview, sometimes a comedy thing. We work in comedy bits we have written and produced, and then we usually do a half hour interview by phone with someone we think is awesome."

—Jesse Thorn, The Sound of Young America

Podcheck Review

Scott Fletcher hosts this podcast from Illinois. If there was an award in podcasting for Best Male Voice, the nominees would be Scott Fletcher, Scott Fletcher, Scott Fletcher, and, oh yeah, Scott Fletcher. You can hear his voice on dozens of promos, bumpers, and sweepers throughout the podcasting world. His show, although listed in the Comedy section, could have just as easily been put in the Technology or News section (sorry Scott, we needed to pigeonhole you somewhere). The show is released a few times a month and is a must-listen for anyone in the podcasting community. The typical length is in the 15-to-20-minute range per episode. This show is PG-rated.

 "It is a show where I have a list of news stories and I make fun of them…. I did not set out to model after Jon Stewart, but now that I have been doing it a while, that is kind of where I am heading with it. It is serious news, so anyone that is interested in podcasting can tune in for 15 or 20 minutes and pretty much get the headlines. But also I don't usually hold back on whether or not I think something has merit

because I do a lot of praising on the show, but I also do a little bit of reality check—you know people who spun up the hype machine a little too early."

—Scott Fletcher, Podcheck Review

Comedy4Cast

Clinton Alvord hosts this very concise podcast. Even though it is one of the shorter podcasts, what it lacks in length it more than makes up for with humor. This show is released about twice a week and is typically about 4 minutes in length. The show is PG-rated.

"Comedy4Cast is a short-form podcast, averaging under 4 minutes an episode. The shows are what I call 'mostly work-safe' and 'kind of family friendly,' insomuch as there is no swearing and 'adult' situations are kept to a minimum. Rather than concentrating on one set format or cast of characters, I try to cover a wide range of styles. One show might feature a short story or monologue, while the next could be a skit or parody of other well-known podcasts. My work is influenced by radio comedy legends such as Stan Freberg and Bob and Ray."

—Clinton Alvord, Comedy4Cast

Why Do a Comedy Cast?

People love to laugh; people need to laugh, and if you are someone who has that gift of comedic timing, you need to have a comedy podcast. Maybe you are someone who dreams of doing an open mic at the local comedy club, but you have not yet worked up the courage or the routine. If so, then starting a short podcast with some selective jokes might be for you. If you have the largest collection of bar jokes or Internet chain mail jokes, you have the content for a good podcast. It is very likely that someone doing a comedy podcast is going to get that big break that will make them the next cast member of *SNL* or the next big standup star—be it Keith Malley, Tim Henson, Wichita Rutherford, or you.

Couple Casts

Although most couple casts could also be described as comedy casts, the one thing that makes these shows a couple cast (other than the fact that the hosts are a couple) is that they feature the personal lives of the hosts. Topics might range from the couple's sex lives to nightmarish stories of traveling the globe. Regardless of the topic, the hosts offer a view into their everyday lives—the good and the bad. On one episode of The PK and J Show (see Figure 3.2), listeners were taken along with Jeanette while she interviewed the person giving her a Brazilian wax. On The Nate and Di Show, listeners found out about the septic system backing up into their storage shed (where they live).

As listeners, you are brought into the daily and weekly happenings of these different couples. The most successful shows are the ones that make you feel like you are part of their family. There are a lot of examples of couple casts, and the ones listed in Table 3.3 do a great job of welcoming you into their families.

FIGURE 3.2

The PK and J Show.

Table 3.3   Popular Couple Casts

Names	Podcast	Website URL
Paul and Jeanette	The PK and J Show	www.pkandjshow.com
Nate and Di	The Nate and Di Show	www.nateanddi.com
Harry and Ziva	The View from Here	www.theviewfromhere.net
Len and Nora	Jawbone Radio	www.jawboneradio.blogspot.com
Jason and Anna	Delta Park Project	www.deltaparkproject.com

The PK and J Show

Paul and Jeanette are a 20-something couple from Columbus, Ohio who are, as they say, "living in sin." (Hey Paul, when are you going to ask Jeanette to marry you?) They release their show roughly once a week, and a typical episode runs about 1 hour. It is very well produced; Paul is one of the most talented audio people in podcasting, and Jeanette has arguably the sexiest voice in podcasting. They often have original skits and spoof commercials. Their "brown phone" segment, where listeners call in and leave messages, is always worth hearing. This show is R-rated.

"I guess sex is part of our show.... We think it is just more interesting to talk about that and it is just something we naturally talk about. If you were on an actual radio show, there is a certain code you need to adhere to in order to keep your job. So in this case it is the fuel that keeps us going. There are no limits, you can say whatever you want."

—Paul, The PK and J Show

The Nate and Di Show

A married couple living in a storage shed on the beach in South Carolina, Nate and Di release their show about once a week with a bonus show thrown in here and there. The typical length of an episode is 30 to 40 minutes. They often have skits in their show, and an early one led to Nate being the first podcaster fired from his job because of podcasting—but more on that later. Their show definitely takes on a political slant: imagine Jon Stewart and Janeane Garofalo married and living in a storage shed on the beach and you have a good idea of what this show is like. They also play listener feedback to end most shows. This show is R-rated.

"The format we prefer to use is reality entertainment. One of our biggest influences is gonzo journalism, particularly Hunter Thompson, and we try to bring that aspect into our show. It is a little bit of comedy and a little bit of politics. We try to place ourselves within every story or skit that we do; it spices it up for our audience."

—Nate and Di, The Nate and Di Show

The View from Here

A married couple originally from the U.S. now living in Israel, Harry and Ziva release their show two to three times a month, and a typical episode is 35 to 40 minutes long. The show is R-rated.

 "What happens to me and Harry in Israel on a daily basis. What we read about, what we hear about, what we do, what we laugh about. It is really like we are sitting at the kitchen table and just talking about things, except everyone else gets to listen and enjoy. Two people living in Israel just shooting the shit."

—Ziva, The View from Here

 "We talk a lot about pop culture in Israel and compare it to America. I think that we offer a very unique perspective of Israeli life, being that we are not religious. We are secular Israelis just living our lives, getting up in the morning, going to work, and just laughing our butts off at the most ridiculous things that we see in Israel."

—Harry, The View from Here

Jawbone Radio

Len and Nora are a married couple from Cleveland podcasting out of their attic. Len is one of the most talented artists in podcasting. His artwork can be found on many podcasters' websites and t-shirts, including the artwork for the Podcast Outlaws network (www.podcastoutlaws.com). They release a show every four to five days, and the typical length is 40 to 45 minutes. The show is G-rated.

"It has been said that our show is about zippy patter. It is a conversation between myself and Lenny and oftentimes involves exploring newfound things, like a brand-new program, or a strange new trend, or something in the pop culture. And then there is a recurrent theme of advice that is tongue in cheek. We also have a fair number of guest interviews, and we encourage a fair amount of interaction with our listeners."

—Nora, Jawbone Radio

Delta Park Project

This show consists of a married couple, Jason and Anna, podcasting out of Beaverton, Oregon. They release a show once a week, and the typical length is 35 to 40 minutes per episode. The show is PG-rated.

"We just kind of talk about what we are watching on TV or what movies we have seen or really anything else that is in the news that is interesting. And then we have little games that we play. Also we are both from Montana, [so] one of the things we try to include every week is the crime blotter from the newspaper from the town where we grew up because it is all small-town crime."

—Anna, Delta Park Project

The Making of a Successful Couple Cast

The one thing all these couples do with their podcast is to open the door to their lives. If you want to have a loyal listener base as a couple cast, it does not matter if you are G-rated or X-rated. If you are not comfortable talking about your sex life, then don't do it. What does matter is that you are open and honest with your listeners and that you come across as comfortable discussing what happened to you and your partner. Also, having a way for listeners to get feedback on to your show was deemed very important to most of the couples we talked to. Having a two-way interaction with your audience is usually important in garnering a loyal fan base for any type of podcast, but couple casts in particular typically require an audience that is allowed to share in the experience.

One last piece of advice for those looking to do a couple cast: Do *not* give out your last names. Some people out there will take you literally when you invite them into your lives. Make sure when you register your domain name that you make the registration private, so that potential stalkers will not be able to track down your Whois information. Best to be safe than sorry.

Educational

This area in podcasting is really starting to take off, with more and more universities, colleges, high schools, and even elementary school classes producing podcasts. Instructional audio is nothing new; it is just that with podcasting the distribution of that audio has been made quite a bit easier and cheaper. Educational podcasts don't have to come just from teachers and professors; they can also come from everyday people who use their podcast to educate their listeners about a specific subject or about random facts. Table 3.4 lists four very diverse examples of educational podcasts that do a great job in educating and entertaining their listeners.

Table 3.4   Popular Educational Podcasts

Host(s)	Podcast	Website URL
Jeff	English as a Second Language	www.eslpod.com
Chris	Digital Photography: Tips from the Top Floor	www.tipsfromthetopfloor.com
Sam and Steve	The SG Show	sgshow.blogspot.com
Mark and Kathy	TechPod Podcast for Teachers	www.podcastforteachers.org

English as a Second Language

The host of this very popular daily podcast is Dr. Jeff McQuillan. Jeff received his PhD in applied linguistics and education at the University of Southern California, and his podcasts last an average of 15 to 20 minutes per episode. The show is G-rated.

"We do a podcast of English that is intended for lower intermediates to advanced students of English. It is not for the rank beginner; that is, if you know no English, this podcast will not be useful to you.... We start with a 3-to-5-minute dialogue or usually just sort of a story

where we talk about everyday things...using lots of vocabulary that will be specific for the particular topic. Then the last 10 to 15 minutes we discuss the dialogue, [and] we discuss the story in more details."

—**Dr. Jeff McQuillan, English as a Second Language**

Digital Photography: Tips from the Top Floor

Chris Marquardt produces this show out of Germany. This is both an educational podcast and a technology podcast. It should be noted that not all tech shows have to be about computers, and Chris puts together what is clearly the leading photography podcast out there. He has a large and loyal listener base that actively contributes to his forum boards. He releases about three shows a week, and the average length varies between 10 to 30 minutes per episode. The show is G-rated.

 "The podcast is about digital photography, but there are many non-digital photographers listening to the show as well, so I think it is more about photography in general. It is photography lessons, it is tips and tricks. I do interviews with professional photographers. I also do soundseeing tours, where I tell people what I am doing while I am taking pictures. It is really being there at the time when things happen, and people still learn something from it."

—**Chris Marquardt, Digital Photography: Tips from the Top Floor**

The SG Show

Hosted by 8-year-old Sam and his father, Steve, this podcast comes out of California. They talk about things of interest to both young children and adults, with the result being a very entertaining and educational show. The show is released about once a week, and the average length is 20 to 25 minutes per episode. The show is of course G-rated.

TIP

This is one of those handful of shows for which you should know the website address by heart. This way, when friends, family, co-workers, or total strangers ask about podcasting, you have one that you can send them to for their first taste.

"We talked about things for families to do, we talked about some books, and a lot of things that kids do."

—Sam, The SG Show

TechPod Podcast for Teachers

Hosted by Mark Gura and Dr. Kathy King, this podcast comes from Fordham University's Regional Education Technology Center (RETC). The show is released about once a week, and the typical length is 25 to 30 minutes per episode. The show is G-rated.

"[The TechPod Podcast for Teachers (PFT)] provide[s] lively conversations about technology and education with leaders and innovators in educational technology with the ambient sounds of the bustling Bronx nearby. From resources and curriculum ideas, discussions about technology developments and roving field reports, to intimate conversations with educators, ed techies, and authors, we are breaking into new areas with mobile technology and hybrid developments for teaching, learning, and professional development.

"My co-host, Mark Gura, and I consider that producing the podcast is a project in which we at Fordham University's Regional Educational Technology Center can help the field extend its uses, significance, and implications further for education and society. TechPod PFT is intended to model the experience of learning to podcast and its potential for other educators."

—Dr. Kathy King, TechPod

The Importance of Educational Podcasts

How important is podcasting to educators? Well, Duke University is already podcasting classes, lectures, and visiting speakers, and Yale University is also looking at podcasting its classes, as are many other universities. One of the first papers on podcasting at the university level came from the University of Missouri's School of Journalism in March of 2005. Early on, universities were able to see the advantages of using podcasting as an educational tool. Podcasting is clearly here to stay in the classroom; the only question is what different and creative ways can podcasts be put to use to help improve the learning experience for the students and listeners. That is a question that many of you reading this book will help to answer.

Gaming

This is a well-represented category, with many podcasts covering computer gaming, console gaming, role-playing gaming and board gaming. Gaming podcasts run the gamut, discussing gaming news, interviews with industry professionals, reviews, or reports from gaming sessions.

The gaming podcasts also run between 15 minutes and 2+ hours. Although many listeners prefer a shorter podcast to a longer one, the longer podcasts often have dedicated listeners who insist that it can't be too long, as long as it's good, as the fans of the Gaming Uncensored podcast insist. A few examples of good gaming podcasts are listed in Table 3.5.

Table 3.5　Popular Gaming Podcasts

Host(s)	Podcast	Website URL
Charlie George	Tired Thumbs	tiredthumbs.blogspot.com
Jamie and Tommy	Gaming Uncensored	www.gaminguncensored.com
Paul Tevis	Have Games, Will Travel	havegameswilltravel.libsyn.com

Tired Thumbs

Charlie George hosts this podcast out of Joliet, Illinois as part of the Tech Podcasters Network. The show is released three times a week (Monday, Wednesday, Friday) with the average length being 10 to 30 minutes per episode. The show is G-rated.

> *"On Monday's show I review a game.... I play a game, I check it out and tell them is it worth it (the sale price), and if it is not worth it, I tell them a ballpark range at what I would buy it at. Wednesday I do gaming news and I do the email bag thing, and I also do my Tired Thumbs gaming tip of the week. And then on Friday I do a podcaster game file where I talk to a podcaster and I ask them what is on their shelf and what are they playing, and we usually have a lot of fun with that."*
>
> **—Charlie George, Tired Thumbs**

Gaming Uncensored

This podcast, which features Jamie and Tommy, two college students from Texas talking about computer and video games, can run anywhere between 1 and 2 hours. The hosts have a good chemistry that allows them to take tangents that may or may not be related to gaming, but still manage to entertain the fans. (One of the best stories features Jamie receiving sales and marketing calls from the local funeral home on the morning of his 26th birthday.) So if you're going to cram a lot of gaming info into one podcast, focus on the entertainment factor.

Have Games, Will Travel

Paul Tevis, a writer and gamer, created this podcast after realizing he preferred talking about games over writing about them. His podcast revolves around reviews of board games and RPG games, as well as industry interviews when he goes to the conferences.

"I've always been better at talking than writing. In the gaming world, however, writing is how you get recognized. I'd been circling the gaming industry for a while, trying to figure out how I fit in, when I discovered podcasting. I listened to a few shows and said, 'Hey, I can talk about games.' So I did. It turns out that I had a bit of a talent for it, but more importantly, I found that I really enjoyed it…. My goal is to provide a short, information-dense show so that people who don't have another hour's worth of time to listen to podcasts are still willing to add me to their playlist."

—Paul Tevis, Have Games, Will Travel

Secrets of Effective Gaming Podcasts

Gaming podcasts are more commonly run by two hosts than one, and the addition of a second host changes the dynamic of the podcast a great deal. One host gives a definite feel of intimacy as well as an air of one-on-one instruction. Two hosts generally bring a lighter mood to the podcast, and the two-host shows are almost always longer.

Doing a gaming podcast requires an almost fanatical dedication to gaming, which almost always requires a sizable budget for game purchases and plenty of free time with which to play them. If you have 10 games in your collection, you're going to run out of podcasts fast. Make sure you're playing a lot of games so you will have lots to talk about over the life of your show.

One thing to remember when it comes to gaming podcasts is that gaming fans are fickle. If you do not have a regular release plan, it is likely that you will lose listeners. Therefore, if a gaming podcast is your goal, you need to consider a regular schedule and stick to it. Most attempt a semi-weekly or weekly schedule. Regardless of that, communication with the fans is important. Adding a forum to your blog is a great idea (see Figure 3.3). Fans love a place where they can get together and discuss their favorite games—and your podcast!

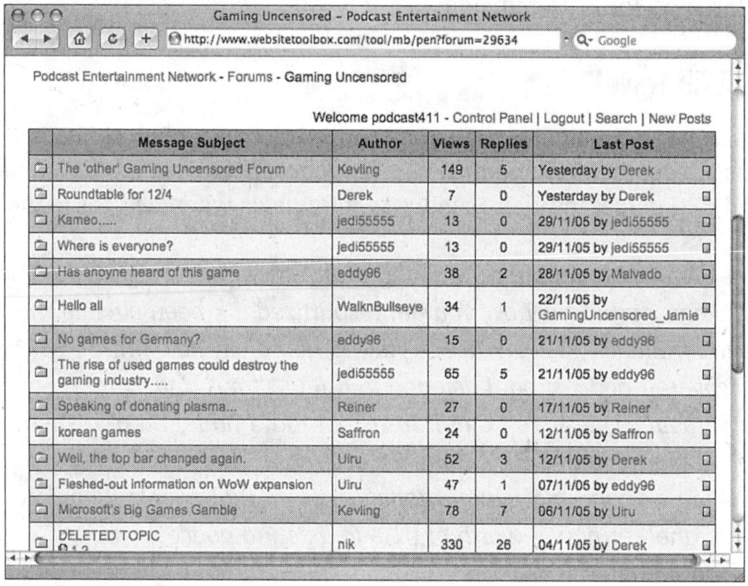

FIGURE 3.3

Gaming Uncensored message board.

Godcasts: Religious and Spiritual Podcasts

You cannot talk about podcasts without talking about religious and spiritual podcasts, or "Godcasts" as they have affectionately been called. This genre of podcasting is the fourth most popular behind audioblogs, music, and technology. One of the best places to find religious podcasts is at the GodCast Network (www.godcast.org), which was the first podcast network and was started by Craig Patchett. Not all religious podcasts are rebroadcasts of a Sunday sermon (although there are more and more of those popping up every week), and most are not even by priests or clergy. Most are just everyday people talking about a subject that they are very passionate about, even if that means doing so in the Klingon language. What follows in Table 3.6 is a very diverse mix of different religious and spiritual podcasts.

Table 3.6   Popular Religious Podcasts

Host(s)	Podcast	Website URL
Steve Webb	Lifespring	www.lifespringpodcast.com
Ron Stephens	Awaretek	www.awaretek.com
Father Roderick	Catholic Insider	www.catholicinsider.com
Rachel Patchett	Rachel's Choice	www.godcast.org
Joel Anderson	Klingon Word	klingonword.blogspot.com

Lifespring

As one of the very first "Godcasters," Steve has been producing Lifespring since early November 2004. The show is released about once a week, and the typical length is in the 30-to-35-minutes range. The show is G-rated.

"I wanted to do some programming that hopefully non-believers might be interested in listening to more than just a sermon. So I try to make Lifespring somewhat entertaining. I put music in there, I talk about some things of faith, and I just try and make it entertaining for people who might be considering the idea of what is the whole God thing."

—Steve Webb, Lifespring

Awaretek

Awaretek was the first podcast for host Ron Stephens, who also hosts the popular Python411 show. This show is released roughly once a week, and the typical length is 20 to 30 minutes per episode. The show is G-rated.

"I cover the big issues of the day, what is really important in life, so it is kind of a philosophy but it has to do with science and technology and trying to find some sort of spiritual angle that is compatible with science and with reason and with logic and then applying that in a

practical fashion to what we might do in the present to try to create a better future."

—Ron Stephens, Awaretek

Catholic Insider

Arguably the most popular religious podcaster, Father Roderick burst onto the scene in the podcasting world in the spring of 2005 by offering listeners around the world a behind-the-scenes view of Pope John Paul II's funeral. A new show is released 3 to 10 times a month, with an average length varying from 10 to 30 minutes. The show is G-rated.

"Most of the time [it] is just soundseeing, so I would just go out and I [would record]. I was very often in Rome, so that is an interesting place to be. There is lots to see, and I could make a lot of audio documentaries about the churches and the places and the people I met there."

—Father Roderick, Catholic Insider

Rachel's Choice

Rachel Patchett is the daughter of podcast legend and founder of the GodCast Network, Craig Patchett. When she first started, Rachel was the youngest podcaster with her own show. Each show has a Bible verse, along with a select music track. A new show is released about two to three times a month, with an average length of about 5 minutes per show. The show is of course G-rated.

Klingon Word

Hosted by Joel Anderson, Klingon Word has a unique concept for a show. This podcast is a great example of how you can bring two things together in a podcast that would never have made it past a program director on radio. In this case, it is the Klingon language and the Bible. The show is released about twice a week and is about 5 minutes in length per episode. The show is G-rated.

Passion for the Godcast

As you can tell from this diverse mix of shows, you do not need to be a priest or clergy member to do a Godcast and have a strong listening base. Also, Godcasts can cover any area of religion or spirituality that you believe in. This is one area in podcasting where if you are not passionate about the subject, the podcast will fail.

The Interview Cast

Okay, so you want to do a podcast, but try as you may, you can't get anyone you know to commit to being your co-host. What are you to do? Well, you could always interview people you do not know. Think Jon Stewart, David Lettermen, *Inside the Actors Studio*, *Fresh Air*, and *Space Ghost Coast to Coast*. There are plenty of examples to borrow from in the broadcast world, and Table 3.7 highlights some of the more popular ones. If done well, the interview cast can be one of the most interesting podcasts out there. If done poorly, it can be the worst (more on that in Chapter 7, "The Art of the Interview"). What follows is a small list of some of those that do it well.

Table 3.7   Popular Interview Podcasts

Host(s)	Podcast	Website URL
Rob Walch	podCast411	www.podcast411.com
Wichita Rutherford	5 Minutes with Wichita	www.5minuteswithwichita.com
Greg Demetrick	5 Questions	www.5questions.net
Bazooka Joe	Small World	www.smallworldpodcast.com
J.A. Donnelly	MadPod	www.madpod.com

podCast411

Hosted by Rob Walch (co-author of this book), this podcast has been described as *Inside the Actors Studio*, except for podcasting. Rob releases two shows a week that typically run 20 to 25 minutes an episode. The show is G-rated.

"This is the show to get the 411 (information) on podcasters, podcasts, and podcasting. I try to mix in the most popular podcasts with up-and-coming or very niche podcasts to learn what makes their podcasts work. Why they are podcasting, how they produce, how they promote, and if applicable how they monetize their shows. The beginning of each show is news and tech tips, and then we get into the interview that lasts about 15 minutes, and at the end play a promo and some listener feedback. While our show is G-rated, many of our guests' shows are not—but that is what editing is all about."

—Rob Walch, podCast411

5 Minutes with Wichita

Although this podcast could just as easily be placed in the Comedy section, it is at its heart an interview show. It just happens to be the funniest interview show anywhere—in broadcast radio and podcasting. Which is why Wichita Rutherford was the first podcaster signed to a Sirius Satellite deal, even

before Adam Curry and Podshow. He releases one show a week and, you guessed it, it is 5 minutes long. The show is G-rated, and Wichita proved that you can be funny (very funny) without using the F-word.

"5 Minutes with Wichita is a 5-minute interview show where I go all over the world and talk to all kinds of famous folks. Bluegrass stars, NASCAR drivers, actors, country stars, and rock stars."

—Wichita Rutherford, 5 Minutes with Wichita

Wichita brings in some incredible guests (Charlie Daniels, Junior Johnson, Ricky Skaggs) and has a unique and hilarious interview style. This show may not be for everyone, because not everyone has a sense of humor. Many podcasters can learn a lot from this podcast—just because you can drop the F-bomb and worse on a podcast does not mean you have to.

5 Questions

Greg Demetrick is the host and producer of this show. Greg releases two shows a week. The first one is a short 5-to-10-minute show that gives the five questions for the week and invites listeners to answer them. The second show is the main show, and it runs 35 to 45 minutes in length and consists of answers from listeners and an interview with one specific guest. This show is PG-rated.

"When you look at Blogger or LiveJournal, a lot of people blog there not so much to get their ideas out but to start a conversation with somebody through notes or through comments. I was like, How do we take this concept and apply it to a radio show? For me, the answer was simple: Take the listener out of the position of being a listener and put them in the position of being the content provider. Because what they

have to say is far more interesting than anything I could make up. So
that is really where the idea was born."

—Greg Demetrick, 5 Questions

Small World

Bazooka Joe hosts this podcast where he interviews everyday people. He releases a
new show about six times a week. The length of each episode varies from 15 minutes
to an hour, but most shows fall in the 20-to-30-minute range.

"I talk to people from all walks of life from all over the world, and that
can be dentists, it can be musicians, it can even be drunken sandwich
makers."

—Bazooka Joe, Small World

MadPod

J.A. Donnelly hosts this podcast with help from Shadoe Steele. They feature podsafe
music and rare interviews. The show is released three times a week, and the length of
each episode is 20 to 25 minutes. The show is PG-rated.

"Our show consists of interviews from the past and present. We have
thousands of interviews that we did with celebrities over the past 25
years. And Madpod is conducting new interviews weekly, sometimes
up to seven. We have everybody, except the Beatles and Elvis."

—J.A. Donnelly, MadPod

Asking the Tough Questions

Wichita shows us with his show that an interview can be funny, entertaining, and
informative in just 5 minutes. Bazooka Joe shows us that an interview done well with
good prep work can turn any average everyday person into a fascinating guest. Listen
to these shows and ask yourself, Does the host sound like he or she is interrogating the
guests or does the host sound like he or she is just having fun with the guests? The goal
for any interviewer should be to inform as well as entertain the audience. When you
can do both, you will capture your listeners' attention.

If you're fired up to put together your own interview-based podcast, be sure to check
out Chapter 7.

Music

If you love music, then depending on your age, you either grew up admiring your local DJ or you grew up despising the program director who was forcing your DJ to play the same old Top-40 crap over and over again. The dividing line here seems to be those born before 1970 and those born after. Either way, you always yearned to be the person choosing and playing the coolest and hippest new tunes. With podcasting, you finally have a chance to live that dream. But it is not just about playing someone else's music. If you are in a band, then the one thing you want more than anything else—well, next to partying all night, women (or men), and sleeping late—is exposure for your music. With podcasting, you can create your own "radio station" that not only plays your music, it plays nothing but your music. For all these reasons, it is no wonder that music podcasts are one of the most popular types of podcasts. Even Senator John Edwards has played some music on his podcast. The Association of Music Podcasting (AMP) located at www.musicpodcasting.org is arguably the best place to find good podsafe (no copyright restrictions) music podcasts (see Figure 3.4). Table 3.8 lists some great music podcasts. Each of them has a slightly different niche they are focused on.

FIGURE 3.4

AMP podcasts.

Table 3.8 Popular Music Podcasts

Host(s)	Podcast	Website URL
C.C. Chapman	Accident Hash	accidenthash.podshow.com
Phil Coyne	Bit Jobs for the Masses	www.bitjobs.net
Brian Ibbott	Coverville	www.coverville.com
Dave	Dave's Lounge	www.daveslounge.com
Aaron	Celtic Music News	www.celticmusicnews.com

Accident Hash

C.C. Chapman podcasts out of the Boston area. There are not enough nice things you can say about C.C. He cares deeply about both the independent musician and the independent podcaster. Music.podshow.com comes from this caring (with kudos thrown in for Chris Rockwell and others at Podshow). He releases about 10 shows a month, and they average about 30 minutes per episode. The show is PG-rated.

"Accident Hash I gear towards trying to play the best mix in podsafe music. My music tastes run the gambit. I'll listen to pretty much anything, and I try to do that on Accident Hash. I'll just play a little bit of everything. I definitely lean more towards the alternative rock, and I also really like the mellow acoustic stuff. I have been trying to play more and more. The only rules I have, other than being podsafe, is that I usually don't talk about timely information, I never put a date on the show, and I try to focus more on the music. The goal was that you could listen to it at any time and it would not be tied to a date."

—**C.C. Chapman, Accident Hash**

Bit Jobs for the Masses

Phil Coyne podcasts out of Birmingham in the U.K. and is a member of AMP. He plays some of the very best unsigned bands from the U.K. and beyond, but in addition to playing independent music he has some selective interviews with these musicians. A new show is released every four to five days, with an average length of 30 to 35 minutes per episode. The show is PG-rated.

"It started off really as an experiment. I just wanted to see if I could do it and how it would sound. Initially I had two Top-40 tracks randomly chosen, but then I did some research and found out that was not a good idea to play licensed stuff on your podcast, so that first show was taken down. But then I did some more research and found a site called UKbands.net, which basically has a really big archive of decent unsigned U.K. bands."

—Phil Coyne, Bit Jobs for the Masses

Coverville

Brian Ibbott podcasts out of Arvada, Colorado. His show is focused on playing covers of other songs. The show is released about three times a week and averages about 35 minutes per episode. The show is G-rated.

"Coverville is usually a three-times-a-week show that features cover songs. Rare and unusual, sometimes comical cover songs.... I am definitely a music geek. I collect CDs, I collect rare music. I really like the way a cover song can transform a song that you are totally familiar with into a whole new meaning or give it a whole new veneer. I especially like the cover songs where the covering artist does it in their style to the point where you cannot even recognize it."

—Brian Ibbott, Coverville

Dave's Lounge

Dave podcasts out of Durham, North Carolina and is a proud member of AMP. His show is one of the best-produced music podcasts, offers incredible podsafe music, and is one where you can listen to the same episode over and over. He releases a new show about once a week, and the typical length is 25 minutes per episode. This show is G-rated.

"Dave's Lounge showcases the best in chill out, trip-hop and down-tempo music. Music that you can relax to and chill out to and sometimes nod your head to if a nice groove is going."

—Dave, Dave's Lounge

Celtic Music News

Aaron podcasts out of Georgia. Celtic music is not *all* about drinking, and this podcast showcases the very best Celtic music. He releases one show a week, and they average about 20 to 25 minutes per episode. The show is PG-rated.

 *"You will hear all kinds of different Celtic music. Mainly I do tend to focus on the Celtic rock mix, but you will hear pretty much everything, from things you will hear in **Titanic** or just almost straight-ahead rock and roll with a fiddle mixed in."*

—Aaron, Celtic Music News

Picking a Musical Style

Music podcasts come in all shapes and sizes. Some have the DJ being the central figure; others are nothing but music with a brief introduction of the date and name of the show. Still others are podcasts for bands where a piece of each song is played and then the story about the song is revealed. That is the beauty of podcasting—there is no magical formula created by a computer back at the corporate office in New York or Atlanta. Music podcasts, at least the ones done right, are all about the experience of the listener, and listener number one is the person creating it. If you are doing a music podcast or thinking of doing one, you need to read Chapter 8, "Music—Issues and Sources."

News

Listening to news is a tricky business with podcasting. Considering that the very nature of podcasting allows you to download podcasts and carry them with you to listen to at your leisure, it doesn't seem as if current events would translate well. However, many people get their news—and even weather—from podcasts, keeping up with the shows and putting them at the top of their listening list.

When NPR began podcasting many of its more popular shows, including its news shows, people subscribed. The major television networks followed closely with podcasts of *Meet the Press* (NBC), *Nightline* (ABC), and *Face the Nation* (CBS), as you can see from Figure 3.5.

FIGURE 3.5

The News and Politics: Featured Podcasts from iTunes lists dozens of different news podcasts.

The corporate podcasters have a monopoly on news podcasts, but it is possible to do your own take on the day's current events. Most podcasters prefer to have a political bent to their news podcasts, but there are a few who focus on current events and weather. Table 3.9 lists a few independent news podcasts.

Table 3.9   Independent News Podcasts

Host(s)	Podcast	Website URL
John Wall	The M Show	themshow.libsyn.com
Ed Roberts	KC Weather Podcast	kcweather.blogspot.com
Russell Holliman	Mobilepodcast.org	www.mobilepodcast.org

The M Show

John Wall hosts The M Show out of Boston. This is a great news and entertainment show that is the perfect length to listen to on a short commute or treadmill jaunt. The show is released five to six times a month, with an average length of 10 minutes per episode. The show is G-rated.

"The format is 10 minutes of news, talk, and entertainment. I try to keep it really tight, and I just start in the first 3 or 4 minutes [with] whatever I have seen in the news over the past 4 or 5 days. And it tends to focus more on either business, marketing, or high-tech kind of stuff, but if there are bigger issues in the news, I'll bring in anything that catches my attention. Over in the talk section I try and include just two or three question interviews with either people I know or anybody of note that I can get that I feel like talking to. That has been the biggest challenge, trying to line up people for that segment. In entertainment I try to close with just a minute or two of a book or DVD that I have seen that I can recommend."

—**John Wall, The M Show**

The KC Weather Podcast

The KC Weather Podcast is hosted by a meteorologist Ed Roberts, and was the first weather podcast. The show is released just about every day, and the average length is around 4 minutes per show. The show is G-rated.

"Basically what my podcast is, is weather forecasts for Kansas City. It is very specific, very localized, so as a result you do not get a whole lot of listeners with regards to that, but it is something I love to do."

—**Ed Roberts, The KC Weather Podcast**

Mobilepodcast.org

A more opinionated and sardonic look at the community (called Podcast Island) comes from Russell Holliman of Mobilepodcast.org, who keeps up with current events and gives his own take on them, including predictions on the future of podcasting, both within and without the community. Russell also covers the current events of Houston, TX, as read from the *Houston Chronicle*, a paper for which he has no qualms in showing his disdain.

"Audioblog I suppose is the best way to describe it. I've always said that it is a technical experiment in totally mobile podcast techniques, but that was mainly to deflect all the criticisms of the content.... I have nothing else to talk about. I mean, people talk (or blog) about the

*things they "know"—and although my shrink would argue that I don't
know myself at all, my opinions are my most constant source for material. But what else could I talk about? I am not into music.... I don't
have a female partner to talk dirty with.... The whole "I love the Treo
[smartphone, his original recording setup]" thing has been done to
death.... Why do people blog personally, and why do others read
those blogs?"*

—Russell Holliman, Mobilepodcast.org

Podcasting About Podcasting

There is one area of the news that hosts several independent podcasts, and that's podcasting news. At first, people scoffed at people who podcasted about podcasting, but a
few shows are starting to stand out as entertaining and useful. Perhaps the most popular of these is the Podcheck Review (www.podcheck.com), hosted by Scott Fletcher,
who recounts the happenings in the community.

Politics

Politics has always been the subject that you are either a) supposed to avoid in polite
conversation or b) have extremely strong feelings about and discuss extensively.
Podcasting allows people who fall into the "b" category to do so at their passionate best.

Political podcasts go all over the spectrum, from the Left Wing Nut Job on one end to
Shelley the Republican on the other, to Free Talk Live (a Libertarian talk radio show that
is also given the podcast treatment). Several talk radio shows podcast now, from Air
America to Rush Limbaugh, letting people who might miss their favorite shows at work
listen at their leisure.

Beyond the talk shows, most of the political podcasters are like everyone else—they just
want to air their political views. That includes Senator John Edwards, former U.S. presidential and vice presidential candidate. The senator's podcast was the first podcast from
a nationally known politician (see Figure 3.6), and since his podcast launched in March
of 2005, politicians from both sides of the aisle have also now started podcasting.

Listeners to political podcasts are much like the hungry readers of political blogs. They
are eager for information, but savvy enough to be able to spot when you haven't done
your homework and are speaking from a knee-jerk reaction rather than an informed
opinion. And they will call you on it. Table 3.10 showcases a small sampling of the
diversity available with political podcasts.

FIGURE 3.6
Senator John Edwards' One America Committee website.

Table 3.10   Popular Political Podcasts

Host(s)	Podcast	Website URL
Senator Edwards	One America Committee	www.oneamericacommittee.com
Shelley	Shelley the Republican	www.shelleytherepublican.com
Ian, Manwich, et al.	Free Talk Live	www.freetalklive.com
Thomas Jeffery	Left Wing Nut Job	www.leftwingnutjob.com

One America Committee

Hosted by Senator John Edwards and his wife Elizabeth, this podcast is produced from their home in North Carolina. The senator has been joined by his eldest daughter, Cate, and she even hosted one show from the College Democrats national meeting. The shows are released about two times a month and average about 25 minutes. The shows are G-rated.

"Our podcast is a conversation. Basically what happens is folks from around the country submit questions to us; they submit them on our website. Elizabeth and I sit together and do this: We sit in our dining room and usually put the recording equipment on our son's blanket, which makes it quieter. And sometimes we have our kids running through while we are doing the podcast. What we do is we just sit at the table, we answer the questions, as many of the questions as we can. It is very conversational. Elizabeth participates and we interact with each other. We talk about not only the questions but what is happening in our lives that day and the preceding few weeks, and it has been a really good experience."

—Senator John Edwards, One America Committee

Shelley the Republican

This show is produced by Podshack and is one of the few conservative shows in podcast land. The shows are released three to five times a week, and they average 15 to 30 minutes per episode. The show is PG-rated.

"Shelley the Republican is a political podcast that is not a Godcast. Although I am a Republican, I am not a mouthpiece for the GOP, tackling a wide range of political issues such as Muslim terrorists, world politics, and partisan politics. Some have described the show as an effort to stop the spin machine of the Democratic party and challenge spoon-fed thinkers; listeners will either love me or hate me. No listener is indifferent."

—Shelley, the Republican

Free Talk Live

Free Talk Live is an on-air syndicated talk radio show that is also released as a podcast. The show comes from a Libertarian slant ("Pro-Freedom") and encourages lively conversations from all sides of the political arena. The show is released six days a week with two shows per day. The average length is 38 minutes per episode. This show is G-rated.

Left Wing Nut Job

This is the companion podcast that goes along with the website LeftWingNutJob.com. This show is released between 6 and 12 times a month, with an average length of 5 to 10 minutes per episode. This show is R-rated.

Although you may think that you'll have listeners who prefer the "other side" to whatever you are podcasting about, the truth is that most of your listeners will be of your same political bent, as Thomas Jeffrey of the Left Wing Nut Job discovered.

"A podcast's title and classification will pretty much attract like-minded listeners, which invariably results in a bit of preaching to the choir, but I'm sure in time I'll get some hate mail or some such thing, but for now nothing major."

However, if you turn to podcasting to discuss politics because you do not like arguments and you want to just have a soapbox, remember that your listeners may want to "discuss" an alternate viewpoint with you.

Then again, if you thrive on political discourse, ranging from polite to argumentative, a political podcast may be the perfect thing for you. Thomas loves adopting the persona of the Left Wing Nut Job, podcasting his own views with a sardonic newscaster tone to his voice.

"The passion that you exude in doing something you love is readily apparent to anyone who is listening. Make it fun and interesting for both yourself and your listeners because, at least in the beginning, you're only going to be doing this for yourself until you get some people subscribed. Don't be afraid to limit your focus initially until you get a feel for what you can handle and then feel free to change or augment your show to polish it. Political opinion is as diverse as there are people on the planet, so you'll undoubtedly find like-minded people who are willing to tune in. Most likely they will be appreciative of you voicing the same opinions that they share and providing an outlet for those opinions."

—Thomas Jeffrey, The Left Wing Nut Job

Radio Dramas

The surprising thing about radio dramas is that there are not more of them. Seeing as podcasting is an obvious vehicle to bring back the nearly dead art form of radio plays, you'd assume there would be more, but there are only a handful of dramas.

Perhaps more people haven't gotten into audio dramas because it is quite production-intensive, much more so than regular podcasts. You need more than simply a microphone and a computer; you will need background sounds, possibly music, more than one microphone (which means also getting a mixer), more than one voice, and a writer to keep the serial going. Very few podcasts have this level of production, so radio dramas still struggle as an art form. Table 3.11 lists two of the most popular radio drama podcasts.

Table 3.11   Popular Radio Dramas

Host(s)	Podcast	Website URL
Grant and Doug	The Radio Adventures of Dr. Floyd	www.doctorfloyd.com
Andy Doan	Spaceship Radio	www.spaceshipradio.com

The Radio Adventures of Dr. Floyd

Created by Grant Baciocco and Doug Price, this show is the clear favorite of radio dramas. The Radio Adventures of Dr. Floyd is a serial drama about a time-traveling adventure told in 5-minute weekly shows. It is a G-rated comedy with enough pop culture jokes to keep the parents laughing while amusing the kids with Dr. Floyd's pursuit of the evil Dr. Steve.

Spaceship Radio

From what sounds like a broadcast straight out of the golden era of radio, this show is actually hosted today by Andy Doan. At first taking old sci-fi radio shows and releasing them over podcast, he then made a call for scripts from writers, wanting to record and release original sci-fi radio dramas. The show is released about six to eight times a month. The average length is 30 minutes per episode. The show is G-rated.

"My show is a journey back to a time when people realized that the best special effects are created inside the mind. When writers had to rely on their skills as storytellers to encourage the imaginations of

the audience. What I'm hoping to create is a bit of a renaissance movement. The old radio plays that I present are timeless, yet we have left them in the past. It's my dream to bring this type of intelligent entertainment back to the forefront in our culture, through the inspiration of new creative minds."

—Andy Doan, Spaceship Radio

Finding a Niche

The good news about the lack of dramas is that there is a niche to be filled. Dr. Floyd is incredibly popular, but there is room for more radio dramas if you have the itch to create a serial drama. The startup costs are substantially higher, but there are undoubtedly listeners who are hungry for more dramas and would pounce on a well-done podcast.

One thing to keep in mind is that even though you can find CDs of sound effects, they *are* copyrighted like music. So you will either need to procure permission to use the sound effects, find free sounds, or record your own. If your podcast drama is going to be an everyday drama with door slams and cars driving off, you can probably do this all yourself. If you're going to need spaceship theremin sounds, that will be more difficult.

One of the best sites for free sound effects is the Freesound Project at http://freesound.iua.upf.edu/index.php This is a site with user uploaded and created sounds that are Creative Commons licensed so that everyone can make use of them.

Q-Podders

Q-Podders is a community of gay, lesbian, bisexual, and transgendered (GLBT) podcasts and those who are friends of the GLBT community. Table 3.12 lists of some of the podcasts from www.qpodder.org.

Table 3.12   Popular Q-Podder Podcasts

Host(s)	Podcast	Website URL
Madge Weinstein	Yeast Radio	yeastradio.podshow.com
John Ong	Ongline	www.johnong.com/ongline/
Wanda Wisdom	Lucky Bitch Radio	www.luckybitchradio.com/

Yeast Radio

This show is hosted out of Chicago by the ever-flamboyant and always opinionated Madge Weinstein. One of the first members of Podshow, this is a show that is often political and always entertaining. The show is released about five times a week and varies in length from 20 minutes to an hour per episode. This show is X-rated.

"I provide an example of what you can do in podcasting that you can not or at least has not been done in traditional media. In that I create a show where I just do whatever the [heck] I want. So it's not anything [specific], I don't have to apply a label. I don't have to be the Howard Stern of this or the Joan Rivers of that. Because one day I can be toilet humor and just [a] disgusting misogynist pig and then the next day I can have an interview with somebody like Kent Bye and talk about the media…. It is completely boundless. Just like podcasting, you can do absolutely whatever you want. I don't really feel like I have to be defined in any way at all."

—Madge Weinstein, Yeast Radio

Ongline

Hosted by John Ong, this show is produced in Kansas City. This is the audioblog of John's life as a gay minority in the United States. He releases about two to three shows a week, and the average is 30 to 40 minutes in length per episode. The show is X-rated.

"Ongline podcast is a series of audio documentations of the life of a Malaysian-born Chinese who lives in the United States. Immerse yourself in the life of a not-so-typical individual. Expand your horizon by experiencing the topics, issues, stories, and simply, the life of a gay Asian man. Until now, the voice of a minority individual has not been this loud!"

—John Ong, Ongline

Lucky Bitch Radio

This show is hosted by Minneapolis drag queen Wanda Wisdom. Wanda will take you "on a journey of self-discovery, the likes of which you'll never forget." New shows are released about four to five times a week, and they have a length that varies between 20 and 90 minutes per episode. The shows are X-rated.

"[The show] is an opportunity for me to get honest with myself and to share my crazy side with other people. I talk about what is going on in my life. It may not seem that unique, but I tell you the act of sitting down and sharing in an honest way what's going on in my head with total strangers, clear across the world, seems to resonate somewhere. Because I don't try to be something I am not. I just try to be me and I know a lot of people who listen relate to what I go through.... I think really the beauty is I am not trying to be anything other than essentially who I am."

—**Wanda Wisdom, Lucky Bitch Radio**

The Makings of a Q-Podder

Q-Podder podcasts are about many different subjects, from the arts and entertainment industry, to couple casts, to others that are unique unto themselves. If you belong to the GLBT community or you have a podcast that you think fits with this community, you should check out www.qpodder.org.

Sci-Fi

Science fiction podcasts are some of the most omnipresent podcasts. Most of the popular podcasts started early in the lifespan of podcasting and have a loyal following. The reasoning seems obvious: Early adopters of most technologies are the kinds of geeks who enjoy sci-fi in the first place. Thus, they flock to the discussions of their genre.

Science fiction is one of the most varied genres of podcasting. From discussions on movies and comic books to dramatic presentations of fiction to advice for hopeful movie producers and writers, those who are passionate about speculative fiction have a lot to say, with a lot of people listening.

You only have to attend a sci-fi convention to realize that there are countless podcasting opportunities for sci-fi podcasts. With all the movies, TV shows, books, games, and comics that exist, there is something for everyone. And, like all the topics covered in

> **NOTE** The popular Escape Pod podcast is covered in the "The Written Word" section, later in this chapter, but could have just as easily been included here instead.

this book, if you find something missing, then perhaps that shows you what your podcast topic should be. Table 3.13 includes a small but diverse list of podcasts that are available, along with information on The Sci-Fi Podcast Network (see Figure 3.7).

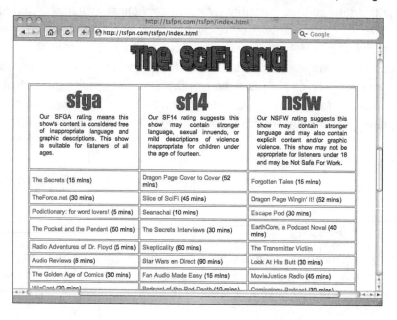

FIGURE 3.7

A listing of shows on The Sci-Fi Podcast Network.

Table 3.13   Popular Sci-Fi Podcasts

Host(s)	Podcast	Website URL
Tee Morris	Morevi: The Chronicles of Rafe and Askana	www.teemorris.com/podcast
Les, Kari, et al.	The Signal	signal.serenityfirefly.com
Michael and Evo	The Dragon Page	www.dragonpage.com
Multiple	Sci-Fi Podcast Network	www.tsfpn.com

Morevi: The Chronicles of Rafe and Askana

Tee Morris hosts and narrates one of the first sci-fi novels to be offered as a podcast, the abridged version of the book he co-authored, *Morevi: The Chronicles of Rafe and Askana*. This podcast is PG-rated.

*"I think the podcast for authors is a wonderful way for promotion and a wonderful, wonderful way of distribution, and also a great way to promote yourself to other publishers in case they are looking for something new. The idea for this came from when I was listening to the Dragon Page and my publisher around the same time said, 'Tee I want you to start thinking about innovative ways of promoting **Legacy of Morevi**,' which is the sequel to **Morevi**. And at that time I was already toying around the idea in my head of doing a podcast of **Morevi**. And I said, 'Here is my idea, what do you think?' And she gave me full permission to do it."*

—Tee Morris, Morevi: The Chronicles of Rafe and Askana

The Signal

This show is hosted by Les and Kari, with major help from a large team of guest contributors. The show's peak was just prior to and during the launch of the movie *Serenity*. They were able to show the power of a grassroots movement through podcasting. The show is released about once every 2 weeks and has an average length of about 1 hour per episode. The show is PG-rated.

*"The Signal is a fan-driven podcast that specifically is working as hard as it can to drum up publicity for the movie **Serenity**. So basically all we talk about is anything that is related to the movie and the [TV] show **Firefly**. The idea for The Signal actually started on one of the **Firefly** guerilla marketing forums; that is where we got our genesis. And we all just really like exploring the **Firefly** universe and things about it. And really the motto of The Signal and our purpose of being out there is to do whatever we can to see that more new **Firefly** is created in any format."*

—Les and Kari, The Signal

The Dragon Page

Michael R. Mennenga and Evo Terra, hosts of The Dragon Page, had two radio shows from their Arizona studios: one local call-in show and one nationally syndicated show that covers interviews with sci-fi authors. They began podcasting both shows in early

October of 2004, which were early hits. After their live show was cancelled by the local radio station, they launched two more podcasts: Dragon Page Wingin' It, a variety show where they drink beer and introduce essays, stories, drama, poetry, and so on, that their listeners submit, and Slice of Sci-Fi, which had the audience backing of the *Star Trek* fandom. Although Slice of Sci-Fi (covered in depth in Chapter 1, "A Brief History of Podcasting") has by far the largest audience, a good many of their listeners are subscribed to all three shows through one feed. They've done much for the community, bringing in other genre podcasters and helping to promote several more.

The Sci-Fi Podcast Network

The Sci-Fi Podcast Network (TSFPN) launched in June 2005 in an attempt to bring all the best sci-fi programming together. Michael A. Stackpole, popular sci-fi/fantasy author and host of the instructional writing podcast, The Secrets (www.stormwolf.com/thesecrets/podcasts/), and writer Kat Klayborne put the network together. They welcome movie discussion, fiction presentation, dramatic presentation, and anything that touches on the spirit of the network. If you create a sci-fi podcast, this network is an excellent place to affiliate yourself with.

*"When I started registering my podcast, The Secrets, I realized that every directory had a different system for categorizing things. The Secrets would be under SF because I'm an SF author, or Education, or Arts & Entertainment, or Audiobooks. As I was looking around I saw content that would be of interest to SF fans likewise scattered around. I decided we needed one place that collected that content. Moreover, we needed a directory that filtered for content. This is why TSFPN and all of the networks under the Podcast Entertainment Network umbrella are **elite** directories. We don't take all comers. We have minimum standards that everyone has to hit before we take them on. This way, anyone who comes to one of our directories knows that they're getting a high-quality, entertaining podcast, not just something chucked together with a bargain-bin microphone, no editing, and crappy sound or content."*

—Michael A. Stackpole, The Sci-Fi Podcast Network

Making of a Sci-Fi Podcast

Sci-fi podcasts are usually longer in nature, spanning around 1 hour. Like sci-fi fans, they reflect strong opinions and encourage community building. Most sci-fi podcasts have forums associated with them, encouraging their listeners to continue the discussion online.

Sci-fi podcasts have been innovative in that they were the first type of podcast to present the reading of original fiction material. The first three books serialized through podcast were all sci-fi in nature.

Sex

*"The title for my show says a lot about why I started podcasting in the first place; at the time I started out, podcasting was just beginning (and there were few women on the playing field), but I could tell that if it caught on the way I thought it would, then we'd have one of the most democratic, accessible audio mediums on our hands **in history**. And that's also something that has been missing from my line of work, sex education: democratic dissemination of accurate sex information. And of course, user input. Thus, Open Source Sex."*

—Violet Blue, Open Source Sex (see Figure 3.8)

FIGURE 3.8

Enter if you are over 18 screen shot from Violet Blue's website.

On one end of the podcasting spectrum there are the Godcasts, and on the other end is audio erotica or sex casts. The beauty of podcasting is that if either one of these groups offends someone, that person has the choice to simply not subscribe. Podcasting is a pull technology that is not censored by anyone. So frank and candid discussions that are often needed with subjects revolving around sex are openly embraced with podcasting.

As with most genres in podcasting, the variety of offerings is very diverse, with some sex podcasts bordering on comical (although they may not have intended for that to be the case) and others that are nothing more than a marketing tool to shill a book. But there are also some very well produced and thought out shows, such as those listed in Table 3.14, that have managed to capture their audience's attention and loyalty. Each of these shows approaches sex from a slightly different perspective. Some emphasize the sexuality of the host(s), others try to educate about sex, and others use erotica to stimulate their audience or do some combination there of. With podcasting, these hosts are able to talk about the things that Dr. Ruth had only dreamed about saying.

Table 3.14   Popular Sex Podcasts

Host(s)	Podcast	Website URL
Soccergirl and Ryan	Soccergirl, Inc.	soccergirl.podshow.com
Violet Blue	Open Source Sex	www.tinynibbles.com
Emily	Sex with Emily	www.sexwithemily.com
Missy and Bee	Suicide Girls	www.suicidegirls.com

Soccergirl, Inc.

Hosted by Soccergirl and often joined by her boyfriend Ryan, this podcast originates from their home in upstate New York. She releases about 10 shows a month, and they average about 30 minutes in length. This show is X-rated.

"It's comedy and a little bit political, and obviously I am very comfortable with nudity and I am very attached to my sexuality and my freedoms. And we have a very eventful sexual life together, and I am really happy about it. I feel that the taboo that surrounds sexuality and especially female sexuality is just silly, and it is unacceptable and I don't think that there is any reason why I should not feel comfortable putting myself out there, so that is a lot of what it is."

—Soccergirl, Soccergirl, Inc.

Open Source Sex

Hosted by Violet Blue, Open Source Sex is the podcast for her Tiny Nibbles website. The typical length of an episode is 20 to 30 minutes, and new shows are released one to three times a month. But they are so worth the wait. Wikipedia described Violet as "an American sex writer, podcaster, blogger, editor, and sex educator." This show is X-rated.

"I have no set format for Open Source Sex, no future plans except to not get bored (or let listeners get bored). I try to keep each show's content unique while staying on topic (sex) within a range of entertainment, titillation, education, and fun. This means I do everything from read erotica and present lectures on taboo sex topics to interviewing porn stars and sperm bank workers. As long as it's hot and fun, and it seems like there's an interest in the material in the wider culture (like threesomes or fetishes), it's fair game.

"What has made my show remarkable for many people is that it's not like any other sex content they've encountered: people are so used to having to settle for bad porn, having their intelligence insulted, having their sexual interests made fun of, or all the usual stereotypes. I think people are a lot more sexually sophisticated than the media considers them to be, and in my podcast I talk about sex with them like we're friends investigating or playing with something really cool. I also think that most of the homophobia, judgmentalism, racism, and male/female sex stereotyping is an irritatingly antiquated thing to include with sex, and I'm over it."

—Violet Blue, Open Source Sex

Sex with Emily

Hosted by Emily, this podcast has the tag line "Saving the world one orgasm at a time." This show is released between one and four times a month, and the typical length of an episode is 30 minutes. The show is X-rated.

"Sex with Emily is a talk radio podcast show about sex and relationships hosted by a 30-something single woman living in San Francisco. The show features not only experts but "real" people sharing the intimate details of their relationships—in and out of the bedroom. Our

goal is to "save the world one orgasm at a time" because who isn't having a better life when they're having honest, open, and (hopefully) mind-blowing sex?"

—Emily, Sex with Emily

Suicide Girls

Hosted by Missy and Bee, this podcast is a rebroadcast of their Sunday night show on 103.1 FM in Los Angeles. This show is released once a week, and the typical length of an episode is 80 to 90 minutes. The show is NC–17-rated.

Keeping It Fresh

An often-quoted marketing report stated that sex- and erotica-based podcasts are the most popular types of podcast. However, that report was hugely flawed in that it took its stats from one of the smaller directories. The truth is, sex sells, but podcasts are free, so for the most part the porn industry has stayed out of audio podcasting. There is, however, a very large male podcasting audience that has found favor with a few well-produced podcasts revolving around sex, and they will be willing to listen to others if they are also well produced and have some real content. We started this section with a quote from Violet Blue, so it is only fitting we end this section with some advice from her as well.

"My overall recommendation for podcasters is this: don't get bored or do something that might get you stuck in a rut. Listeners can tell when you're going through the motions, and because podcasting is a listener-driven market, they can just go elsewhere. Don't be afraid to break your own rules — listeners really enjoy the immediacy of podcasting, so if you do something unplanned, they'll love it. Also, don't fall back on a gimmick: a girl podcasting naked is interesting for just about a minute — unless what she's saying is really cool, funny, shocking, sexy, or enlightening. Then she's interesting for a lot longer."

—Violet Blue, Open Source Sex

Sports

We mention multiple times in this book to podcast about something you are passionate about. And with the possible exception of Mac-heads, no one group is more passionate about their hobby than sports fans. After all, *fan* is short for *fanatic*. This is evident in the sports podcasts that are out there. One great place to locate a wide variety of quality sports podcasts is at the My Sports Radio podcast network (www.mysportsradio.com). One of the things you will notice with many sports podcasts is that they are often-times "buddy casts," where you have two or more buddies (and Budweisers) sitting around and bantering back and forth about sports. Table 3.15 provides a small sampling of some of the best sports podcasts, and you would be well advised if you are doing or thinking of doing a sports podcast to check these out.

Table 3.15 Popular Sports Podcasts

Host(s)	Podcast	Website URL
Multiple	My Sports Radio Network	www.mysportsradio.com
Andy and Matt	The Skinny on Sports	skinnyonsports.podshow.com
Dave and John	RaiderCast	www.theraidercast.com
Scott and Steve	Extra Points	www.extra-points.com

My Sports Radio Network

Sam Coutin has put together one of the best sports podcast networks. MySportsRadio.com (MSR) is a not just a podcast network, it is also a sports content production company. MSR has created a community where listeners interact with podcast hosts on a daily basis. MSR's mission is "to produce and broadcast the largest catalogue of quality sports radio programming for the most interactive sports community on the planet." Founded in December 2004, MSR has more than 500,000 downloads of the shows on its network every month.

 "Digital music distribution shook up the music industry and leveled the playing field in the music industry because music fans chose file-sharing of MP3s as a prominent method of music acquisition and consumption. Similarly, sports fans are thirsty for a different content consumption model—one that satisfies their craving for an edgy,

*bite-sized, Tivo-like listening experience. MSR strives to satisfy that
thirst with a healthy catalogue of quality, niche, sports podcasts supported by a tight-knit community of sports fans."*

—Sam Coutin, My Sports Radio Network

The Skinny on Sports

Hosted by brothers Andy and Matt Skinn, The Skinny on Sports is one of the founding
podcasts on the Podshow network. They release about 6 to 10 shows a month, and a
typical show runs about 10 minutes in length.

*"The Skinny on Sports is the fastest 10 minutes on your iPod and the
sports stories that matter! Each week, Andy and Matt Skinn (The
Skinnies) take a look at the biggest stories and issues in the world of
sports. Rather than simply reporting on the outcomes of various sporting events, we express our opinions and dig deeper into the stories.
We keep you up to date on the biggest news in the world of sports
and give you the information you need to form your own opinion and
sound knowledgeable with your friends. You'll always have 'The
Skinny'!"*

—Andy Skinn, The Skinny on Sports

RaiderCast

Hosted by Dave and John with help from Shawn and Jodi, this fearsome foursome produce what is clearly one of the best pro sports team fan-based podcasts. They release
two to three shows a week during the season and offer a slightly less frequent release
schedule in the off-season. The shows average 30 to 40 minutes in length per episode.
The show is PG-rated.

*"Our show is about the Oakland Raiders through the eyes of the fan.
When we first started this show, we wanted to create a place for all
the good Raider fans to express how they feel about their team. It has
turned out to be a place for fans to vent, musicians to play Raider
music, and a place to get up-to-date information from the players
and coaches. It also has become a place for fans to find out about*

upcoming Raider events that they would have never known about before. It is a lot of work keeping up with all the events, but that is where you meet the people and we wouldn't have it any other way....

"To start a team cast like ours, you have to be involved. Go to signings, go to camp, go to all the games, but most important get out there and talk to the fans. Make your fans feel important; appreciate their opinion whether you agree or not. Offer the fans many avenues to talk to you (emails, voicemails, face-to-face meetings). They are what is important. One other thing that helps is, go where the team is and keep letting them know who you are then they will start being available more (or at least we hope). Share links with all the other fan websites. The more people who know about you, the better. Last, but definitely not least, get out and cross-promote. Meet great people like yourself [Rob] and Keith and the Girl."

—Dave, RaiderCast

Extra Points

Hosted by Scott and Steve, this podcast is from New England. Shows are released weekly, and the typical length of an episode is about 40 minutes. This show is PG-rated.

"Every week, we break down the important fantasy football news... and answer listener questions for advice with their fantasy football teams. If you're looking to conquer your league, salvage your season, or just figure out what the big deal is about this fantasy football thing, Extra Points is the show for you!"

—Scott and Steve, Extra Points

No League Is Too Small

The world of podcasting includes numerous podcasts about specific sports, sport teams, and celebrity athletes. But you do not have to limit your podcast to professional, college, or major high school athletics; you can just as easily podcast about the local rugby club. Granted, a podcast about the Johnson County Sundogs may not bring in thousands (or even hundreds) of listeners, but for all the current and past Ruggers, they will find it very relevant. Or maybe you want to do a podcast on the Bayport/Bluepoint Little League, where each show you wrap up the scores from the past week and interview the MVP for each age group. Hey, instead of yelling at your child's coach now, you can interview him, and as the late Billy Martin would have told you, nothing is worse than facing the press.

Tech Podcasts

Not surprisingly, one of the most popular genres in podcasting is technology-focused shows. After all, anyone creating a podcast is already pretty comfortable with tech, and most of the early listeners of podcasts were also very tech savvy. Over time, there will be more "flashing 12's" listening to and creating podcasts. But there will always be a hungry base of listeners eager to hear about the latest in tech news and development. Table 3.16 offers a small and diverse sampling of what is out there in the way of tech podcasts—from PC focused to Mac focused, to all tech issues in general to tech issues for teenagers, or to those interested in digital photography. The variety of tech podcasts is vast.

Table 3.16   Popular Technology Podcasts

Host(s)	Podcast	Website URL
Victor Cajiao	Typical PC User	www.typicalpcuser.com
Christopher	Tech4GenY	www.tech4geny.com
Leo and friends	This Week in Tech	www.thisweekintech.com
Adam	MacCast	www.maccast.com

Typical PC User

Victor Cajiao hosts this podcast from California. Like his tag line, "help for the rest of us," states, this is a podcast where the typical PC user can come to learn about new ideas and to share and hopefully get answers for his or her problems. Victor is a friendly host, and you can really feel his passion for his listeners. The show is released about three times a week, and the average length is 30 minutes per episode. The show is G-rated.

 "I had a 70-year-old aunt of mine, who had never used a computer as of January of 2005. We gave her an old computer and I got her an Internet connection. She loves Morgan horses. I spent 3 hours one

afternoon just showing her what was available on the Internet around Morgan horses. And I saw this woman's face light up in a way I had never seen before, and at that moment between that and listening to some podcasts, I said, you know if I can do that for some other people who are not the über geeks, where I can bring them to a show where they can learn the basics and then also do some intermediate stuff, I think I can get my heart into that. And to me that is the first thing for podcasting—you have to have heart for it before you can have brains for it."

—**Victor Cajiao, Typical PC User**

Tech4GenY

Christopher produces this podcast out of New York City. Not all podcasters have to be between the ages of 30 and 44, and Christopher proves that by podcasting while he is still in high school. He is normally joined by a cast of other teenage podcasters, or he is out interviewing the biggest names in technology. Additional hosts include Alexander, Anthony, Eugene, Jack, and Mike. This show is released about once a week, and the typical length varies from 15 minutes to 1 hour. The show is PG-rated.

*"The focus was that [we] would deliver tech news from the younger generation with punditry. It is basically the younger voice.... We are kind of like a kid show on **The Screen Savers**."*

—**Christopher, Tech4GenY**

This Week in Tech

Hosted by Leo Laporte of TechTV/ZDTV fame, and joined with a cast comprised of the who's who in TechTV reporting, this show is released every Sunday at midnight, because that is basically the only time the Internet can handle the strain of all their loyal listeners downloading the show at once. The typical length of the show is 1 hour per episode. The show is G-rated.

MacCast

Adam Christianson has one of the most popular Mac podcasts, with a loyal audience of well over 12,000 subscribers. If you are at all interested in the Mac platform, then this is a must-listen-to podcast. Six to eight shows are released every month, with an average length varying from 30 minutes to 1 hour. The show is G-rated.

"The MacCast [is] for Mac geeks by Mac geeks. It's pretty much an every-Mac-user-type show. I actually have a lot of PC users, and a lot of new switchers. Some of them were thinking it was going to be very technical with the geek term. That it was going to be over their head, and [they] got to listening to it and realized it really [was not over their head]. I kind of cover all ends of the spectrum, and when I do get really technical I try and make sure that I explain to other parts of the audience what I am talking about, so that people don't get lost, but not try and talk down to them in a way that the more tech-savvy guys are bored."

—**Adam Christianson, MacCast**

Thriving as a Tech Podcaster

Ninety-nine percent of people who podcast will never reach the size audience that Leo Laporte has been able to reach with TWiT. If that fact bothers you, then you should give serious thought to why you're podcasting to begin with. Victor articulated it very well when he said that you have to have heart for a subject before you can have brains for it. There is plenty of room for additional RSS feeds in the tech genre; you just need to make sure that the subject you decide to podcast on is something you would want to subscribe to yourself.

The Written Word

Although most podcasts are original material of the podcaster, only a few hosts actually choose to read their own writing in podcast form. This is beyond just writing a script for the podcast; considerable work must go into the production, reading, and sometimes even sound effects. This area goes into reading your own essays, stories, or even novels (see Figure 3.9).

We cover the detailed reasons for and history of podcasting one's writing later in the book in Chapter 9, "The Audible Written Word," but for now we'll just discuss those writing podcasts listed in Table 3.17.

FIGURE 3.9

Scott Sigler's website for Earthcore and Ancestor is much more than just a site dedicated to promoting his books.

Table 3.17   Popular Writing Podcasts

Host(s)	Podcast	Website URL
Scott Sigler	*Earthcore, Ancestor* and *Infection*	www.scottsigler.net
Mur Lafferty	Geek Fu Action Grip	www.geekfuactiongrip.com
Paul S. Jenkins	The Rev Up Review	www.rev-up-review.co.uk

Earthcore, Ancestor, and Infection

Author Scott Sigler was the first person to podcast a story that had not seen publication elsewhere. His novel *Earthcore* rocked the podcast world, an adventure/sci-fi novel that held nearly 10,000 listeners entranced through the half-year production. He followed it up by reading *Ancestor*, his second podcasted novel, and then his third, *Infection*.

Geek Fu Action Grip

Mur Lafferty (co-author of this book) was a writer who was unable to find an outlet for her essays that focused mostly on her geeky lifestyle. Most essay outlets were not interested in her view of the world through *Star Wars*–colored glasses, so she decided to start podcasting her essays in December 2004.

*"Geek Fu is part audioblog and part game or comic review podcast, with an essay thrown in at the end. It's usually covering something geeky like how it is extremely odd to be pregnant when you're a sci-fi fan and all you can think about is **Alien** and the radiation-inspired sci-fi of the '40s, but I've branched the essays into whatever is on my mind, including how it was surprising that liberals lashed out against each other after the 2004 elections. I have even branched out into podcasting my own fiction. My listeners are very involved with the podcast, and lately I've been featuring guest essays."*

—**Mur Lafferty, Geek Fu Action Grip**

The Rev-Up Review

Paul S. Jenkins has a well-thought-out podcast that features everything from his review of the latest sci-fi (either on page or screen) to pod-safe music. His views are polite, honest, and unapologetic of the things he sees and reads, from the newest Hollywood movie to the latest serialized fiction from other podcasters. Each podcast ends with a piece of his original fiction.

"I read speculative fiction, and I also write it. I continue to include my own fiction in The Rev-Up Review because I feel it adds value and variety to the show, and it gives listeners some insight into my preferences as a reviewer. It also reminds them that I'm a writer, which is one of the essential purposes behind the show. It may sometimes be blatant, and sometimes subtle, but The Rev-Up Review is a vehicle for promoting myself as a writer, while at the same time providing useful, engaging content. The fiction installments create continuity from one show to the next, encouraging listeners to stay subscribed."

—**Paul S. Jenkins, The Rev-Up Review**

The Microphone Is Mightier Than the Sword

The number of people recording and releasing their writing via podcast has grown greatly (well, like podcasting has in general). Authors are getting more comfortable with releasing their work, in part due to the Creative Commons License (see Appendix B, "Creative Commons Explained"). Professional authors such as Cory Doctorow and James Patrick Kelly are also getting involved, paving the way for more professionals to give away their work via podcast for greater gain in the long run. We discuss this topic more in Chapter 9.

Others Genres

Frankly, the list of other genres of podcasts goes on and on. If you're feeling particularly inspired (and lucky), you might even successfully create a new genre with your podcast.

We could go on for quite some time with the many different types of podcasts available. But we won't. There are so many different, unique and talented people podcasting that new subjects are popping up daily. If you did not see a podcast that is similar to the one you do, then consider yourself lucky because you likely have a good niche for yourself. And just because you do see one that is similar to what you want to do, it does not mean you have to change. After all, *Bewitched* inspired *I Dream of Jeannie*, and *The Addams Family* inspired *The Munsters*. Think about what a loss it would be not to have *I Dream of Jeannie* and *The Munsters*.

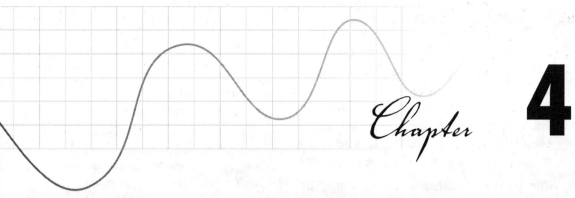

Chapter 4

FINDING YOUR PASSION

"The first edition of The Rev Up Review was entirely experimental. I'd had my iPod for two weeks, and had been listening to podcasts for less than a month. But I thought, "I could do this, let's give it a try." So I put everything into that first show: me rambling on, sound effects, a Skype call, some sound-seeing. And to finish off I read some of my fiction."

—Paul S. Jenkins, The Rev Up Review

Why Passion Matters

Whether you're a new podcaster with high hopes or a veteran who wants to polish tarnished subscriber numbers, the same rule applies: You must podcast what you are passionate about. Choose a topic you love. If you're already podcasting, switch gears. It's better to lose listeners because of a voluntary change toward a direction you're passionate about than to lose them because your interest (and therefore your podcast) has gone stale. In the first case, you'll undoubtedly attract new listeners; in the second case, you'll just keep losing them. If you don't podcast about something you are passionate about, your podcast will crash and burn.

Before you set yourself in front of your mic, sit down and think. What are you passionate about? Seems like a silly question—you know what you're passionate about, of course. However, can your passion sustain a podcast that will go on for (hopefully) years?

The podcasting team that makes up The Signal, a podcast dedicated to the cancelled TV show *Firefly* and its movie, *Serenity*, had a finite number of shows planned. The TV show died after 15 episodes, despite a rabid cult following, so the discussion topics were limited to those episodes and the movie. The podcast ran as a marketing technique (independent from the movie studio) for the movie, and ended after the movie was released. The following was so intense that the podcasting team planned a second season, but—and this is the important part—they took some months off to plan the content.

> ### The Burned and Battle-worn Podcast
>
> When Mur decided to podcast, she toyed with the idea of doing a cooking podcast, as cooking is a hobby of hers. It is not, however, an incredibly passionate hobby. She had set up a gmail account for the podcast, recorded the first one (thankfully lost to the recycle bin), and realized immediately that it was halting and poor. She honestly had no idea what she would podcast about in the area of food. Her heart just wasn't in it. What she was passionate about was her writing and her geek identity. So that's what she podcasted about, her passion shone through, and she got listeners who shared in her passion.

The Signal is a perfect example of people acknowledging that their passion has limits. If your passion is the NFL, then you are assured limitless topics. If your passion is the career of Lawrence Taylor from the New York Giants, then you might want to present it as a podcast in three or so parts and then call it a day or move on to another topic.

Regardless, examine your passion to discover whether it has legs. And don't discount something you think might not appeal to the public at large. The Knitcast (www.knitcast.com) is simply a podcast about knitting, but it has an impressive following. There are people at home with fringe hobbies who lack entertainment or information centering on their hobby, except for perhaps an expensive quarterly magazine. If you make a podcast about it, these people will come.

So find your passion. Look at your hobbies, what you read, what you watch, what excites you. Search for that passion on one of the many directories online and see what's already out there. Listen to the podcasts. Are they missing anything you'd like to see discussed about the topic? Is it something you can talk about? Find the holes that need to be filled. If there's something you want to hear about, it's likely someone out there wants to hear it too. Is someone not presenting your political point of view? Is your favorite sports team not represented? Are people completely ignoring your hobby? And if not, are they ignoring your favorite part of it?

Think about your likes—or even your dislikes—and think of all the things associated with them. You can use the time-honored bubble method here (see Figure 4.1). Write your topic down on a piece of paper and then draw several lines out from it. Each of the lines should point to another subtopic.

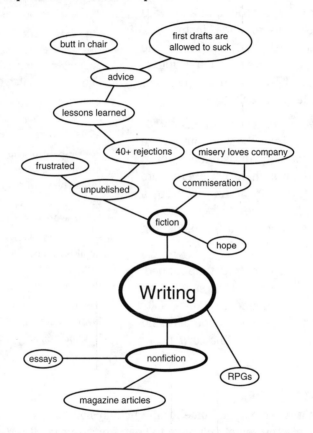

FIGURE 4.1

An example of using the bubble method to illustrate the podcast I Should Be Writing.

For example, you could say your passion is gardening. But gardening encompasses an entire range of topics, so what aspect of gardening do you enjoy? Maybe you like orchids, tomatoes, Venus fly traps, azaleas, pyracanthas, petunias, forget-me-nots, and bonsai. You could have a general gardening show, focusing on each of those topics for one or two shows each. This gives you 16 show topics right from the start.

On the other hand, someone may already be doing that, and you think they do it better than you ever could. Or it may happen that one of those subcategories really entrances you. Either way, you can form a highly focused podcast based on just one plant. Your tomato (or vegetables in general) podcast can start in the early spring and go through the growing season, and afterward you can discuss preservation techniques, planning for the next year, or even go into history, anecdotes, or, heck, take a couple of months off. Most TV shows don't go every week, you can take a break, too.

You can use your podcast to interact with your audience, inviting them to join you in your passion. Instruct your listeners to each buy an orchid from a chain hardware store and teach them how to nurture it, using a blog or mailing list to keep up with the listeners' progress. (More on using blogs and mailing lists later in the book.)

Of course, you don't want to get too refined. If you take more subcategories, such as an entire podcast built around the foods a fly trap will and will not eat, then you may find you've podcasted yourself into a corner.

> ### Possible Passions to Podcast
>
> Here's just a handful of subjects and some subcategories within them that you might feel compelled to podcast about:
>
> - **Exercise**—Hints on your chosen exercise, weight loss tips, a training audioblog, professional sports information or commentary, and so on.
> - **Cooking**—Recipes, history, hints, focus on one food, following festivals or state fairs for award winners, and so on.
> - **Your job**—Not your job in particular, but the kind of work you do, your career, news within the world of what you do, tips on how to get into your line of work, and so on.
> - **Family discussions**—Again, not your family's info personally, but tips on child raising, spousal communication, dealing with familial stress, and so on.
> - **Books**—Your favorite authors, your favorite genre, book reviews, industry information, and so on.
>
> See Chapter 3 for more ideas.

Passion Pitfalls

Don't you hate it when you go home for the holidays and you know that, for whatever reason, you have some secret you have to keep from your family? You don't want your grandmother knowing you're dating someone outside your faith. You don't want your mom to see your tattoo. You, a Red Sox fan, can't discuss baseball with your uncle, a Yankees fan. Or you have an even worse secret?

Issues like this don't just come up with your family. You may refrain from discussing politics, sex, sports, or whatever appeals to your particularly nonaverage sense of humor with people for myriad reasons.

We can say whatever we like on podcasts (within legal reason—more on this in Chapter 6, "Your 'Script'"). We may forget that even though the government can't come after us, we can still get into trouble with our family, our spouse, our minister/priest/rabbi, or someone else we hadn't even considered.

Understand that we're not telling you to be all goody-two-shoes and make friendly, nonoffensive podcasts. You can tell that many people have succeeded admirably in making podcasts that are decidedly *not* sunny skies and fluffy bunnies. Howard Stern became a household name for his off-color radio shows. But there are dangers.

Nate Fulmer of The Nate and Di Show (www.nateanddi.com, see Figure 4.2) discovered this when he and Di podcasted a skit where they were in a church, making fun of the sermon. Two days later he was fired (mind you, Nate never mentioned where he worked or even what type of company he worked for). The infamous "Episode 5" was never mentioned, but since a vice president of the company had prayed over Nate during a lunch a couple of weeks before, Nate had a pretty good idea that their podcast was the breaking point. Nate will always be known as the first person to be fired over his podcast.

FIGURE 4.2

An episode of The Nate and Di Show got Nate fired.

This concern is one to consider—sure, you are free to say what you like, but others, such as your boss, are free to act on what you say. When planning your podcast, seriously consider what you're going to say about your boss, co-workers, or clients, because if they hear it, your career could suffer.

Repercussions from spouses and families loom as well, depending on how much infor-mation you give out. Several people say that their spouses don't understand what they do or why they do it, so they are able to get away with more. Corby from The Twisted Pickle Show (www.thetwistedpickle.com, see Figure 4.3) plays off the fact that his wife has no knowledge of his podcasting and therefore the podcast is layered with the ten-sion of what will happen if his wife ever finds out. He calls it "ninja-casting." Of course, when his wife finally does find out and listens to past shows, she might call it "divorce-casting."

FIGURE 4.3

The creator of The Twisted Pickle Show podcast hides his podcasting from his wife, and that's always a messy proposition.

The spouses and family who do listen to podcasts usually don't want family laundry aired, as the saying goes. Your sister's mental illness issues over Thanksgiving may make for a bittersweet anecdote, but your mom might disagree.

You never know who is going to be listening. That is something you must remember. Mur was shocked when she realized that her husband's uncle listens to her podcast, and was yet again happy that she doesn't talk much about her family or her in-laws.

Some people don't care. If the things you put in your podcast are the kind of things you wouldn't mind saying to your boss and your grandmother, or if you simply don't care, then go on with your bad self; that is one of the beautiful things about podcasting.

So Many Passions, So Little Time!

Some ambitious people decide they simply have too many important hobbies in their lives to ignore any of them. This is not an odd thing. Many of us find that we are not so one-sided as to have one or two important things in our lives. However, if you're so passionate about several things, there's nothing that says you can't do more than one podcast.

Well, that's not exactly true. There *is* something that says you can't: time. It's an uncomfortable realization in adulthood that we just don't have enough time for fun stuff as we once did. Those darn mortgage payments! And, man, that demanding family!

There is also the sad truth that podcasting about a passion takes you away from that passion. There are, of course, exceptions. More than one podcast about running is recorded while on the road, for example. Rob's passion happens to be podcasting, which is what his podcast is about. But for the most part, podcasting takes us away from our passions (take the irony that Mur's writing podcast, I Should Be Writing, takes writing time away from her).

But as always, there are a handful of podcasters who make it work. Notable podcasters

Privacy and Your Family

Other worries are more pervasive and frightening than simply losing your job or angering your dad. Most podcasters keep information about their children out of their podcast for safety reasons. Some will list their children's names, but some won't even go that far. But going as far as mentioning where the kids go to school, linking to their wish list, and so on, is treading in dangerous waters.

We all know that we live in a dangerous world. When you begin podcasting, you become a public figure. Are people going to gossip about your marriage like they do about Hollywood celebrities? Not at that level, no. But the minute you get one listener, you are a person putting your personal life out for the public to hear. And it only takes one weirdo to ruin everything. So even if you have 75 listeners, remember that you have a responsibility to protect your children.

Ten years ago the saying was "On the Internet, no one knows you're a dog." Nowadays, it's much easier to find out who people are, where they live, and how to find them. So stay aware. We have more on privacy later in Chapter 13, "Using Your Site as a Marketing Tool."

who sink hours and hours into their many passions are Evo Terra and Michael R. Mennenga (Dragon Page: Cover to Cover, Dragon Page: Wingin' It, and Slice of Sci Fi, three different science fiction podcasts), Marc Gunn (The Brobdingnagian Minute, with partner Andrew McKee, The Cat Lover's Podcast [see Figure 4.4], Irish and Celtic Music Podcast, Pub Songs Podcast, and Renaissance Festival Podcast), and Chad Barnard (The Locals Only Show, The Church of Pod, and Me and the Bean). Others dedicate time to their podcast(s) as well as produce others'. Michael Geoghegan hosts Reel Reviews as well as serves as one of the producers of Grape Radio. Both of us aid Senator John Edwards with his podcasting efforts as well as some others.

FIGURE 4.4

Marc Gunn's Cat Lover's Podcast is one of many he produces on a regular basis.

Producing several podcasts can be difficult, but it's rewarding. Chad Barnard, who works on three podcasts of varying production value, recommends, "Do not burn yourself out! This is something that happens to people with one cast much less multiple ones. If you feel that you are beginning to phone it in, scale back immediately. There's nothing that can hurt your show and your audience size more than putting out rushed and half-arsed material."

There are few better qualified to speak on the topic of producing multiple podcasts than Marc Gunn, who ran five.

"I'm psycho. I started exploring podcasting in March (2005). That's when I was scouring the Net for all the different styles of podcasts. I found some cool ones. Then I started thinking what I could do.

"…I had tons of ideas going through my mind. So the first one I decided to do was a Cat Lover's Podcast (www.catmusicblog.com)…. It was well received. And more importantly I had fun doing it.

"The next one I started was the Renaissance Festival Podcast (www.renaissancefestivalmusic.com). I started it because I thought it would be cool to promote the music at Ren Faires.

"Rennies loved the Renaissance Festival Podcast. That's what really gave me the buzz. When I started working for myself in July, I was finally able to do the first Brobdingnagian Bard's podcast—A Brobdingnagian Minute. Then I started the Pub Songs Podcast, which was designed to keep the folk tradition alive and educate people about a lot of the cool Irish pub songs out there. I'm still meaning to update that podcast, but alas, that's the only one I've done thus far. Last out was the Irish and Celtic Music Podcast.

"What drove me to it? Most of it began with a desire to promote certain aspects of my professional musical career or something I'm passionate about, like preserving traditional Celtic folk music.

"The Irish and Celtic Music Podcast though has become something more. I've published the Celtic MP3s Music Magazine for about 5 years now. Each week, I featured two bands with free Celtic MP3s. That was all well and good, but I found I couldn't promote those artists enough. Now I've found my Celtic podcast is much better at sharing music I love with others. I can help more people. So it's highly rewarding."

As passionate as Marc is about his podcasts, he has some strong opinions of others who may wish to follow in his footsteps.

"Don't!

"No. Just kidding. I don't think it's bad doing more than one show, but if you're decent at organizing and setting time tables, I think you'll find it much easier. And if you can do them without editing, you'll be better off as well. That's where it can get time-consuming. The great thing about the music podcasts is the editing is just between songs. But the spoken ones can really take some time. Just make sure you have time available to do it or can make a time schedule that will give you that flexibility."

—Marc Gunn, Podcasting Psycho

Does Anger Equal Passion?

Several political talk shows show us that a good, healthy (or unhealthy, according to some cardiologists) temper can make for some entertaining watching and listening. And everyone remembers the newscasts where the normally calm and cool newscaster got angry and lost his temper, yelling at someone or simply walking out. The riot on Geraldo Rivera's talk show set will live in many people's minds. People have a fascination with intense emotions, especially those emotions that the watchers or listeners don't feel comfortable showing in public.

Still, intense anger is also seen as an unprofessional face to show the world. Podcasting is a hobby for the majority of podcasters, and therefore they don't care whether they start their podcast with, "Man, I'm pissed off today" over "Welcome to My Podcast! I am your host...." However, when you think about what you want to present to the world, you might want to consider what face you show people.

Starting out angry will automatically turn some people off, and even if they enjoy the rush they get from disagreeing with your passion, they will likely let you know how much they disagree with your vehemence. Some people think that you haven't "made it" in podcasting until you get an email that someone doesn't like your show, and if you focus your podcast on your angry opinions, you're likely to make it quickly. When you present loud, strong opinions, you're inviting others to do the same. So be prepared. (Then again, if that's what you want, you don't need to worry about this warning!)

False Starts

One of the things that a lot of people don't get about podcasts is that they can be forever changing. Granted, if you change all the time, your regular listeners are going to get frustrated and stop listening, but the fact remains that you have the prerogative to change something that you don't like.

Podcasts are unlike any broadcasted or printed medium. You can start something, identify that it doesn't work, and change things with little to no repercussions.

When podcasting was new, there were several podcasters who were excited about podcasting, but were unsure of what they wanted their shows to be. People would start a podcast, then switch gears effortlessly. This is one of the few reasons you would want to start your podcast off the cuff, because there's little to worry about if you need to change something (for example, opening music, bumps, show format, and so on).

Other issues with false starts can be realizing that your podcast is too much like another well established and popular show; in that case, you don't have to give up. You can reexamine your passion and look for a different angle. Keep the topic and change the focus. There are several ways of looking at a topic—just find a new one.

If your well-produced podcast needs considerable tweaking, for whatever reason, it can be discouraging. You may need to change core banding elements of your podcast, such as theme song, website, logo, or any number of other things that make the faltering podcast what it is. In extreme cases, you may need to change the title and even the feed. Alert your listeners to this; people don't like it when you drop off the face of the earth. If you are keeping the general feeling, you simply need to alert your readers that things are changing and then implement the changes. Never be afraid to start over if the podcast isn't working for you and you're not having fun.

> **NOTE** In October of 2005, Luria Petrucci and Neal Campbell created The Crappy Christian Show, which is an audio podcast best described as a couple cast. Initially they were trying to be like Dawn and Drew, except they did not feel very comfortable in that role because it was not who they truly were. As such, their listener base was small and the show was basically lost in the crowd. Then, in December of 2005 they had an idea for another show—a video podcast. This one was more in touch with who they were and what they were passionate about. They quickly captured thousands of viewers. Their new podcast is GeekBrief.TV (www.geekbrief.com).

If you don't have a lot of listeners, you can change all you want. Change the format, change the opening music, or change the entire topic. The difficulty comes when you do have listeners, because you will need to examine what they're listening for and see whether that is something you need to change. If you change your mind entirely about what you want to podcast about, you will likely have to buy a new domain, launch a new blog, get a new RSS feed, and tell all current listeners to resubscribe, which will annoy some and alienate others. Finally, if those who do follow you to the new format end up not liking it, you're likely to lose those subscribers too.

Although this may seem like a lot of stuff to change, and you may fear losing your listeners, the cliché is still true: You can't fit a square peg in a round hole. You don't want to put your new cooking podcast at www.japanese_anime_forever.com. For such dramatic changes in format, relaunching your podcast from scratch is worth the effort in the long run. False starts can seem irritating and defeating, but that doesn't mean you should fear change. If you're not doing what you want, then why podcast at all?

Why We Podcast

It's passion that keeps us podcasting. We love it. Podcasting is more than narcissistic, although you do need an ego to assume that hundreds (or thousands!) of people want to hear your view on something. It's not all about you; it's also about your passion. Many people have said their podcast has turned people onto whatever their subject is; people listened to their podcast without being familiar with the subject! So you'll be getting people excited about the same things you are excited about. And that's where the narcissism comes in.

Part II

REFINING YOUR PODCAST AND YOUR SKILLS

Chapter 5

GETTING STARTED

The first few minutes you share with your listeners are the most important time you have, but so many podcasters treat it as the least important. They dawdle, they thank their friends, they play promos (of other shows), they talk about things that new listeners won't know or care about. Always give your listeners what they came for within the first 5 minutes. Remember that on every show, someone's going to be listening who's never heard you before. Make them care.

—Steve Eley, from Escape Pod

Choosing a Title

In the last chapter, we talked about picking a subject you are passionate about, which is clearly the number-one piece of advice from current podcasters. In this chapter, we are going to talk about first impressions. The old saying is, you only get one chance to make a first impression. With over 30,000 (soon to be over 100,000) podcasts to compete with, listeners will have less and less time to spend when looking at a new podcast. And they almost certainly will not give you a second chance with so many others to yet explore.

The very first thing any potential listener will ever learn about your show is the title of your show. How you choose a name will go very far in setting up that first impression. Let's look at some great names:

- Catholic Insider
- Chess Is Cool Podcast
- K9Cast

- MacCast

- MommyCast

- RaidersCast

- The Kansas City Weather Podcast

We bet most people can tell what each of these podcasts is about as soon as they see the titles. It is often important to pick a title that clearly lets potential listeners know what your show is about. This is especially true for niche shows and shows that are about a specific subject. You want to make sure people looking for that subject can easily connect your show with the subject (see Figure 5.1).

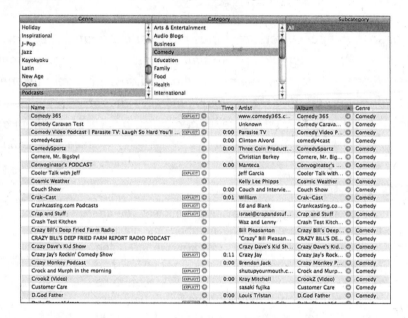

FIGURE 5.1

Searching for "Comedy" podcasts in iTunes narrows the pack a bit, but there's still a huge number of podcasts from which to choose.

Chris at Tips from the Top Floor, a podcast about Digital Photography, renamed his show Digital Photography: Tips from the Top Floor, after the release of iTunes. That simple change helped his subscriber numbers to increase drastically from about 1,000 to over 10,000.

The English as a Second Language (ESL) Podcast launched in July of 2005, and by October of that year had over 10,000 subscribers. Jeff, the host of the ESL Podcast, did not do any promoting of his show; he simply listed it in iTunes and people searching for that subject signed up in droves. His only real marketing was the name of his podcast.

For shows where the subject matter is a little more gray (comedy or entertainment), a catchy unique title may be more appropriate. Yeast Radio, The Twisted Pickle, and The Evil Genius Chronicles really tell you nothing about the content, other than that the creators of these shows at least have some creativity. And if a listener is searching around the Comedy section of a directory, a name that jumps out at them may be more likely to be clicked than a boring name like The John Doe Show.

Let's try something: You are looking for a show that is likely to make you laugh and entertain you. You are also looking for something a little different than standard fare. Which of the following would you click?

- Mutant Cheese Doodle Podcast
- KCRW's Le Show

Granted, if you are French and don't like puffy orange junk food, you may go with the latter. But most people would go for the former.

If you already have a blog or a website with some sort of following, oftentimes you are best served to play off the name of the site or blog. Some great examples are TheForce.Net Podcast, Suicide Girls Podcast, iLounge.com Podcast, and, of course, The Diggnation Podcast. All these used the popularity and traffic from their sites to spur traffic to their podcasts. But this really only works if you have established traffic. If your blog has a strange name and no traffic and you are looking for the podcast to help bring traffic to the blog, you may be better suited picking a new name for the podcast that might attract attention.

Once you have some potential names picked out, go into iTunes, Yahoo!, Odeo, and Podcast Alley and do a search for those names and derivatives of those names. Early on in podcasting there were podcasts with the following names:

- She Said, He Said Podcast
- He Said, She Said Podcast
- She Said, She Said Podcast

Talk about confusing! You can practically hear the potential listener base dropping through the floor. It is very important to look at the other names of podcasts out there so you don't create unwanted confusion. The couple of hours of work you spend now researching good names and looking at what is out there will save you tenfold that amount of time and frustration later on if you have to change your podcast's name.

Once you have narrowed down potential names, go to your favorite registrar and see if you can register, at a minimum, the .com, .net, and .org web domain names. You want to make sure you protect your namespace. There is nothing worse than having a podcast about religion located at www.*yourdomain*.com and then having a porn site register www.*yourdomain*.net or .org. And if your podcast/website takes off and those names are available, trust us, someone will register them and you'll end up wishing you had done it when you had the chance.

Your Intro

If your potential listeners like the name of your show and have decided to check it out, we have now reached phase two of what affects your podcast's first impression—the show itself. At this point you can assume that the person listening has some sort of interest in what you are podcasting about. It is not like with channel surfing on the TV. The listener actually had to take the time to download your show (chances are they are not yet subscribed, so they are listening as the show is webcasted or played on a flash player). This means you should have a little more than the 5 to 10 seconds a typical channel suffer would spend evaluating a show before moving on. You probably have as much as 45 seconds to a minute to make a good first impression. No pressure.

In the next few sections, we'll take a look at some of the ways you can lead off your podcast, starting with the pre-intro.

Pre-Intro

Before the intro, many podcasters have a "pre-intro" for lack of a better term. This is usually something where they state one or more of the following: the date, the show number, the guest star, the cast's rating, or something else specific for that episode. This is done for numerous reasons, and it's considered in good "podiquette" to do so.

One of the most important reasons this is done has to do with playing the device on a mobile MP3 player and not being able to see the screen for one reason or another. These notes are important especially if the listener has a player without a screen (for example, iPod shuffle) or if they're using it in a car (driving and trying to navigate through the menus on an iPod are a big no-no). Having this information at the beginning of the show lets the listeners know right away if they are playing the correct episode. Another important reason to do this is to help those who are sight impaired. Audio podcasts are very attractive to this segment of the population, and having a pre-intro helps in their listening experience.

A pre-intro can be done many different ways—such as Adam Curry's "Delta Sierra Charlie One Niner Niner" to signify DSC-199, or the show name and date, as is done on the MacCast. podCast411 does the date, show number, and the guest's name. For interview shows, we would suggest including the guest's name up front. But no matter how you decide to do it, the pre-intro is the very first thing the listener hears and usually is no more than 5 to 10 seconds. Although the pre-intro is not intended to set the tone for your show, this does not mean it has be so monotone that it sounds like something from the Emergency Podcasting System.

Celebrity/Guest Show ID

Celebrity/guest show IDs at the beginnings of a podcast are also very common—for example, "This is Jane from the Jane Doe podcast and you are listening to John Smith on my favorite show, the ACME Crowbar Podcast." The use of celebrity show IDs are a great way to let potential listeners know what type of person listens to your show. If you are able to get someone who is very popular to do a show ID for you, it gives a nice message that your show is essentially endorsed by that person and helps bring credibility to your show. Sending an email to other podcasters asking for a show ID and telling them to be creative will often result in some great sound clips.

Message

When it comes to your introduction, you need to ask yourself the following questions: What type of tone am I trying to set? What type of information do I want to convey to a new listener? Knowing the answers to these questions will greatly improve the quality and effectiveness of your introduction. Many times your title itself will already convey the message of the content so it is fine to have an introduction that just sets a tone. For other shows, especially ones focused on a specific subject, but where the title is not very clear on what that subject might be, you need an introduction that not only conveys the tone and feel of the show, but also clearly spells out what the show is about. Now, that does not mean if the title is clear you are forbidden from spelling it out for the listeners. The MommyCast has a very well produced 40-second intro that conveys the feel of the show while also introducing what the show is about.

This brings us to the question of whether you should get outside help to produce your introduction. With some hard work and help from your significant other, friends, or family, chances are you can produce a very good introduction on your own. That said, Tips from the Top Floor and the Kansas City Weather Podcast both turned to Scott Fletcher for help with their introductions. Scott Fletcher, from Podcheck Review, has probably helped more podcasters with introductions, bumpers, sweepers, and promos (see Chapter 14, "Using Promos to Hype Your Podcast,") than any other podcaster. Wichita Rutherford and Paul with Barefoot Radio would probably come in a close second. Using outside help from any of these three will clearly give your introduction a professional, but yet very fun feel.

NOTE Bumpers and sweepers are essentially the same thing. They are prerecorded audio segments consisting of sound effects, voice, or voice over music that serve as a transition between two different sections of a show. They are usually very quick—10 to 15 seconds in length or less. They can be used to transition from one song to another, from a news section to a comedy skit, or anywhere else you might have a hard transition that you want to soften.

Sometimes with your introduction, you want to bring the listeners up to date with past shows. With the K9Cast, Walter and Tara have a great introduction format where they start with a short show identification, then do a recap of the past show's content, then give a preview of this show's content (see Figure 5.2). They complete this all in typically less than 45 seconds. If you have a podiobook, this is also a good way to recap what has been talked about in previous chapters.

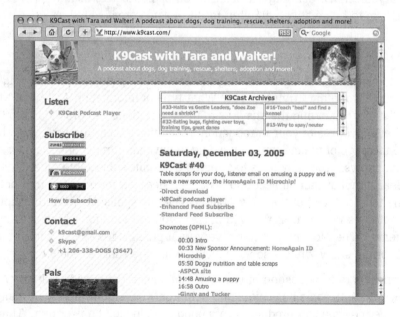

FIGURE 5.2

The K9Cast provides listeners with a quick recap of the previous show before setting off on a new topic.

Sponsorship

If your show is sponsored or underwritten by someone else, you really should point that out upfront. First, I am sure your sponsor would appreciate it. But second, you need to think about fair disclosure. Your listeners, by and large, aren't stupid. If you spend your entire show talking about how great XYZ service is and you never mention XYZ paid you to do the show, it will come back to haunt you. There is an issue of trust between a podcast's host(s) and the listeners, and not pointing the sponsorship out will break down any trust your audience had with you. Worse, losing your audience will almost certainly make you less attractive to your sponsor.

It's also a mistake to assume that listeners won't find out if a sponsor supports your podcast. Podcasting is a "community," and people talk and post on forum boards. Listeners will eventually find out if someone is sponsoring you, so make it clear right from the outset.

Commercials

Commercials are a little more formal than quickly mentioning a sponsor, and they usually involve hawking some product or service. There are two main ways to deliver a commercial on your show. One is to play a "canned," pre-produced slick commercial that is supplied to you from your advertiser or is inserted with one of the ad-insertion systems. If you go this route, you need to look out for the "nails on the chalkboard" effect. This happens when the volume levels or general sound of the commercial is so different from that of the rest of podcast, it instantly turns off the listeners. The second one is where you, the podcaster, read the commercial. This is less grating on your listeners and is much less likely to drive away potential listeners.

To learn more about the difference between sponsorships and commercials, **see** "Advertising and Sponsorship," **p. 299** (Chapter 18, "Generating Revenue").

We are not against advertisements in podcasts, but you need to remember not all podcast listeners are going to put up with commercials. Part of the appeal of podcasting is the lack of commercials. We highly suggest for this reason that you not have a commercial in the first 2 minutes of your podcast. There is no reason to risk driving away new potential listeners before they even get a chance to make a decision about your show.

Some advertisers are going to insist that the advertisements be placed early in the show. It is your job to point out to them the differences in podcasting and commercial radio and let them know you want to make sure you have as large a listening base as possible. Hooking new listeners is all about making the best possible first impression, and having a commercial upfront will never achieve that goal.

Length

Given the choice between a 3-minute introduction and no introduction, most listeners, especially those who have subscribed, would pick no introduction. You need to pick some balance between having a full-fledged promo to start your show for the new listeners and the desires of your current listener base. The length of your introduction will vary depending on the type of show you are doing and its overall length. You do not want a 1-minute introduction on a 5-minute show, but for a show that is over an hour long, a 1-minute introduction may not be out of the question.

Looking at over 50 of the more popular podcasts, we noted the following breakdown concerning the length of show introductions (see Table 5.1).

Table 5.1   Average Length of Podcast Introductions

Show Length	Avg.	Min.	Max.
<15 min	0:21	0:00	0:47
15 to 30 min	0:33	0:13	1:08
>30 min	0:43	0:15	1:45

As would be expected, the length of the shows correlates to the length of the introductions. Although there is no hard-and-fast rule for what the length of your introduction should be, you should take into consideration that if your introduction is much greater than the averages listed here, you run the risk of turning off potential new listeners and current subscribers. It is always best to err on having an introduction that is too short rather than one that is too long.

Chapter **6**

YOUR "SCRIPT"

"I feel like I need to know what I'm talking about. With comics there are lots of rumors and what not, so I can't always 'know' if something I'm saying is for real, but I always use prep time to try to separate the signal from the noise. If I don't take the time to prep well then I'll end up saying something that is totally bogus and lose credibility. It is hard enough to gain credibility in the podcasting world (at least I think it is), and if you lose it then I think it will be really hard to get it back."

—**Neil Gorman, Comicology**

Preparation

Preparation is one of the most important things you will do once you set up your podcasting rig. It's not quite as easy as just setting up the rig and then talking into the microphone, of course. But your preparation is going to show in the quality of your podcast.

What are you going to talk about? Are you going to stick to certain subjects, or choose just one and ad-lib? Now, don't get us wrong; there's nothing wrong with ad-libbing, but turning on the microphone when you have nothing to say is one of the nails in the coffin of your podcast.

Prep work can include simply writing down a couple comments to stick to, or surfing the Web for a topic to give your opinion on. This is, of course, if you're doing a personal audioblog and you just want to keep track of topics that interest you. If your podcast has a focused topic, whether it is sports or politics or movie reviews, then you definitely need to do your homework before starting.

Given that you are very likely recording your podcast on your computer, your access to the Internet is at your fingertips. Be sure to have a browser up with windows open for the news, sports scores, or odd fad that you want to talk about.

If you want to do an interview show, a fiction show, or a music show, then your prep work takes a bit more planning. You absolutely have to know something about someone before you interview them. You need to listen to their podcast, read their book, or at least visit their website to become familiar with them before asking questions. Rob will listen to a minimum of two to five shows before he interviews the guests for his podcast (more about this in Chapter 7, "The Art of the Interview.")

The amount of prep time varies with what kind of podcast you are doing. Consider your preparation as the important first step before you begin recording—without it, you're likely to just go on and on without a plan, and no one likes to listen to that.

Jason Adams from Random Signal (www.randomsignal.com, see Figure 6.1), a podcast featuring independent music from Chapel Hill, NC and other areas of the South, uses the Internet and brief notes to keep his show straight.

"I decide which songs I'm going to play, [then] I make sure that I've got all the info about the songs/bands/albums at my finger tips (usually by having the bands' websites up). I usually jot down rough notes about things that I want to be sure to mention in the podcast, but sometimes, I just take notes as I go. Without notes I usually forget at least one thing that I wanted to talk about, but more often than not I end up veering away from my notes anyway. I guess I like to at least feel prepared, when I can."

—Jason Adams, Random Signal

One pitfall some podcasters encounter is thinking that if they have a co-host, they can just bounce off each other without planning anything. It is possible that certain people out there can completely ad-lib a 20-minute (or more!) show, but they are rare. Sadly, the majority of podcasts that attempt this end up podcasting a normal conversation between two people, often uncomfortable and giggly when they can't think of something to talk about. Although you may get a voyeuristic thrill listening to it, the novelty soon wears off and you're wondering why these boring people are wasting your time and space on your MP3 player.

Prep is vital to any podcast. Even if your notes just say, "I want to talk about Harry Potter this podcast," that is at least a launching pad. But what about Harry Potter? The books? The movies? Speculations on the future stories or perhaps a discussion of J.K. Rowling's prose styling? And after you decide what you want to talk about, you'd better make sure you're up on all the topics before you open your mouth. If you get something wrong, someone *will* let you know about it.

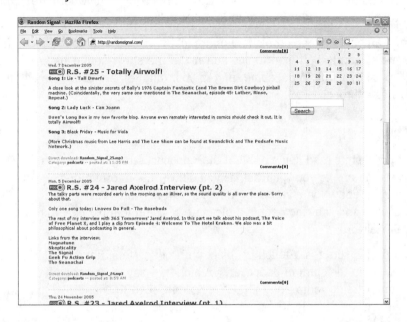

FIGURE 6.1

Random Signal uses a casual show notes form, somewhat chatty with pertinent links.

Outline or Free Form

Many podcasters, usually the "old-school" people, believe that podcasting needs to be unscripted and spontaneous. Just get in front of a mic and go! Although the people who can do this are admirable—and we certainly wish we were that talented—we believe those people are few and far between. Content rarely erupts from people that easily, and most of us need some sort of outline to follow.

If you have no outline prepared, it's difficult to stay on topic, remember everything you wanted to talk about, and stick to a time schedule (more on that later). Once the RSS feed is updated with the latest podcast, you can't modify it if you forgot to add something important to your file. Well, you *can* add something new, but uploading an edited file means your listeners might download two copies of your podcast—the good one and the bad one—and that annoys some people. They don't know which one to listen to, and if they've already listened to the wrong file, it's unlikely they will want to listen to it again to hear the new stuff you put in. Podcast listeners' time is valuable.

Not to mention that uploading a file and then realizing you've forgotten something to put in it makes you really want to kick yourself. Trust us.

Preparing an outline keeps the show on topic. By considering your topics carefully, you can segue smoothly between topics and make the show sound better. You can go off topic (especially if you forget something in your outline), but using the outline is a good bare-bones approach.

Reading from a Script

Several podcasters read some or all of their podcast straight from a script. This can add a professional tone to your podcast, as you deliver the information in a smooth and pre-pared way. It shows you've done your homework, and your podcast is free from the dreaded "um" and "ah" factor. It is a pleasure to listen to a podcast that is well-scripted and well-delivered.

Reading from a script is a touchy subject with podcasters, however. Many believe that a script is not in the spirit of podcasting, which they say is raw and off the cuff. Podcasts are not mainstream radio, they argue, and don't need to sound like mainstream radio. The argument holds only if you want the raw, conversational sound to your podcast. Podcasting is whatever you want it to be, and if a script works for you, then great.

Other arguments state that few people actually work well with a script and instead read the text from a script like a sixth grader reading a book report. When absolutely every-thing is scripted, even the jokes and the apparently off-the-cuff comments can sound sterile and without soul. A dry reading of a script can kill whatever passion you wanted to get across to the listener with your podcast.

If you do decide to go with a script, read it out loud a couple times before recording so you don't have any odd phrases you will stumble over (Mur has this problem with her essays a lot). The brain will often have no trouble reading a sentence that the tongue can't handle. Have you ever gotten tripped up just reading tongue twisters silently? No? That's our point. Get acquainted with the text, and deliver it with a conversational tone.

Scripting jokes is also a touchy subject. It's difficult to pull off reading a joke and deliv-ering it properly. This is another reason to get well-acquainted with the text—put the joke in, but be familiar enough with it to ad-lib it, thus making it sound more nat-ural. Whatever you do, however, don't read it word for word; it will sound forced and unnatural.

Going off Bullet Points

Bullet points are perhaps the nonscripted podcaster's best friend. They lack the slightly anal detail of a full outline, and they don't take up as much time as a script. You can jot down your thoughts before you podcast and keep your notes with you.

Bullet points are also an excellent reference when building your show notes. Although we believe you should listen to the final version of your podcast after you are done with it, you don't have to worry about building your show notes through that final listen if you already have them in front of you.

The third thing bullet points do for you is allow you to put your show into a logical order. If you jot down the things you want to talk about, you might realize that your topics are in the wrong order. This enables you to reorganize your show ahead of time. Trying to do this in the middle of recording is possible, but it often shows up in the quality of the podcast, with clumsy segues, your best topic coming second instead of last, and so on.

> **TIP**
>
> Remember to keep your best part for last, just as grocery stores put the milk in the far corner. If you make your listeners wait for the best parts, they will listen to the whole thing. Put the best part early and they might turn off the podcast when they are done listening to just that one part.

Editing Versus Live

In the early days of podcasting, there was a sense of pride in the gritty amateur quality of it. It was just you, your mic, and the Internet. It was *real*. It wasn't polished and fake like the radio and TV announcers' teleprompted speeches. Like real conversation, you were talking with your listeners, not at them.

But because some of us were not schooled in announcer-speak, we sat in front of our microphones and stuttered, paused, and said "um" way too much. Sometimes coughing or sneezing would cause unpleasant spikes in the audio file. And we realized that cutting out these occasional gaffes made the podcast better to listen to.

The Pitfalls of Editing

Although we advocate editing your podcast, there are legitimate reasons for going "raw."

We have spoken with several podcasters who, like ourselves, have uploaded an unedited file that they thought they had edited and were mortified when listeners started asking, "What gives?"

Now, if none of us worried about editing, this would have been fine, because listeners would have been used to the consistent flubs in our podcasts, but a habit of editing makes an unedited podcast stand out like a nihilistic teenage writer at a baseball game. So whatever you choose, stay consistent.

The line separating the editing podcasters from the live podcasters is drawn definitely... in sand. Some podcasters feel that if they edited, they could not do their shows as frequently as they manage. Others want to keep the conversational feeling and think that editing will remove that from their show.

For the record, both of us edit our shows extensively, removing mistakes, slow parts, any and all bodily noises (no Senseo burps on our shows), and household interruptions such as dogs barking and phones ringing. We cover this topic in depth in Chapter 10, "The Great Editing Debate."

Time Limits

What you will hear throughout this book, and anything else you read on podcasting, is that it's a "free" medium, meaning that you can pretty much do with it what you want. Do you want 5 minutes of swearing non-stop? You can do that. Three hours of reading soup can labels? You can do that too. Not a lot of people would listen, but you're free to do this.

> **TIP**
>
> We do not, of course, expect you to know exactly how long your podcast is going to be straight out of the gate. Your first couple podcasts are going to be experiments, and when you get comfortable, you can pinpoint your ideal length and make that your goal to work toward.

There are no time limits on podcasting. You can go as short or as long as you like, which is another yoke of traditional radio we have thrown off. We are not hindered by a schedule to fill exactly 25 minutes of airtime. If you have 2 minutes of stuff one week and 2 hours the next, it's not going to matter from a publishing perspective.

The only thing is, it does matter from an audience perspective. Your audience listens to you for a variety of reasons, and one of which is they like your content. If they like your content, they will learn to expect the same kind of content from you in the future. They will expect consistency, and when you go from one end of the spectrum to another, listeners will get annoyed.

So although you don't need to adhere to any restrictions set by an outside establishment, like radio, you still should consider how long you want your podcast to be and keep to within ±25% of that target. Planning your podcast, as mentioned previously, will help you keep on this target.

Forcing a Constrained Time

Regardless of what people think about radio and its pitfalls, there is something to be said for order. It's challenging to keep every show on the same schedule to the second, and make sure that every show is comfortable and predictable (not in plot or content, but in structure). For the same reason that people can see beauty in the constrained poetry styles of sonnets and haiku, some podcasts can shine if placed under a strict time limit.

Time limits allow you to prepare the same amount of content per week and give people something they can look forward to. Although many people like the anarchy of podcasting, there's no denying that the podcasts that stick to a time limit sound more professional than those that do not (see Figure 6.2). Whether or not this is a good thing, the listener must be the judge.

If setting a time limit seems to be right for you, try it out a couple times before adopting the limit.

Although we advocate editing your podcast, this practice may actually put a kink in your plans for keeping to a schedule. You can record for your set 30 minutes, but when you cut out the pauses, the time you had to answer the door, the "ums," and the sneezing fit you had, you may be left with 25 minutes. Rob solves this by recording long, knowing he's going to edit down, and then cutting to his desired length. Mur is a little more free with her shows, but still manages to hit her target marks within 5 or so minutes on a normal week.

Exceptions That Prove Rules

One of the universal truths in podcasting is that whenever you come up with a rule, a successful podcast shows up that proves it wrong. We believe that editing is the way to go with podcasting, but there are many podcasts—The Daily Source Code, Evil Genius Chronicles, and Radio Free Burrito, to name a few—that do just fine without any editing.

So we must also make the caveat that some podcasts may do quite well with unpredictable lengths. Dave Winer's Morning Coffee Notes can be 2 minutes of him singing or 30 minutes of content. And he still has quite a few subscribers. Although we warn later in the chapter that excessive swearing may turn off some listeners, the truth is, some of the most popular podcasts are also those with the foulest language.

This doesn't mean our advice is bogus; people are, by practice, lovers of predictability and routine, and when they know that they can fit your podcast into, say, their 15-minute morning commute or their 1-hour workout, they will plan accordingly. If your podcast gets to be longer than normal, or if you need to put out a 5-minute public notice, be sure to mention at the beginning that it's not going to adhere to the normal length.

There is one more reason to consider keeping your time consistent: If you have any intentions to move your show from podcast to radio, you need to keep your "half-hour" show to 26 minutes, for example. Moving your show to KYOU radio or satellite radio creates more need for dedicated attention to your length.

	Name		Artist		Album		Time	Size
1	SoSF_020_Gigi Edgly		Michael & Evo		Slice of Sci-Fi		59:23	27.3 MB
2	SoSF_021_Excaliber		Michael & Evo		Slice of Sci-Fi		56:09	25.8 MB
3	SoSF_022_Richard Hatch		Michael & Evo		Slice of Sci-Fi		52:34	24.1 MB
4	SoSF_023_Dragon Con		Michael & Evo		Slice of Sci-Fi		50:50	35 MB
5	SoSF_024_Serenity Giveaway		Michael & Evo		Slice of Sci-Fi		55:49	25.6 MB
6	SoSF_029_Tim Brazeal		Michael & Evo		Slice of Sci-Fi		50:55	23.4 MB
7	SoSF_030_Peter Mayhew		Michael & Evo		Slice of Sci-Fi		59:03	27.1 MB
8	SoSF_031_News Show		Michael & Evo		Slice of Sci-Fi		56:24	25.9 MB
9	SoSF_032_Paul in Studio		Michael & Evo		Slice of Sci-Fi		56:26	25.9 MB
10	SoSF_033_Back At It Again		Michael & Evo		Slice of Sci-Fi		55:30	25.5 MB
11	SoSF_034_Giveaways Galore!		Michael & Evo		Slice of Sci-Fi		56:06	25.7 MB
12	SoSF_035_Chris & Mat		Michael & Evo		Slice of Sci-Fi		54:05	24.8 MB
13	SoSF_036_Evo's Gone		Michael & Evo		Slice of Sci-Fi		55:16	25.4 MB

FIGURE 6.2

Note the consistent show lengths in this list of Slice of SciFi podcasts.

"In order to maintain the integrity of podcasting, I always tell show producers, 'When you feel you've said what you wanted to say or played enough music, that's when you end the show.' Make it organic, essentially no time constraints.

"Radio is run on very tight and extremely restrictive program "clocks" and since part of the appeal of podcasting is that it is somewhat anti-radio, I try not to impose traditional methodology. However, if some-one has hopes of actually getting into radio through podcasting, then 26 and 52 minutes would be standard times for a 30- and 60-minute program."

—Stephen Page, Station Manager, KYOU Radio

Length Matters

Before you decide how much time you think you want to fill, think about this: How much do you have to say? And how much of that is quality content?

Media Artist Secrets is a very popular podcast that stays below 15 minutes. It's short, sweet, full of information, and exemplifies the truism that you should always leave your audience wanting more. If the only complaint you get about your podcast is that it's too short, you're doing something right.

TIP

Not every MP3 player has a screen that shows how long a file is going to go. Most listeners will likely appreciate the fact that when Dragon Page: Cover to Cover comes on, they know they will be listening to an hour-long show, rather than another podcast that they may not be able to hear the whole thing in one sitting.

Don't worry about sticking to a per-minute schedule; however, keeping an eye on the clock while you prep and record may benefit you.

College professors bemoan the fact that the attention span of their students is about 45 minutes, which is why most college classes don't last longer than an hour. Although many popular podcasts are an hour or longer, most listeners you talk to will say an hour is too long.

> **TIP** If your audience thinks your show is just a little too short, there is little doubt they'll be back for your next program.

When it comes to really long podcasts, you need to make absolutely sure that the content is top notch and will keep your listeners entertained. As we've mentioned before, most listeners think the ideal length of a podcast is their commute time. So people who have 1-hour or longer commutes might think that a podcast that lasts 90 minutes is ideal, but the rest of the people may think it's too long.

What do they do when they decide your podcast is too long? At best, they'll get bored and stop listening to that episode, but continue to download. They may listen all the way to the end and then send you some feedback. At worst, they'll unsubscribe. There are a lot of podcasts out there, and a listener can choose to download three 20-minute-long podcasts or your hour-long podcast. Therefore, your content had better be compelling enough to keep people's attention.

Swearing

When podcasters get behind the mic on their first podcast, it often occurs to them that they have the freedom, perhaps for the first time ever, to say anything they want. They can say words that they would not say to their grandmother or their boss, and that are certainly unutterable over the conventional radio waves.

It's true: Podcasting is over the Internet, which is not regulated in any way. The Federal Communications Commission has no say over what can and cannot be said online, inside the law. Podcasters have no one to answer to, and if they swear, they will not get fined thousands of dollars like Bono and they won't have their show pulled if a listener complains.

For example, although Dawn and Drew are notorious for having one of the most unflinchingly honest and crass podcasts online today, there are still some lines they won't cross. But even self-censoring may not turn out to be enough because where the dreaded "line" is varies from listener to listener.

TotPM: What gets aired? Are there things that you just say, "We can't do that; that just crossed the line"?

Drew: Hell no!

Dawn: No, that is not true, Drew, sometimes I am like, "We can't do that."

Drew: That's very, very, very rare.

Dawn: It is very rare, but sometimes I will say something, that even I can't say that, like I know that is going to be [trouble]....

Drew: Yeah, but out of, like, 114 shows that we have done, we have done that, what, twice, maybe three times.... You know what is really crazy, though, is the stuff that we think we are on the verge of not putting it out, where we expect people to slam us and give us all kinds of flack and all kinds of hate mail, [but] we never get any and nobody says anything. But then all of a sudden something we both think is so tame and not a big deal, people will give us all kinds of flack over it.

What You Can and Cannot Say

The list is short on what you can't say. You can't say things that are against the law, such as threats to anyone, slanderous material, or copyrighted material. But swear words? You can go to town. And many people do. If Lenny Bruce were still with us, he would be a podcaster.

The realization that they may swear often makes people go a bit overboard with the freedom. Many podcasts seem to be nothing but swearing. If you listen closely, you might be able to catch a topic here and there, but they often merely sound like drunken sailors on shore leave.

What a lot of podcasters have to learn the hard way is that there is a reason the FCC puts limits on what you can and can't say over the air: Many people are offended by swearing. There are people who would normally be very interested in your podcast, but they will be turned off if you swear a lot. Others will cheer your use of free speech.

Keep your listeners in mind. For example, although swearing does not turn us off, we are both parents to young children. If we want to listen to podcasts when our children are around, we prefer not to listen to ones that include heavy swearing. Other people listen to podcasts at work, but don't want their boss to wander by and hear your four-letter descriptions of what you think your malfunctioning PC should do with itself. Keep in mind that not everyone listens to podcasts alone.

There is also the subject of oversaturation. Swearing is intended for an effect, a shock, a harsh word to make people sit up and take notice. If you use swear words as often as you say the word *is*, then these words lose their shock value and even their meaning, and people will be straining to hear your message through the barrage of pointless cursing.

Many podcasts have adopted a quick courtesy message ahead of their podcast to warn of adult language. Listeners appreciate this. A 5-second message stating that the podcast is not work- or child-safe can keep your listeners happy and keep you from losing subscribers.

iTunes "Explicit" Tag: Friend or Foe?

For those listeners who subscribe via iTunes, they have another flag available to them to warn of colorful language: the dreaded iTunes "Explicit" tag.

Most iTunes users know that iTunes often offers the "radio" (clean) version of a song, without swear words, as well as the "album" (unedited) version. The album version is labeled "Explicit" in bright red letters.

Now, if you slip up in your 30-minute podcast and say some objectionable word, you may think you're not terribly offensive, but you still qualify as explicit. Mur didn't think her podcast was explicit because she doesn't talk about sex or violence, but her essays do sometimes edge into the more colorful areas of speech, and she realized that she needed the Explicit tag before iTunes would accept her into the directory.

Some people believe the Explicit tag hurts their numbers in iTunes subscribers, but on the other hand, Dawn and Drew have been at or near the top of the podcasting mountain for months and months, and their podcast is quite explicit. The question comes down to providing content that people want. If you do that, listeners will come, Explicit tag or no.

Experienced iTunes users will know that "Explicit" can mean anything from one word that rhymes with *hit* or an hour of dirty jokes, so you're not likely to push those users away.

E? G? NSFW? X?

Because there is no regulatory commission set to define podcasts beyond the iTunes Explicit tag, podcasters take on the responsibility of rating their own podcasts. Seeing as how we have not accepted an across-the-board ratings system, the ratings may be anything.

The SciFi Podcast Network (www.tsfpn.com) rates its members' shows in three categories: SFGA, meaning it's safe for general audiences, children, even bosses, SF14, the equivalent of a PG rating, meaning there may be some swearing here and there, and NSFW, standing for Not Safe For Work. These podcasts usually contain swearing, sexual situations, violent imagery, and more.

Most podcasts with explicit sexual situations leave clues either on their website, making you confirm you are 18 or older before viewing, or in their podcast titles. It's pretty clear you don't want your 4-year-old listening to Open Source Sex (violetblue.libsyn.com).

Although the movie industry created the MPAA to regulate movies and the computer game industry created the ESRB to regulate video games, the podcast world still has no ratings system. This may be confusing for some listeners. Therefore, as a conscientious podcast host, you will want to seriously consider making a note either on your blog, in your show notes, or in your podcast itself that you have adult information.

Podcast Ratings

In this book we use movie ratings: G, PG, R, and X. G has no swearing or adult content, PG may have a swear word or two, R can use the full range of swear words and most adult content, and graphic sexual descriptions get the X rating.

These ratings are simply for the listeners' information and do not represent any restrictions placed by an official organization.

We're not trying to tell you not to use adult words or sexual content; one of the best things about podcasting is the freedom it allows hosts. We just believe that the listener has a right to know what he or she is getting into before downloading your show. Therefore, if your show's title doesn't make the adult content obvious (such as Open Source Sex), it is good form to let people know either in the show notes or in a quick comment at the beginning of the show. If that Explicit tag was not there, think about how shocked someone might be listening to Yeast Radio for the first time, especially if they were expecting it to be a cooking show.

Chapter 7

THE ART OF THE INTERVIEW

*Respect the listener as much as you respect the person
you're interviewing. Neither is an idiot.*

—Wichita Rutherford, 5 Minutes with Wichita

David Letterman, Oprah, Larry King, Barbra Walters, Johnny Carson.... The list goes on and on of famous people who became famous by interviewing other famous people. If we said you have 60 seconds to write down as many names as possible of different programs based primarily on conducting interviews, there is a good chance you would run out of time before you ran out of shows. By and large, people enjoy watching someone being interviewed if the interview is done well. So what does it take to make a good interview? As Wichita stated to start this chapter: R-E-S-P-E-C-T. If you respect the listener and the guest, both will enjoy the interview. In addition to respect, you also need to have fun with the interview, and you need to share that feeling of fun with the listeners and the guests.

Wichita went on to say the following:

In their own words

"The people who listen to my podcasts are very smart, and they have figured out there are several levels of humor going on in my interviews. For example, when I finish an interview, I ask the interviewee to read a couple of sentences from a physics book. I put that at the end of the next interview

when the artist says, "Come back next week and hear Charlie Daniels say, 'As an object approaches the speed of light, the energy of motion is converted into mass.'" It sounds funny to hear somebody famous say something like that.

NOTE

To learn more about the 5 Minutes with Wichita podcast, see, "5 Minutes with Wichita," p. 64 (Chapter 3, "Podcast Genres").

"These things sure don't sound very important one at a time once a week. But string them together, and I'm telling you how to build a particle accelerator. And out of the 200 to 300 emails I get every day at least one person every other week says "Oh yeah, the particle accelerator is coming along nicely." That's how I found out I have a pretty big cluster of subscribers over at MIT."

Even if the interview is only a small part of your show, an interview done well can really improve the overall feel of your show. In this chapter, we go over those items that we feel will help improve your interviews.

Finding Guests

It is really hard to have an interview show if you have no one to interview. Luckily, finding guests is a lot easier than you might think. Andy Warhol is quoted as saying, "In the future, everyone will be world-famous for 15 minutes." We would follow that up with, "but most people are really looking for at least 15 hours." Truth be told, you as a podcaster definitely fall into this group, and there is nothing wrong with that. As a host of a show where you will be doing interviews, oftentimes you will be offering people a chance to extend that 15 minutes. You will find the hard part is not convincing people to come on your show, but rather it is letting them know you have a show to come on to.

One podcast that really exemplifies extending those 15 minutes of fame for the everyday person is the Small World Podcast, by Bazooka Joe. He goes out each day and interviews everyone from the guy next door to the person who claims to have dated the person that saw Elvis being abducted by aliens. Joe offered us this advice on where to find guests:

"One of the ways I have been finding people to interview is that there are two news services that I have started using, and one is called the PR News service (www.prnewswire.com), and that is how I found out about Space Adventures when I interviewed them.

*"And another one I am using is based out of San Diego, and I am using it as a trial basis. It is called Flash News Wire (www.flashnews.com). They offer a service for news that is a little quirky. To give you an idea of how quirky it can get, TV shows like the **Daily Show** or the **Late Night Show** when they do the little news bits or bring on some guests, chances are they got them from Flash News Wire.*

*"People I am going to be interviewing in the near future would be this one woman. She has written a book called **The Gospel According to Oprah**. There is also a hair technician out of Florida, and he has put out a press release where he wants to help Chief Justice John Roberts with his hair. Because apparently he [Chief Justice Roberts] is going bald and he specializes in hair transplants and toupees…. This is working out so well I am actually considering purchasing it [a paid subscription to the Flash News Wire Service]… but just using the trial membership has been fantastic."*

We mentioned earlier that it is easy to get guests, and if you are looking for noncelebrities, this is really true. However, if you are looking to get someone you might see on the cover of *People* magazine, it is going to take a lot more work and either a lot of luck or a really good job of networking.

Erich Bergen, host of Green Room Radio (www.greenroomradio.com), has had some great guests on his podcast, including such celebrities as Donny Osmond and Don McLean (who wrote the song "American Pie"). We asked Erich how he was able to get some of his guests. Here is what he said:

 "I have been fortunate enough to have a lot of friends in the entertainment industry whom, while they are not well known, know contacts and… so a lot of it is just word of mouth."

No, our advice is not to hit Erich up for his contacts, but rather to hit up the contacts you already have. Talk to your friends, relatives, and coworkers for possible leads for guests (now, if you are doing a show about bondage and sexual role playing, you may want to skip hitting up your relatives and coworkers for leads). Each time you do an interview, ask the guest (off the air, of course) if he or she knows of anyone else who might enjoy coming on your show. If you do a good job on the interview and treat the guest with respect, there is a good chance that person will mention your show to some friends or associates.

Finally, make sure the guests you pick fit the framework of your show and fit the mold your listeners expect. Don't jump the shark. It would not make much sense to interview Paris Hilton on a show about interviewing sports celebrities (unless she suddenly decides to became a tennis star or something). We are sure she would make an interesting guest, but would she really fit on that type of show? Make sure you stick with guests that fit your show and don't bring on someone famous just for the sake of it. Make some guidelines for what constitutes a good guest for your show. Later on down the line, if you think you want to go outside this guideline, present it to your listeners and let them know that you will be bringing on some new types of guests.

Dr. David Van Nuys from Shrink Rap Radio, a podcast where he interviews other psychologists, had this to say about what he is looking for in guests:

"In my show, I'm looking for guests to not only inform but also to reveal something of their inner selves and something about whether their expertise in psychology has been of any use in dealing with their own personal issues. I want to know the ways in which they have been able to apply their academic learning to their own lives. I believe that this sort of self-disclosure will hook my listeners and give them something they can identify with. My goal is to bring it from the academic or professional level down to the universal human level."

Table 7.1 contains a good list of places to look for potential guests of all flavors. If you are looking specifically for celebrities, the Internet Movie Database (IMDB Pro) site is a great place to start. The hosts of The Signal used IMDB Pro to get Ron Glass, Gina Torres, and Adam Baldwin on their show. Because you only get a free 14-day trial (see Figure 7.1), figure out a long list of potential guests before you sign up and then spend as much time looking through the site and printing out as much contact information as you can before the 14 days are up.

Table 7.1   Places to Find Guests for an Interview Podcast

Type of Guest	Site	URL
Authors and topical experts	Authors and Experts	www.authorsandexperts.com
Strange topical experts and newsmakers	Flash News	www.flashnews.com
Celebrities, sports figures, and newsmakers	Guest Exchange	www.guestexchange.com

Type of Guest	Site	URL
Authors and topical experts	GuestFinder.com	www.guestfinder.com
Celebrities	IMDB Pro	www.imdb.com
Topical experts and newsmakers	PR News Wire	www.prnewswire.com
Authors and topical experts	Radio-TV Interview Report	www.rtir.com
Authors and topical experts	Radio and TV Guests	www.radio-tv-guests.airtalents.com
Authors and topical experts	Yearbook.com	www.yearbook.com

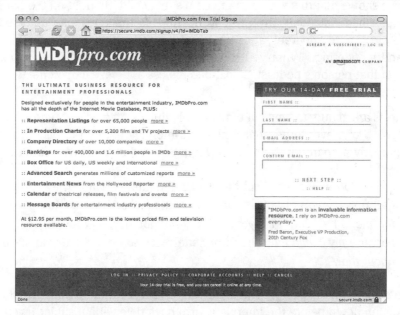

FIGURE 7.1

The site IMDB Pro includes a free 14-day trial and can be useful in recruiting celebrity guests.

Prep Work for Live Interviews

We started out this chapter by talking about respecting your guests. The best way to do that is by showing them you took the time to do prep work for the interview. If you are interviewing someone who wrote a book, then read the book. If you do multiple interviews in a week and do not have the time to read the whole book, make sure you at least researched the book's topic a little, read any reviews about the book, and find out what other works the author has done. If you are interviewing the CEO of a company, make sure you research the type of product or service the company offers. And if you are interviewing a podcaster, make sure you have listened to a few of his or her shows. If that person has a blog, read some of his or her blog postings too.

Rob remembers being interviewed in late October of 2005, when one of the first questions he was asked was, "Do you have any children?" Just one week earlier Rob had played the heartbeat of his unborn son on his podcast. He had also mentioned on numerous shows that this was going to be his first child. So right off the bat, Rob knew this person had not done any prep work. And as the questions unfolded, this fact became even more apparent, and Rob found himself looking at the clock on his computer and wondering, "When will the hurting stop?" When the interview was finally posted on that person's podcast, it sounded lifeless and very monotone, which was not good for either party.

Your guests are giving up time out of their daily life to come on your show and are doing you a favor. Don't ever forget that. You as an interviewer need to take time out of your life to properly prepare for the interview. Wichita had this to say on the subject:

> *"I want to know a lot about the person I'm interviewing. They expect that from me, and I have to be respectful for the time they are allowing me to help further **my** career. I'm not doing them any favors because my name isn't Oprah or Letterman. So I don't ever kid myself about that."*

To help smooth things along, make sure you have a handful of well-thought-out questions written down before the interview. Also have notes about subjects you would like to talk about. Not so much additional questions, but rather a subject matter you would like to explore. You can even relate a story that pertains to something the interviewee said in the public domain. For example, if interviewing another podcaster, you might use something like the following:

> *"On your November 14th show you talked about leaving the toilet seat up. Well, there was this one time when I was not paying attention and...."*

This lets the interviewee know you took the time to research him or her, and you can always edit out the story later on if it does not flow well.

Prep work is not just about respecting your guest, it is also about making the final production of the show easier. Bazooka Joe had this to say:

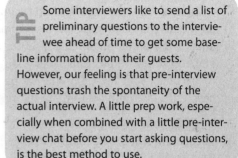

"I found out really early on that if I want to do a quick and concise show, I have to be on the ball. So I have about five questions I am going to ask and then after that I will go off on different tangents."

By having a general roadmap of what you want to ask and where you want to go with the interview before you start, you will make it easier come post-production to edit the show the way you like.

Using Skype and Other VoIP Services

When it comes to conducting the interview, in most instances you will be at one location and your guest will be at another. One way to record the conversation is to go to RadioShack and pick up a $20 phone recorder adapter. And if you do this, then guess what? Your interview will sound like you recorded it with a $20 phone adapter. This is not a good thing.

If you are lucky enough to be interviewing someone who is technically savvy, you should have the option of recording a Skype-to-Skype conversation (www.skype.com) using Voice over Internet Protocol (VoIP) technology. Skype offers digital voice communication, which means you will be getting the full spectrum of your voice, making for a warm sound. Some podcasters have gone out and purchased $700, $800, and even $2,800 phone hybrid recording setups. In our opinion this is not money well spent. These hybrid systems run over standard phone lines, known as POTS (Plain Old Telephone System). Because POTS limits the bandwidth of the voice (which causes that tinny, hollow sound you are used to when you talk on the phone), even with a $2,800 Blue Box you won't get as good a sounding recording as you will with a good Skype-to-Skype call.

Unfortunately, no matter how good your phone setup is, Skype or otherwise, the quality of the call will always be limited by your guest's phone. With a Skype-to-Skype call, you are getting the full spectrum of the voice and you can use much better microphones on each end than are found in a traditional phone mouthpiece. A good Skype-to-Skype call and recording sounds almost as good as having the person in the studio with you, and many times your listeners will not be able to tell the difference. That will never be the case with even the best phone hybrid, no matter how much you are willing to spend.

What if your guests are not technically savvy and most, if not all of your interview guests will be on a standard landline phone or cell phone? Should you then look at getting a phone hybrid? The answer in our opinion is still no. You can use "Skype Out" to make the calls to their landline or cell phone. Skype Out is a pay service (about $0.02 per minute), whereas Skype-to-Skype is completely free. But even at $0.02 per minute, it is going to take over 500 hours of calls to equal the cost of a low-end phone hybrid system. Plus, if you are not someone who has unlimited long distance, at $0.02 a minute you will actually be saving money each phone call.

It should also be pointed out that software phone hybrids are available, but these will also suffer the same limitations as the hardware hybrids in that they also use POTS to transmit the call and you will still be limited by the quality (or lack thereof) of the guest's phone.

Recording an Interview with Skype

Podcasters record Skype calls using a few different techniques. Some do it completely on the computer using software such as Audio Hijack Pro (Mac) or Hot Recorder (PC). But the method we like to use is to take the audio out of the computer and use a mixer to record on an external digital recorder. Figure 7.2 shows Rob's setup for recording Skype calls. There are numerous reasons for using this kind of setup:

- It is very reliable. Computer crashes are a fact of life, and a crash during a recording can be fatal for your interview.

- It does not take up any additional computer overhead, leaving more CPU

CAUTION

After you connect with the guest, feel you have properly matched up the levels, and are ready to start the interview, pan your channel all the way to the left and the guest's all the way to the right. This allows you to split the audio during post-production if you need to adjust the volume levels for a better match.

When you are doing Skype Out calls, panning left and right is really important, because what you think is a matching volume level oftentimes is not even close when you hear the final version. Plus, with the person on the other end being on a phone, there is usually a low-frequency buzz you will want to filter out.

power for the Skype call, thus giving you a better connection. It also means your computer will run cooler if fewer applications are active, thus keeping system fan noise down.

▓ It is easy to adjust levels and monitor the audio during the interview. You will learn early on that everyone talks at a different volume level, so you are always adjusting the settings for each new guest.

▓ This method works with any computer, Mac or PC.

▓ This method works with any VoIP software, such as Skype, Gizmo Project, iChat, Google Talk, and the others.

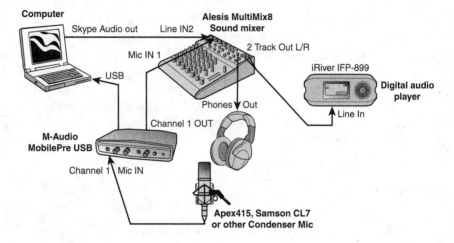

FIGURE 7.2

The Skype recording setup Rob uses for podCast411.

List of VoIP Services

Up to this point, we have talked mostly about Skype, and there is a good reason why. It is the *de facto* standard for VoIP communication in the podcasting community. It offers some very nice features, including IM (instant messaging) and the ability to transfer files. At any given point in time at least 2 million people are online with Skype. But Skype is not the only VoIP software; we will quickly talk about a few others in this section. This is not a complete list, just the ones most popular in the podcasting community. We are also only listing those services that are free, so we will not be talking about Vonage, Packet8, Lingo, or any other similar service.

■ **Skype (www.skype.com)**—A lot of great features come with Skype, such as Skype Out (discussed earlier). With Skype In, you can sign up for a phone number where people can call in to your computer from a landline or cell phone. This is a nice option to have if you are going to be interviewing celebrities, because many times they will not want to give out their number. Skype 2.0 also adds video calling, which can be nice in that you can see your interviewee's reactions. One thing clearly missing from Skype, however, is its own built-in recorder.

■ **Gizmo Project (www.gizmoproject.com)**—As with Skype, Gizmo also offers free calling to others using Gizmo (see Figure 7.3). Additionally there is Gizmo Call Out and Gizmo Call In, where you can also make calls out to any landline or cell phone or where you can receive a call from any landline or cell phone. One of the features that Gizmo has that Skype does not is a built-in recorder. Although the recorder is good (not great) for Gizmo-to-Gizmo calls, we have found the sound levels on Gizmo Out and Gizmo In calls to vary between you and the person to whom you're speaking. The one thing that Gizmo does not have (yet) is the same size user base. Skype has many times the number of users. But if you are only going to be making calls out to landline and cell phones, then Gizmo is just as good a choice as Skype, and with the additional feature of being able to set up a conference call-in number at no cost, it can actually be a better choice.

FIGURE 7.3

Gizmo Project is a quality VoIP service that rivals Skype.

- **iChat (www.apple.com)**—This comes free with Mac OS X and is only available for computers running OS X. So you can only talk directly to others on a Mac running OS X or to those running Windows XP using AIM from AOL. On the plus side, it has great videoconferencing capabilities. On the con side, it does not allow you to make calls out to traditional landlines and cell phones. Nor is there the call-in option that is available with Skype and Gizmo. This is not a good standalone VoIP solution, because you will also need to get Skype or Gizmo if you really want to talk to the rest of the podcasting community.

- **Google Talk (www.google.com/talk)**—At the time this book was written, Google Talk was still in beta. That said, it has a long way to go before it reaches the level of functionality and features of Skype or Gizmo Project. Additionally, it is only available for PCs, so just like iChat it really is not a good standalone VoIP solution. In the podcasting community, about half the podcasters are on Macs, so you need to get Skype or Gizmo Project if you want to talk to the rest of the world. As with iChat, there is no option to make calls out to landlines or cell phones.

> **NOTE**
>
> Google is not one to release a service and have it be second-rate (although right now Google Talk is not even third-rate to be quite honest), and we do expect Google to put in the resources necessary to make this service equal to Skype and Gizmo in the near future.

Double-Enders

One of the best ways to record an interview with good sound quality, where the guests are at two different locations, is to do a double-ender. No, a double-ender is not something you are going to hear about on shows such as Open Source Sex. A double-ender is when both parties each record their end of the conversation and then the two pieces are brought together, synced up, and then edited. Great care needs to be taken to make sure that both ends are indeed matched up correctly.

This method is used by many podcasts where the hosts are in two locations. The biggest advantage of this method is the great sound quality you get when you go this route. You can both be talking via cell phones and it will not matter, because all people will hear at the end is the recording through each mic directly into the computer. You get audio quality equal to having the

> **TIP**
>
> One trick to match the files is for one person to place the headphones over the mic and then have the person on the other end do a quick countdown. This way, his or her voice is recorded on your end and their end at the same time. Then in post production you get two tracks that are very easy to match up.

guest in your studio, but you and your guest are relaxed because both are in familiar surroundings.

There are some major and minor reasons double-enders are not used more in interviews. On the technical side, you need to make sure you sync up both files correctly,

TIP

To send very large files (up to 1GB), use yousendit (www.yousendit.com). This free service allows you to upload your files to the server. The service then sends a link to the email address you supply, for the recipient, to download the file.

and you need to get the guest's end of the recording sent to you, which requires at least a modicum of computer savvy. It also requires a broadband Internet connection because an interview recorded to an uncompressed audio file is sure to generate a very large file.

Another problem with doing double-enders is that you can pretty much forget about this method if you are going to be interviewing a lot of people, especially if any of the guests are not podcasters. There was zero chance that Rob was going to ask Phil Gordon, Larry Kudlow, Walt Mossberg, or Senator John Edwards to record their end of the conversation and then spend half an hour uploading it to the Net for him. It all comes back to respect of your guest's time, and doing a double-ender takes additional time and effort on your guest's part that can be avoided using the recording method mentioned earlier in the Skype section.

Face-to-Face Interviews

There is something different about a face-to-face interview. You get to see the facial reactions of the guests when you ask them a question (for better or for worse). You can also tell by their body language if they are into the interview or disinterested. Conversely, the guests can tell the same things about how you are reacting. Doing a face-to-face interview is also very intimidating for someone new to doing interviews. At least with a Skype interview there is some security in knowing the other person cannot see you sweat or realize how nervous you really are. However, some podcasters really love doing live face-to-face interviews. Andrew from Exit 50 is one of these people, and he had this to say about doing these types of interviews:

"Enjoy what you are doing, enjoy the people that you are talking to. Get out there, do it. The more that you do, the better you get at it. Yes, it is hard as hell to go up to somebody and say can you [do] an interview, and then you get scared. The more you do this, the more fun you will have.... Don't be scared. Talk to them like you are having a conversation. Don't worry about what you are going to say.... Just be

yourself and have fun with it. Do it in a setting that is not so like, 'Okay you sit here, and I sit there.' Do it in a restaurant. Think outside the box."

Also remember that depending on the surroundings, the audio quality can vary from the best to the worst. If you and your guest are face to face in your recording studio office, chances are the audio will be pristine. However, if you are face to face in a sports bar on a Sunday afternoon in Kansas City with the Chiefs playing in the background, there is a high probability that the audio will be barely understandable. So when you pick a location outside of your normal studio setting, if at all possible you should scout out potential interview spots to see what type of background noise you will be dealing with. There is nothing wrong with a good man-on-the-street-type interview as long as it is more man and less street.

Time-Shifted Interviews

Let's say you and a potential guest both want the interview to happen, but you just cannot work out a time when you are both available. A method a few podcasters use to get around this problem is to conduct what's called a *time-shifted interview*.

> **TIP**
> We recommend that you have the interviewee read the questions out loud before answering each one. Not only does this help you keep track of where he or she is in the list of questions, but it can also make that person sound more natural when answering.

How this works is simple: You send an email to the guest with some questions. The guest then records his or her responses to the questions and sends you the recording.

You then record the questions and mix together the two. You can even do follow-up questions this way. Like a double-ender, this method is pretty much limited to those who are comfortable doing a recording on their end and have the time and desire to put it together and send it to you. This is not something you would be asking Paris Hilton to do for your show. Another downside to this method is that there is no real interaction with the guest and no chance to bond. Most interviews done this way have a clear lack of chemistry between the guest and the host.

Interview Flow

Prior to the official start of the interview, it is always a good idea while you are getting the sound levels matched up that you use the time to bond with your guest. Tell a joke, ask how he or she is doing, ask what the weather is like where your guest lives, and so on. Then start the recording and let your guest know that the recording has started but that you are not yet into the interview.

Next, let him or her know what the basic format of the interview will be like. If you edit, let your guest know that. This way, if your guest messes up answering a question, he or she can always start over. Make sure to ask the guest if he or she has any questions before you start the interview.

Now that you have done all the hard work of finding a guest—researching about that guest, picking a method to record the interview, and letting the guest know the ground rules of the interview—you are finally at the point of actually conducting the interview. If you can get the interview to flow well, it will sound more like a conversation between two old friends than it will a stiff formal interview.

We asked Wichita what he does to get his interviews to flow so well. Here is what he said:

> **TIP**
>
> It is important to keep the full, unedited version of the interview with the recording of you telling your guest the recording started. We would recommend you tell the guest something like this:
>
> "I have started the recording, but we are not yet into the interview. When I say, 'John, welcome to the show,' from that point on all material is fair game for the interview. I do edit the interviews, and only about xx% of the interview will typically make it on the finished podcast. Do you have any questions before we start?"
>
> This clearly lays out the ground rules for the interview and records you laying them out. Although it is unlikely you will ever be sued by a guest, it is better to be safe than sorry. Think of this as your audio release form.

"I've found that getting everybody I'm not interviewing out of the room makes the atmosphere a whole lot more intimate. That way, the person I'm interviewing, usually a performer, doesn't feel like he or she needs to perform for their friends or manager or publicist. They're just talking to me, and I'm just talking to them.

"Since they don't know me, but usually know of me, they don't know what is going to happen, but they're ready for it to get a little weird and fun right off the bat. That's because they know for sure I'm not going to attack them with surprise questions or try to make them look bad to their fans.

"I tell them before we start that if in the middle of what we're doing they decide they don't want to do this or it's too 'out there' for them, its not too late. Just tell me and we'll stop right there, and I'll let them erase all of the interview themselves so they'll not have to worry

about anything they've said later on. Nobody's done that yet, but the option of 'getting out of it' is always on the table for them. I think that really helps a lot.

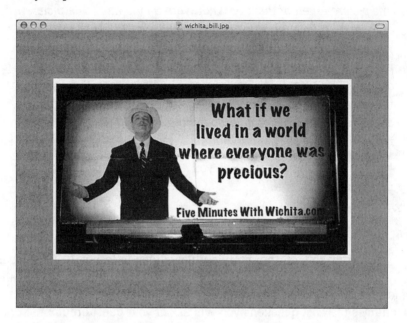

"I also try to stay away from the questions they get every time they do an interview, such as: 'What is it like on stage?' 'When did you real-ize this was going to work?' 'When did you start singing, playing guitar, etc?' They've heard these so many times they literally have stock answers ready and waiting. So I ask things I really want to know, like 'What do you call your grandparents?' and 'Did you ever get in trouble on the bus on the way to school?' 'Were you fat when you were little?' 'What was your dog's name growing up?' 'What size shoes do you wear?' Things that you'd never think to ask but you'd want to know if somebody said, 'Hey, did you know Eddie Van Halen had a dog named "jo-jo" when he was little?' People can relate to that. Something they had or did growing up.

"I try to ask questions that let the listener see that the person I'm inter-viewing is really just like them. The only difference being he/she is a great guitar player, or can act really well, or sing really well, or drive really well, or whatever. When the artist gets really comfortable and is

*feeling loose and is really just talking to me and not worrying about the interview, I show them some pictures and ask them if they recognize anybody in them, or is it really them in the picture or when was this picture taken of them or what were they doing? The picture isn't of them, of course, or anyone they would ever know or recognize, and you can hear that in their voice when they answer. And they **always** play along and say something like, "Yes, that **is** me. Long before I got a haircut" or "Yes, that's back when I had friends in the circus" or in the immortal words of Bluegrass legend Bobby Osborne before he could figure out what was happening in the picture: 'It looks like he's milkin' a cow... but I know that ain't right.'"*

"What are the pictures of? Well, you'll have to ask somebody I've interviewed."

Staying Focused

Another way to make sure the interview flows well is to put 100% of your attention toward what the guest is saying. Listen to your interviewee. Don't look ahead to the next question. Don't look at your web browser. Pay attention to what he or she is saying. Oftentimes the best questions you will ask of your guest are not the ones you prepared before the interview started, but rather the ones that come up from something the guest said answering a previous question. There is also no faster way to put the whole interview into tilt then when a guest asks a question back of you, but you are not paying attention because you were busy reading the next question.

If you edit, you need to edit out the "ums," the "ahs," the "you knows," and the dead spots. This will make your interview seem snappier and will make both you and your guest seem more articulate. Your guests will not only appreciate the effort, they will be more likely to link to and mention the interview if they think they sounded good.

 "I only have one rule when it comes to questions: I don't ask a question that I am not able to answer myself."

—Greg Demetrick, 5 Questions

Your listeners get to hear you every show, but they will probably only get to hear your guests one time. Therefore, make sure that when you do the interview there is less of you and more of your guest. Rob tries to keep his part of the conversation to under

3 minutes total time for 15 minutes of edited interview. His first rule of editing: When in doubt, edit Rob out.

Getting More Detailed Answers

Not all guests will give detailed answers. After your guests think they have answered the question, there will be a pause as they wait for you to ask the next question. If you say nothing, it will cause a pause, and chances are they will continue talking. Most people do not like dead air. If you edit, this is a great way to get people to talk more. Also, by doing this you are making sure that you are not talking on top of your guest and that you are giving them enough time to answer the questions. Your guests might be pausing just as a way to gather their thoughts.

Conversely, some guests will go off on a self-pontificating rant. In these cases, the most polite thing to say is, "I would like to change the subject a little here and talk about…." Then go to another question that is not at all related to what the guest was talking about.

At the end of the interview, remember to ask your guests whether there is anything else they wanted to talk about that you did not cover. This gives them the chance to talk about something you might have overlooked as a possible question or simply forgot to ask once the interview was in full gear. Additionally, this shows your guests some additional respect. You want your guests to leave the interview feeling good about coming on your show and then promoting the interview with all their contacts.

Dealing with Dull Interviews

Sometimes an interview is going to go completely south even though you did nothing wrong on your end. With all the advice we have given you in this chapter, it still does not really help if your guest is just not very personable. Rob once did an interview where all the guest would give was basically yes or no answers, even for the multiple-choice questions. Normally, it takes Rob about 45 minutes to get through all his questions. On this interview, he was done in less than 8 minutes.

So what do you do when this happens to you? The first choice is to just flush the interview and move on. No reason to torture your listeners with a yes/no interview. However, if the guest is a friend or someone famous, you may feel obligated to put up the interview. In this case, it is time for some creative editing. If the person has a podcast or other audio material available, edit in some clips from him or her throughout the interview. If no audio material is available, you can edit yourself in saying, "That reminds me of something that such and such said on a previous show," and then edit in that clip. Finally, you could have someone you know comment on the answers and then edit that into the show. Yes, this takes much more work, but the alternative is to put out a sub-par show or to throw away the time you already invested in the prep work and the actual interview. When you get one of these pigs of an interview, sometimes putting a bow on it is not such a bad thing, and if done well you can turn the interview into one of your better episodes.

People love a good interview. This is evident when you look around TV and radio at all the different talk shows and late night shows that either are built around guest interviews or have a guest at some point in the show. If you respect your guests, respect your listeners, and offer interesting guests and interesting questions, you will build a good-size audience.

MUSIC—ISSUES AND SOURCES

"Looks to me like podcasting is the replacement for radio…. People want a huge amount more diversity and interesting music and taste, that the airwaves by their very nature can't accommodate. So we are going to see a massive democratization of broadcasting of music, I think, through podcasts."

—John Buckman, CEO Magnatune

Not everyone agrees with what John Buckman said with regards to podcasting leading to a democratization of broadcasting music, but we think he's a pretty smart guy and are inclined to agree. Besides John is hardly a lone voice in the wilderness.

"What really attracted me to it [Garageband.com] was the idea, fairly idealistic idea, of democratizing the music industry, and helping make a merit-based system for music to be discovered and promoted. And what I learned pretty quickly was that the music industry was extremely dependent on the radio industry, and you can't really democratize the music industry without somehow also doing something about the radio industry. And so it is very exciting to have podcasting come along as a trend which really proves that there is an opportunity to democratize the radio industry."

—Ali Partovi, CEO of Garageband.com

Both John and Ali understand the tremendous potential of podcasting to democratize (open up for the masses) the music and radio industries. By contrast, here is a quote from a *Wall Street Journal* article (October 10, 2005) on podcasting:

"All podcasting is about is making it easy for the small percentage of the population that owns an iPod to record to a specific device.... People have been recording their favorite radio shows since the age of cassette."

—Bob Neil, President/CEO of Cox Radio Inc.

To which we can only say, "Wow!" We could understand that comment if it was made in October of 2004, but by October of 2005 one would expect the CEO of a major radio broadcasting corporation to know about podcasting and understand it is so much more than just putting content on an iPod. The democratization of the music and radio industries will be a battle, and you as podcasters will be the ones carrying the muskets.

In this chapter, we introduce you to some great resources that can supply you with the ammo you will need most: independent music. But first we address the issues involved with playing major record labels' (copyrighted) music on your podcast.

Licensing Madness

Let's start with a quick quiz.

Question: What do the following four things have in common?

- Putting your hand on a hot stove.
- Entering your username and password into the link provided in an email claiming to come from PayPal.
- Giving your bank account and social security number to that nice widow from Nigeria.
- Playing RIAA music on your podcast.

Answer: They are all really stupid mistakes you don't want to make.

We understand the temptation to use "big media" music on your podcast. Maybe you want to play the Village People's "YMCA" during the intro for your podcast to help set a tone for the show. Perhaps on your show you are telling a news story about a man stowing away on a plane and getting ripped apart by the landing gear with his remains falling to the ground and you want to play a clip of "It's Raining Men." Or you just dreamed of having your own show where you play a different Led Zeppelin song on each episode.

Stop! Don't do it!

Don't even think about doing it!

There is a reason why in November of 2005 Adam Curry cleaned up his show and changed to only playing "podsafe" music on The Daily Source Code. The lawyers were coming, and Adam did not want to be sued. Make no mistake about it—as a podcaster you are going to be looked at as a file sharer, and the RIAA has had no problems going after grandmas and 12-year-olds for sharing music. Surely you didn't think podcasters would be treated any different?

Unfortunately, even if you just want to secure a couple of licenses, this issue is not as simple as just filling out a couple of forms and being good to go. We asked John Buckman, CEO of Magnatune, if it was even possible to get licenses for a podcast so that you could play any big media music on your show. Here is his response:

"This came up at a conference, The Future of Music Conference, *when there were ASCAP and BMI people there. And they are happy to sell you a license for podcasting, but it is not the entire license you need. So all they are doing is promising not to sue you, but they are not saying no one else will.*

Because podcasts, if you take the entire song and put it on a MP3 stream, that is seen as essentially a pirated copy. That is how these people see it. They see it as a mechanical copy, and so you really need a license from the record companies in order to podcast a piece of music. It is actually no different than selling it through iTunes as far as the rights situation is concerned. When you buy a song from iTunes, they transfer a copy of the music file to you. That is legally what a podcast is."

OK, we realize some people will not be satisfied until they put their hand on that hot stove and are looking for a little more than simply, "Don't do it!" Let us explain the whole issue John was talking about. Say you are dead set on getting the licenses to podcast any song no matter the cost. First, you need to look at the two groups that represent a song. On one side you have the songwriters and publishers (the composition group), and on the other side are the record labels and the artists (audio recording group).

So if Sum 41 did a cover of a Willie Nelson song, Sum 41 and Island records would fall into the audio recording group, but Willie Nelson would be covered under the composition group as the original writer of said song. In the composition group, you have ASCAP, BMI, and SESAC representing the songwriters, and you have the Harry Fox Agency representing the publishers for the mechanical license. Right off you need to get four different licenses just for the composition group. Let's assume for the sample costs breakdown shown next that you make no revenue from your site, you release two shows a week, each show has four songs, and you average 1,000 downloads per show.

> **NOTE** We talked to the Harry Fox Agency about the amount shown in this example and they confirmed that the number was correct. They then stated that they were in the process of releasing a new license structure for podcasting that makes more sense. At the time this edition of the book was written, they had not yet made that new structure public. We are not sure if it will be closer to ASCAP and BMI, or if it will be $10,000 instead of $38,000.

- $288—ASCAP, "Non-Interactive 5.0"
- $283—BMI, Website Music Performance Agreement
- $168—SESAC, Internet License
- $37,856—Harry Fox Agency, Mechanical License ($0.091 for first 5 minutes per Song)
- $38,595—Subtotal

No, there is not a mistake in our calculations. We checked them multiple times. Shocking, isn't it? But with four songs in a show, that is $0.364 per download, times 1,000 downloads per show. With two shows a week and 52 weeks in a year—Bam! It is almost $40,000. Remember, with a podcast, each download is looked at as a single transaction. So if you want to be legal, this is the minimum you would pay, and we have not even gotten to the record labels or the artists yet.

Over on the other side, the audio recording group, you would normally have the Sound Exchange for Webcast licenses to deal with, except, their license does not cover podcasts. So instead of getting a single license to cover all the labels, you will need to go to every label and get licenses with each one. In addition to the amount shown earlier, you would also have the cost and time associated with negotiating a license with each and every record label.

As for Sound Exchange offering up a podcast license in the future, according to them it would literally take an act of Congress for this to happen. So this is one part of the book we will not need to update in future revisions. We talked to Derrick Oein, currently President of AMP and former COO of MP3.com. Here is part of the conversation with regards to the cost of a license from the audio recording group side:

TotPM: With Comfortstand is there any specific podcast license or policy for podcasters?

Otis Fodder: No licenses needed. The only policy would be that podcasters could not compile, say, a compilation on CD and sell it for profit. If a podcaster wanted to have a subscription for a podcast featuring our material, that would be perfectly okay. It is only when it enters an area selling the music for profit—for example, a standalone track on a compilation or putting it into advertising or a film or another vehicle.

The line is basically if money is going to be made off a track, then the artist would be contacted and then with the artist's permission I'm sure it would be a-okay. But in the end it is the artist's decision as the head of the label, and the way it is currently run is that all artists have creative control over their art.

Why should podcasters come to Comfortstand?

They can play anything and everything. And the site has a page. If someone plays our music on a podcast, we will link the podcaster [http://www.comfortstand.com/radio.html].

Anything else of interest about music and podcasting that you

I'm just a big lover of music. Vinyl, cassettes, media of all types. I see podcasting fit right snug into the whole landscape. I continually upgrade however, and I still have not owned an iPod yet. I listen to podcasts and Internet radio music. Being a musician in a few bands, all of my stuff is in sharing networks and encourage others to share. I've found that in one instance, with my band The ... have increased.

I'm an incredibly strong supporter. It's the idea that pirate radio is dead, not at all, but for everyone and that's the way it should ... for everyone to create podcasts you ... to find what you really love, but you ... looks and music anyhow, so it's really

TotPM: Have you heard of anyone who has actually received a license from a major record label for podcasting?

Derrick Oein: Not for podcasting, no. What they [the major record labels] would tell you is, well, if you want to [offer to] download a song you should pay wholesale. To them it is basically a digital download, so you should pay arguably the wholesale price of a download.... Generally you are talking a wholesale cost on the sound recording side between 60 some odd cents and low 70 cents if the wholesale price was a dollar. And they would say that is great, just pay us that.

TotPM: How do you think the whole interaction of advertising in podcasting is going to affect music podcasts?

Derrick Oein: It will be problematic. When the [independent] artists sense there is going to be some commercial aspect to it, they will say, "Well, how much are you going to pay me?" As you roll out more and more commercial aspects to what happens, I think that [independent] artists will be less and less friendly about the licensing and will demand some sort of payment.... I think that you will have to give something back to the artists.... It may not be in the level of paying eight and half cents per download, clearly, but some sort of payment that makes sense.

After reading all that, if you still want a license, here are some sites you should visit:

- ASCAP (www.ascap.com)
- BMI (www.bmi.com; see Figure 8.1)
- SESAC (www.sesac.com)
- Harry Fox Agency (www.harryfox.com)
- Sound Exchange (www.soundexchange.com)
- IMH (www.mentalhealth.com)

Finally, we do find it very ironic that Sony BMG music in July of 2005 paid $10 million and agreed to stop bribing radio stations to feature artists—this stemming from an investigation by New York Attorney General Elliot Spitzer. Additionally, in November of 2005, Warner Music agreed to pay $5 million to settle an investigation by Spitzer into payoffs for radio airplay of artists. Unfortunately, we as podcasters, who are more than willing to help promote some hot new artist or even just some classic artists, cannot get any help from the major record labels. Luckily for podcasters, there is a plethora of free pod-safe music available that we can play on our shows today.

In the future, we do believe that podcasting will reach a tipping point with regard to listeners that will cause the record labels to flock to podcasts as a way to promote new music from their artists. What that number is and when it will happen is anyone's guess, but until then we highly recommend you keep your hand off the stove.

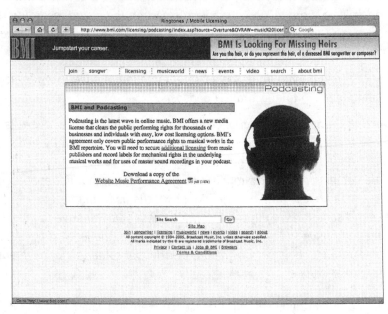

FIGURE 8.1

BMI is trying to generate revenue from podcasters

Free Music Services

Quite a few free legal music services are available on the Net, where listeners can download music for their own enjoyment. But just because the music is free to download does not mean it is free to include in your podcast for distribution to the world. This is where the term *podsafe* comes into play. For the most part, podsafe has come to mean that the music is free to download and use on your podcast and that you do not need to get permission from the musician prior to playing the music on your show. However, it is considered proper etiquette to contact any and all musicians whose music you do play and let them know you played it.

The following sections, sorted alphabetically, discuss sites that of have shown themselves to be friends of podcasting. In several see references to Creative Commons licensing. If you're not fam find a detailed discussion of this important licensing schem Commons Explained."

ccMixter.org

Launched in the summer of 2004, ccMixter.org has sand music tracks from which podcasters can choo Creative Commons about ccMixter.

> **TotPM:** *What is ccMixter?*
>
> **Jon Phillips:** *ccMixter is a project fur tries to encourage a social commun*
>
> **TotPM:** *Can you explain the type*
>
> **Jon Phillips:** *Right now the pr is also hip-hop, rock, and pu munity is about 2,000 indiv to be the underlying musi*

The music on this site has var follow the guidelines when you cannot use songs lab labeled as such. The user This is a great site to fir news, or anywhere yo

Comfortstand.com

Launched in 200 munity-driven free. This site genres to ch available. W of Comforts to podcasting:

The Links page on this site is an incredible resource if you are looking for niche sources of indie music. All music podcasters should have this Links page added to the bookmarks for their browser.

Garageband.com

Garageband.com is the granddaddy of independent music for podcasters. When podcasting first started, the number-one place where podcasters went for independent music, hands down, was Garageband.com (see Figure 8.2). No one else was even close.

FIGURE 8.2

Garageband.com is now offering production services for podcasters

Garageband still has one of the largest offerings of independent music on the Internet and has been rolling out new services and features that are podcast friendly. Here are a couple questions we asked Ali Partovi, the CEO of Garageband.com:

> **TotPM:** *Roughly how many songs are available on Garageband.com?*
>
> **Ali Partovi:** *There are actually different rights levels depending on what the musicians choose to allow when they put their song up. So from a podcasting standpoint, not every song is available for podcasting.*

Essentially we give the musician control over how their music can be redistributed. Some opt for Creative Commons, which is perhaps the most permissive license; it essentially says you can not only download my music for free but you can redistribute it, and that is essentially available for anyone to podcast and redistribute.

At the other end of the spectrum some people say, "No downloads at all." They only want their song available for streaming, and that is really not available for podcasting by anybody unless someone gets special consent directly from the musician.

The middle, which is where the bulk of our catalog is, is licensed for unlimited downloads off of Garageband's servers, but not going as far as Creative Commons. And so you couldn't just take that song and stick it into your podcast, unless your podcast is hosted on Garageband's servers. And in fact the bulk of the music falls into that category, and that is why we thought it makes sense to host podcasts on our servers....

Now that you can host your podcasts on Garageband, you do not need to go through that extra step of asking for permission and waiting to see if the musician responds.

TotPM: *What advice would you like to offer to someone looking at starting a music podcast?*

Ali Partovi: *Remember to keep your content as honest and real as possible. I think listeners are increasingly aware when something is not real, when it is censored, produced, and/or sort of feels like it's not the honest real truth. I think that some of the most successful broad-casters in traditional media, people like Howard Stern or Oprah, have gotten there because of being as honest and true to themselves as possible. I encourage you to just do what is honest and sincere, and you will find some audience. Better to do that than to sell out and try to guess what people want to hear.*

One of the biggest issues with Garageband.com, according to almost every podcaster we talked to, is that you need to contact most of the artists to get permission to include their music on your podcast. You will need to plan accordingly. Do not assume that you

TotPM: Have you heard of anyone who has actually received a license from a major record label for podcasting?

Derrick Oein: Not for podcasting, no. What they [the major record labels] would tell you is, well, if you want to [offer to] download a song you should pay wholesale. To them it is basically a digital download, so you should pay arguably the wholesale price of a download.... Generally you are talking a wholesale cost on the sound recording side between 60 some odd cents and low 70 cents if the wholesale price was a dollar. And they would say that is great, just pay us that.

TotPM: How do you think the whole interaction of advertising in podcasting is going to affect music podcasts?

Derrick Oein: It will be problematic. When the [independent] artists sense there is going to be some commercial aspect to it, they will say, "Well, how much are you going to pay me?" As you roll out more and more commercial aspects to what happens, I think that [independent] artists will be less and less friendly about the licensing and will demand some sort of payment.... I think that you will have to give something back to the artists.... It may not be in the level of paying eight and half cents per download, clearly, but some sort of payment that makes sense.

After reading all that, if you still want a license, here are some sites you should visit:

- ASCAP (www.ascap.com)
- BMI (www.bmi.com; see Figure 8.1)
- SESAC (www.sesac.com)
- Harry Fox Agency (www.harryfox.com)
- Sound Exchange (www.soundexchange.com)
- IMH (www.mentalhealth.com)

Finally, we do find it very ironic that Sony BMG music in July of 2005 paid $10 million and agreed to stop bribing radio stations to feature artists—this stemming from an investigation by New York Attorney General Elliot Spitzer. Additionally, in November of 2005, Warner Music agreed to pay $5 million to settle an investigation by Spitzer into payoffs for radio airplay of artists. Unfortunately, we as podcasters, who are more than willing to help promote some hot new artist or even just some classic artists, cannot get any help from the major record labels. Luckily for podcasters, there is a plethora of free pod-safe music available that we can play on our shows today.

In the future, we do believe that podcasting will reach a tipping point with regard to listeners that will cause the record labels to flock to podcasts as a way to promote new music from their artists. What that number is and when it will happen is anyone's guess, but until then we highly recommend you keep your hand off the stove.

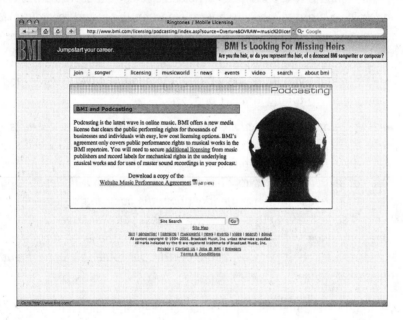

FIGURE 8.1

BMI is trying to generate revenue from podcasters

Free Music Services

Quite a few free legal music services are available on the Net, where listeners can download music for their own enjoyment. But just because the music is free to download does not mean it is free to include in your podcast for distribution to the world. This is where the term *podsafe* comes into play. For the most part, podsafe has come to mean that the music is free to download and use on your podcast and that you do not need to get permission from the musician prior to playing the music on your show. However, it is considered proper etiquette to contact any and all musicians whose music you do play and let them know you played it.

The following sections, sorted alphabetically, discuss sites that offer podsafe music and have shown themselves to be friends of podcasting. In several of these sections, you'll see references to Creative Commons licensing. If you're not familiar with the term, you'll find a detailed discussion of this important licensing scheme in Appendix B, "Creative Commons Explained."

ccMixter.org

Launched in the summer of 2004, ccMixter.org has over 2,000 users and a few thousand music tracks from which podcasters can choose. We talked with Jon Phillips from Creative Commons about ccMixter.

> **TotPM:** *What is ccMixter?*
>
> **Jon Phillips:** *ccMixter is a project funded by Creative Commons that tries to encourage a social community around remixing.*
>
> **TotPM:** *Can you explain the type of music people can find at ccMixter?*
>
> **Jon Phillips:** *Right now the primary style is electronic music, but there is also hip-hop, rock, and punk rock. It is interesting because the community is about 2,000 individuals that are fairly active, and that seems to be the underlying musical style people will find here.*

The music on this site has varying levels of licensing, and you need to make sure you follow the guidelines when picking songs. If you have a podcast with any advertising, you cannot use songs labeled as NC (noncommercial), although most songs are not labeled as such. The user interface on this site is nice, and downloading music is easy. This is a great site to find background music for a promo, for an intro, for reading the news, or anywhere you want to lay down a music bed under spoken vocals.

Comfortstand.com

Launched in 2003, Comfortstand is a community-driven label where all the music is free. This site offers a wide variety of music genres to choose from, with over 600 songs available. We asked Otis Fodder, the founder of Comfortstand, a few questions with regard to podcasting:

> **TIP**
>
> As an example, Nate and Di (Nate and Di Show) often lay down a music bed under the listener feedback. This gives a warmer sound to the listener feedback and helps set a tone to the feedback.

TotPM: With Comfortstand is there any specific podcast license or policy for podcasters?

Otis Fodder: No licenses needed. The only policy would be that podcasters could not compile, say, a compilation on CD and sell it for profit. If a podcaster wanted to have a subscription for a podcast featuring our material, that would be perfectly okay. It is only when it enters an area of selling the music for profit—for example, a standalone track on a compilation or putting it into advertising or a film or another vehicle.

Bottom line is basically if money is going to be made off a track, then the artist would be contacted and then with the artist's permission I'm sure it would be a-okay. But in the end it is the artist's decision as the way I started the label, and the way it is currently run is that all artists have 100% creative control over their art.

TotPM: Why should podcasters come to Comfortstand?

Otis Fodder: They can play anything and everything. And the site has a page where if someone plays our music on a podcast, we will link back to the podcaster [http://www.comfortstand.com/radio.html].

TotPM: Anything else of interest about music and podcasting that you would like to add?

Otis Fodder: I'm just a big lover of music. Vinyl, cassettes, media of all sorts. And music and podcasting fit right snug into the whole landscape. I'm not one to continually upgrade however, and I still have not found the need to buy an iPod yet. I listen to podcasts and Internet radio and download music. Being a musician in a few bands, all of my own work I share on file-sharing networks and encourage others to download, and have found that in one instance, with my band The Bran Flakes, our CD sales have increased.

In regards to podcasting, I'm an incredibly strong supporter. It's the pirate radio of this century—not that pirate radio is dead, not at all, but podcasting gives a voice to everyone and that's the way it should be.... Of course with the ability for everyone to create podcasts you have to wade through the muck to find what you really love, but you have to do that with films and books and music anyhow, so it's really no big thing.

The Links page on this site is an incredible resource if you are looking for niche sources of indie music. All music podcasters should have this Links page added to the bookmarks for their browser.

Garageband.com

Garageband.com is the granddaddy of independent music for podcasters. When podcasting first started, the number-one place where podcasters went for independent music, hands down, was Garageband.com (see Figure 8.2). No one else was even close.

FIGURE 8.2

Garageband.com is now offering production services for podcasters

Garageband still has one of the largest offerings of independent music on the Internet and has been rolling out new services and features that are podcast friendly. Here are a couple questions we asked Ali Partovi, the CEO of Garageband.com:

> **TotPM:** *Roughly how many songs are available on Garageband.com?*
>
> **Ali Partovi:** *There are actually different rights levels depending on what the musicians choose to allow when they put their song up. So from a podcasting standpoint, not every song is available for podcasting.*

Essentially we give the musician control over how their music can be redistributed. Some opt for Creative Commons, which is perhaps the most permissive license; it essentially says you can not only download my music for free but you can redistribute it, and that is essentially available for anyone to podcast and redistribute.

At the other end of the spectrum some people say, "No downloads at all." They only want their song available for streaming, and that is really not available for podcasting by anybody unless someone gets special consent directly from the musician.

The middle, which is where the bulk of our catalog is, is licensed for unlimited downloads off of Garageband's servers, but not going as far as Creative Commons. And so you couldn't just take that song and stick it into your podcast, unless your podcast is hosted on Garageband's servers. And in fact the bulk of the music falls into that category, and that is why we thought it makes sense to host podcasts on our servers....

Now that you can host your podcasts on Garageband, you do not need to go through that extra step of asking for permission and waiting to see if the musician responds.

TotPM: *What advice would you like to offer to someone looking at starting a music podcast?*

Ali Partovi: *Remember to keep your content as honest and real as possible. I think listeners are increasingly aware when something is not real, when it is censored, produced, and/or sort of feels like it's not the honest real truth. I think that some of the most successful broadcasters in traditional media, people like Howard Stern or Oprah, have gotten there because of being as honest and true to themselves as possible. I encourage you to just do what is honest and sincere, and you will find some audience. Better to do that than to sell out and try to guess what people want to hear.*

One of the biggest issues with Garageband.com, according to almost every podcaster we talked to, is that you need to contact most of the artists to get permission to include their music on your podcast. You will need to plan accordingly. Do not assume that you will be able to spend Saturday morning cruising the site for new music and then include those songs when you record Saturday afternoon.

Magnatune.com

Magnatune.com is not a music network; rather, it is an independent online record label that is very pro-Internet and pro-podcasting. The company was started in 2003, and now over 250 artists and over 500 albums (totaling more than 5,000 songs) are available to choose from. Magnatune has a no-cost podcast license for both noncommercial and commercial podcasts, and even has a podcaster account where you can download high-quality versions of the songs for your podcast at no cost. Magnatune wants to have its music played on podcasts and goes out of its way to help podcasters. We talked to John Buckman, CEO of Magnatune, about his company.

> *TotPM: Can you describe what Magnatune is?*
>
> *John Buckman: Magnatune is an attempt to do a record label that actually gets the Internet. Which means Internet community; it means some sort of open-source focus; it means enabling radio and podcasts and remixes. It also means actually paying artists. None of these things exist in any other record company today. So that, in essence, is what it is.*
>
> *TotPM: How much of the music on Magnatune can podcasters use on their shows?*
>
> *John Buckman: We make all our music available with a Creative Commons license so that people can make all sorts of interesting uses of it. For example, remixes—and a lot of podcasters feature really interesting remixes—through ccMixter. And I see podcasts as kind of part of the remix community; you are just repurposing the music in new creative ways. Sometimes talk shows, sometimes music shows, sometimes hybrids.*

When it comes to record labels, these guys get podcasting. They understand podcasting and the potential to use it to promote music. They treat podcasters with respect and want to partner with you to help promote the music they have on their site.

Opsound.org

This site is a project of artist Sal Randolph. Musicians are invited to submit their work to the Opsound site using a "copyleft" license from Creative Commons. Podcasters are free to download, remix, and add the music to their podcasts as they see fit. The site has been up since 2004 and has a large collection of artists covering almost every genre you can think of. This is a great site to find something out of the ordinary, even as measured in the world of independent music. Here are some comments from our conversation with Sal Randolph:

> **TotPM:** *What is Opsound's policy for podcasters using the music on your site?*
>
> **Sal Randolph:** *All Opsound music is offered under the Creative Commons Attribution-ShareAlike license (except a few pieces which are placed in the public domain). This means anyone is free to copy, share, and even make commercial use of the music as long as, 1) the original artist is given attribution, and 2) any derivative works are released under the identical license.*
>
> *I recommend reading the actual text of the license and consulting the Creative Commons website for a fuller understanding [http://creativecommons.org/licenses/by-sa/2.5/ and http://creativecommons.org/licenses/by-sa/2.5/legalcode].*
>
> *I believe most podcast uses would be considered "collective works" under the licensing definition, rather than "derivative works," in which case the only requirement would be to identify the music's author, and provide a link to their site and to the license information.*
>
> *I'm not a lawyer, and can't give you or your readers any specific legal advice! But in general I'd consider all the music on Opsound quite "podcast safe." It is certainly the intent of the participants that the music be freely downloaded, shared, and broadcast.*
>
> **TotPM:** *Do podcasters need to contact the artists before playing their music on their podcast? Or do they simply download, add to the show, and then give proper credit and links?*
>
> **Sal Randolph:** *It's the latter! That's exactly what's so cool about the Creative Commons licenses—the whole point is not having to ask!*

Of course, artists love to know when their music is being used, and
telling the artist might allow them to promote the podcast among their
own friends and fans, but it's strictly voluntary.

The music on this site is a little different from what other podcasters are playing. If you are looking for an "art" feel for your podcast, this is the site for you. You have to love a site whose genres include Abstract, Avant Garde, and Psychogeography. This site even has individual RSS feeds for each genre so as new songs are made available, they are delivered right to you.

Music.podshow.com (The Podsafe Music Network)

The Podsafe Music Network (PMN) was built from the ground up to connect podcasters and independent musicians. Although PMN is part of Podshow, its heart and soul is really C.C. Chapman from the Accident Hash podcast. C.C. truly cares about making it easier for podcasters to have access to podsafe music. And his passion is greatly responsible for the rapid success of this site (see Figure 8.3).

FIGURE 8.3

The Podsafe Music Network is the new go to site for music for podcasts

PMN was launched in July of 2005, and just 8 months later the site had over 15,000 songs available for download and over 5,000 podcasters using the service. We talked to C.C. Chapman about PMN.

> *TotPM: Can you explain what the Podsafe Music Network is? And what is its goal?*

> *C.C. Chapman: PMN is the one-stop shop for podsafe music. The goal is that an artist can come in and submit their music to one site, and by submitting they have a terms of agreement that they have to sign off on that says by uploading this song or however many songs they want, any podcaster has their permission to podcast this song. And on the flip side, podcasters can come in and register, and they know that every single song and every single artist on this website they don't have to get permission for because it has already been granted.*

> *The biggest problem with doing a music podcast or any podcast that you want to include music in legally, is just the back and forth email game... educating the artist what a podcast is, getting the permission to play the music on the podcast, and it is a back and forth game.... So now we are just making it easy that you go and you register, whether you are an artist or a podcaster, and you hook up instantly.*

PMN offers a quick and easy way to find a wide variety of podsafe music to play on your podcast. Almost every genre of music you can think of is represented, and it is easy to preview the music on the site while you are searching for new songs to use.

Others

The sites we've listed so far are by no means the only places to find independent music on the Net. In this section, we've included a small alphabetized list of some other sites for you to check out. Some of these sites are very good, others are not exactly podsafe, and some make it difficult to locate new music. But overall they offer some unique music as well as a chance for you to learn about new artists. Remember, even though you cannot use the music directly from some of these sites, you can still contact the artists directly and ask for their permission to play their music in your podcast.

- Acme Noise (www.acmenoise.com)
- AMP (library.musicpodcasting.org)
- CD baby (www.cdbaby.com)

- Electronical (www.electronical.org)
- Indie Heaven (www.indieheaven.com)
- Intuitive Music (www.intuitivemusic.com)
- Lost Frog (www.lostfrog.net)
- MySpace (www.myspace.com)
- Ninja Tune (www.ninjatune.net)
- Pure Volume (www.purevolume.com)
- Sound Click (www.soundclick.com)

Local Indie Music

Music-based podcasts don't have to be all about finding music online. There is more than likely a wealth of independent music in your own backyard. Every community has local musicians, and there are some extra perks for promoting them. Finding these local musicians is easier than you think. First, you can go to your local guitar store and talk to the people who work there—most are either in a local band or are friends with many of the local bands. Second, you can look in the local arts and alternative lifestyle newspaper that is often found near the front door of bars. In the paper is usually a listing of local concerts. Go to the concerts and meet the bands. Get there early, bring your recorder and business cards, and find the manager of the band. Ask him or her about playing the band's music on your show. You may find yourself having to explain the entire concept of podcasting, but if done correctly, most bands will appreciate you playing their music. After all, next to partying all night and sleeping late, what musicians really want most is to get exposure for their music.

Which brings us to the added perks of focusing on local musicians. Sure, you can play a song from some band halfway around the world, and the thanks you get might be a couple of nicely worded emails and maybe a signed CD. But with local bands, you will often get free tickets to their shows, great seats at concerts, backstage passes, and invites to private parties. Okay, so oftentimes there will be more people at the party than were at the concert, but does it really matter? You just made some new friends, one or two of whom might even remember you if they ever make it big.

Playing Your Own Music

You are not just relegated to playing other peoples' music; if you are in a band, you have access to your own music to play on your podcast. One of the best examples of a band creating a podcast to help promote themselves and their music is the podcast for The Reverse Engineers (www.thereverseengineers.com). Every band out there needs to check out what they did with this podcast. It is probably the best format for a relatively unknown band to promote themselves and connect with their fans. We asked The Reverse Engineers some questions regarding their podcast and podcasting in general:

TotPM: What are people going to hear when they listen to your podcast?

The Reverse Engineers: The idea that we had was to take the songs from Max Q, which is the record we put out last year, and just talk about each one of the songs, and then play each song. We had a lot of people from all over the world that were wanting us to play in their town, and it's kind of neat when you hear a band you want to see them live or talk with them or somehow interact with them. So the podcast for us was a way for us to kind of connect with people in a different way and actually talk about what the music means....

The first 12 podcasts, each one was about a different song on our record.... We covered every song on the record, and now we are going to try and do some live performances and put them on our podcast. And just have people find out a little more about our daily activities and stuff as a band and just as people.

TotPM: I [Rob] used to listen to only one radio station growing up on Long Island—WBAB. I just do not see that kind of loyalty anymore. Do you think podcasting will fill that gap?

The Reverse Engineers: Isn't it wild though, everybody has like [their favorite old radio station, where] they know what the FM station was they used to [listen to]. That was their station. And nowadays people don't give a damn because radio sucks so bad. And that is what is exciting about the podcasts....

So hopefully this next generation will be talking 20 years from now about "I remember xyz podcast," and they will hold it in that kind of esteem, because radio has completely lost that. No one cares about their radio station anymore.

TotPM: Why should independent musicians be interested in podcasts and podcasting?

The Reverse Engineers: One of the things that is our job as independent musicians is to find out ways to get airplay, because it is still really the way to get heard is for someone to actually run across your music through some other means instead of just going into Amazon and maybe finding it or going to your website. FM radio long ago kind of stopped being accessible to independent artists and then college radio was the way for you to get heard. And now college radio is also pretty much inaccessible to independent artists because they are being just hounded by the [major] labels as far as pushing their product. So podcasts are providing a valuable service for bands. [They] are replacing college radio for that type of task that we [as bands] have to do, which is show people [our] music. And the great thing is it is worldwide accessible.

TotPM: What advice would you like to give out to any bands that are not podcasting?

The Reverse Engineers: Regardless of what the podcast is about, as long as it is an audio documentary of the band they are in, they should get involved. Podcasting can be as cheap as buying an MP3 player that has a mic on it [for example, the iRiver IFP 890 series]. When you are at a gig or before a show and you want to record it, record it. It is a great way to even do an audio diary of your band, even record your shows and play live songs on your podcast. It is just another way a band can promote in a much more personal way.

When you are in a band it takes a while between records, so if you turn somebody on to your record immediately, they will turn around and go, "When are you coming out with something new?" Well, it takes a while to do one of those, so it [the podcast] allows you to go ahead and quickly and inexpensively get something out to your listeners to keep them aware of you and give [them] a little different side of your band or introduce [them] to the personalities behind the music and just kind of deepen the experience and really make them more than just a passive fan.

It's also a really great way to actually build our fan base in ways we never thought possible. The fact that within 3 or 4 months we have gotten 1,600 subscribers, it is a great way to really build a fan base and communicate with our listeners. Each episode we make sure to tell them to email us questions so that we can talk about it on the show, so there is that whole interactive thing with the fan that I think is a really cool thing.

March to Your Own Beat

When it comes to putting music on your podcast, be creative in picking that music. What good is it to feature independent musicians if all everyone does is play the same 10 or 20 songs from a dozen musicians? Don't play it safe, and don't emulate what radio has become. You will find listeners of podcasts expect more than that. Don't just use the sites listed in this chapter. If you go out of your way to find new and interesting music, you will grow your listener base. If you are continually the first one to play new music that is enjoyable to listen to, word of mouth will quickly spread about your show. Finding new songs and artists who have not yet been featured on other podcasts will take quite a bit of work, but for anyone doing that kind of podcast, it is sure to be a labor of love.

"When you look at podcasting specifically, outside of a 10-mile radius of San Francisco… everybody in the U.S. and that I know of in the world buys [MP3] players to listen to music. And so there is a really golden opportunity to provide that music to podcasts and to people that want to listen to podcasts. So it is just going to take time and effort to make that happen. But ultimately that is why people have MP3 players—to listen to music. There is a great opportunity here; it is just going to be a lot of work."

—Derrick Oein, President of AMP

Chapter 9

THE AUDIBLE WRITTEN WORD

"For me, The Seanachai is practice. It's the orchestra warming up. A noise that has a kind of beauty to it, but certainly not a symphony. Someday, I'll really try to write something. Something big, something that scares me to attempt. But until then, it's all just practice."

—Patrick McLean, The Seanachai

Science fiction writer Harlan Ellison has a mantra when it comes to beginning fiction writers attempting to get published: Always get paid! At conventions he has fledgling writers chanting the mantra, encouraging writers to never, ever give away their work. Even if you only make $5, you are still getting paid for your hard work, whereas giving away your work cheapens it.

This made sense. You wouldn't give away accounting services for free, or emergency room surgery, or computer programming, all in the hopes that someone would eventually pay you money to do these things. Writing is work. Why shouldn't writers expect payment for the work they do, like anyone else?

This was all before the advent of podcasting.

Starting in early 2005 with Tee Morris and his novel *Morevi: The Chronicles of Rafe and Askana,* authors began releasing serialized versions of their novels, harkening back to Dickens' time with the gradual release of a novel. Only these authors didn't charge for their books the way Dickens did.

The response was staggering.

What Writing Is Podcasted

The original novel is not the only type of podcasted written work out there. Although it's popular, several people release their short stories, essays, poetry, and public domain works. The following sections examine the podcasting potential for different kinds of writing.

Fiction

The popularity of audiobooks is one of the things that helped drive the popularity of podcasting. With audiobooks, you don't have to put down your book to do dishes, exercise, or drive to work. So novels, or "podiobooks" as Evo Terra of Podiobooks.com calls them, became a logical podcast idea. But would it be worth the authors' time and possible publishing snafus that could come with giving a book away for free?

It all depended on what people were trying to get from it.

Original Material

Original fiction is by far the most popular podcasted writing these days. There are countless novels collected at Podiobooks.com, a website dedicated to the serialization and (free) hosting of podcasted books.

Novels aren't the only fiction content podcasted, however. Several websites podcast short fiction, reading their own original work and distributing it for free:

- The Rev Up Review (http://www.revupreview.co.uk)
- Brief Glimpses of Somewhere Else (http://seeker.libsyn.com)
- The Seanachai (http://www.goodwordsrightorder)
- The Voice of Free Planet X (http://www.planetx.libsyn.com/)
- James Patrick Kelly's Free Reads (http://www.jimkelly.net)
- Lies and Little Deaths (http://www.virtualantho.blogspot.com)
- Cory Doctorow's Podcast (http://www.craphound.com)

Most podcasters have a PayPal (http://www.paypal.com) button on their site for voluntary donations from listeners (see Figure 9.1), but that's not why they do it. For Patrick McLean of The Seanachai, the donation button is not at all important financially. He explains that the donations serve another purpose:

"Emotionally it's tremendously important. People can lavish you with praise, but when someone donates I know, beyond the shadow of any doubt, that they really got something out of The Seanachai, and that's tremendously gratifying."

FIGURE 9.1

A creative donation request from The Seanachai.

In late 2005, several professionals got into the podcasting game, including James Patrick Kelly (http://www.jimkelly.net) and Cory Doctorow (http://craphound.com). They saw something in podcasting that could serve their career, while widening their fan base and supporting a new medium at the same time.

James Patrick Kelly enjoys podcasting a great deal (Figure 9.2). Here's what he has to say:

"I do like it—a lot. I started recording stories in MP3 format and posting them on my website a couple of years ago. Podcasting takes those readings to a whole new level. And even though I'm not quite on the bleeding edge of podcasting, it's a kick to be one of the first SF writers to wrestle with this hot new tech."

Kelly is honest with his future in podcasting, however, because he is not sure if he's in it for the long haul.

*"What am I going to read when I finish [the podcast novella] **BURN**? It occurs to me that I could also read some of the columns that I've written for **Asimov's Science Fiction** magazine. I started my podcast with recordings of stories I had already posted on my website, and I can continue offering those. I have a couple of out-of-print novels that I'm proud of, that I might consider reading. But if I keep pumping out a podcast a week, I'll run through my entire output in three, maybe four years. So that's one concern. The other concern is the amount of time it takes to record and post and troubleshoot a podcast. Podcasting tech needs to get way more user-friendly and transparent to the non-geek. Okay, maybe I'm just a geek wannabe but I **am** the guy who family and friends call when they need help with their computers. I'm here to say that some of this stuff makes my head spin. I mean, I'm a science fiction writer—I'm not sure I want to sign on to learn audio engineering as a second career!"*

FIGURE 9.2

*James Patrick Kelly's podcasted novella, **BURN**.*

The much-loved fiction magazine format has also translated to podcast. At least one literary magazine, *Escape Pod*, is in podcast-only format. Although it commonly podcasts reprints, it does accept unpublished work for publication. It is a paying market that relies on the donations from its listeners to pay its authors.

All these podcasters share a love for the written word, whether it is their own or others'. None of them regrets making the decision to podcast their fiction, and each is gratified with the response their fiction has received from listeners.

It's clear that fiction in podcast form is an area that a lot of listeners want to see more of, so if you're a writer and feel your work is ready for hundreds or thousands of listeners, consider podcasting your fiction. You may get a better audience than you would have had you sold your story to a small magazine. You never know.

Public Domain Material

Not everyone who is podcasting stories is doing his or her own work. Although that might raise the flags of copyright infringement, the actual practice is typically far from it because these people are reading works that have passed into the public domain.

LibriVox (http://www.librivox.org) is a podcast that offers books for free. It gets volunteer podcasters to read a couple of chapters at a time and releases the book when it is done. The goal is to get all the public domain books available in podcast form.

On a smaller level, the gang from The Science Fiction Podcast Network (http://www.tsfpn.com) is releasing the works of Edgar Allen Poe as podcasts in the Poe Podcast Project. Several people also podcast their favorite books that are in the public domain, such as *A Christmas Carol* and *The Wizard of Oz*, as a simple exercise or homage and not part of a greater project.

As you can see from Figure 9.3, with so many books in the public domain, there is nothing stopping you from podcasting your favorite classic. But you will need to be careful and make sure that no one holds the intended work's copyright. More on this later.

"I missed out on being a podcast pioneer. But I was intrigued by the idea of podcasting, and so I set out to try it. As I write this, I am reading a new novella on my own podcast, Free Reads [http://feeds.feedburner.com/freereads], a chapter a week for 16 weeks. But by the time you read this, I will have long since finished. And I must say that, while I certainly don't regret creating my podcast, I'm not sure just how devoted I am to it. I'm a writer, not an actor or a sound

engineer or a webmaster. You may very well click over to Free Reads only to find that it's a ghost site that hasn't been updated in months.

"And that, I fear, may be the fate of much of the first wave of podcasts. Podcasting is a lot of work for little or no pay or recognition. Because I expect a major shakeout, I haven't a clue yet as to where this brave new tech is headed or what it means.

"But I have my ear on it."

—James Patrick Kelly, *Asimov's Science Fiction,*
June 2006 (used by permission)

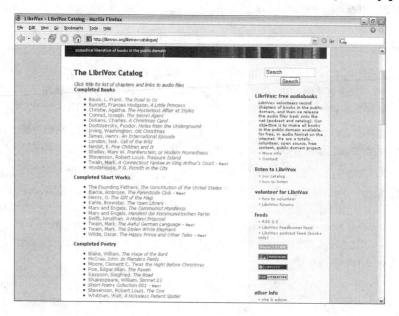

FIGURE 9.3

The growing LibriVox library.

Fan Fiction

As you may or may not know, there are a number of thriving communities online that publish so-called *fan fiction*, or *fanfic*. This is a label given to fan-written work based on an existing franchise, such as a popular TV show, movie, or series of books.

Unfortunately, writing original stories in established fictional worlds such as *Harry Potter* or *CSI: Crime Scene Investigation* is always a gray area. The fans consider it homage to their favorite world and giving people the answers to questions the author hasn't answered (popular plotlines include romantic entanglements between characters that hasn't happened in the author's stories). Many writers, however, consider it a violation of the copyright they hold on their world and their characters.

Legally, fanfic is a violation of copyright, because it involves using someone else's copyrighted characters, even if it's an original story of your fabrication. Although fanfic is very popular throughout the Web, it serves you well to remember it's not strictly legal.

Because podcasting costs more money than blogging does, the desire to make some money through donations or advertising is attractive to help recoup server and equipment costs. However, profiting from copyrighted material, which is what soliciting donations for podcast fanfic is, is very dangerous.

See "Copyright Concerns," **p. 175** (this chapter).

Other Written Work

Fiction—short or long—is the most popular type of writing podcasted, but it's by no means the only writing. Poets, essayists, and script writers are finding podcasting to be an excellent way to publish their work.

Poetry

Most poets write to have their works read aloud; the mere notion of poetic feet (the different rhythms and emphasis on certain syllables) means nothing if the piece is not spoken aloud. Podcasting seems to be the natural outlet for poets to present their work, and several have taken advantage of it.

"I think that [podcasting is] going to be a great boon for writers who rely as much on the sound of words as in their meaning."

—Bill Wadman, The 365 Project and The 52 Project

The general rules for podcasting poetry are similar to the rules for podcasting fiction. Pay attention to quality and don't read too quickly or too slowly—if you make every line a dramatic pause, you lose the drama quickly. As with fiction, you can read your own work, work under the Creative Commons license (see Appendix B, "Creative Commons Explained"), or present poetry that is in the public domain. Whatever you choose, make the poetry something that is close to your heart; poetry is about passion, and audible presentations can release the intensity the author intended.

Essays

Along the same lines, essays are written to portray a point or tell a story from the heart of the writer, making it an ideal type of work to be podcasted. If you have ever been a fan of the essays on National Public Radio or any other radio station, you realize quickly how podcasted essays can be performed to great effect.

In November of 2004, Bill Wadman created The 365 Project (http://www.billwadman. com/365/), a website dedicated to producing something creative every day for a year. "In an effort not to be consumed by the state of the world…. The idea is to create something new every day for a year," he says on the site. Because he's a photographer, many of the creative efforts showed up in photography, but he did post poetry, music, and essays. When he discovered podcasting, he began releasing his audio.

"For me, podcasting was an easy way to get my work out there, as well as a way to keep myself honest by creating an audience so that I couldn't be lazy and skip a day on The 365 project…. There were also several essays which I read as well, figuring that my listeners might rather hear me talk trash than read it."

Currently, Bill is working on The 52 Project (http://www.billwadman.com/52), a project similar to the 365 Project, only he creates larger-scale projects weekly instead of small projects daily.

Bill's advice to fledgling podcasters suggests a more proactive approach to a problem many of us have: dealing with the sound of our own voices.

"The one thing I never liked was reading my work because I don't like my voice. So for me [my advice] would be to get some voice talent to come read it. But I definitely think there is something to hearing words read out loud versus reading them from the page, which is the great thing about podcasting."

Scripts

Like fiction writers, script writers have considerable hurdles to clear before their work ever gets in front of the public. Podcasting removes most of those hurdles, giving the writers, directors, and voice actors a ready audience.

Audio dramas released over podcast are growing in popularity, starting with Spaceship Radio (http://www.spaceshipradio.com) soliciting scripts from authors, to other original dramas produced such as The Falcon Banner (http://www.darkerprojects.com/falconbanner.html).

The audio drama production takes considerably more effort than simply reading a story over a podcast, but a team will usually take on the project, leaving the writer able to create the drama without worrying about the actors, direction, and so on.

> **CAUTION**
>
> In many instances, people posting unlicensed copyrighted material to the Internet think they've found a get-out-of-jail-free card by including a notice that says you shouldn't download the copyrighted work unless you already own it. It's very important to understand that this tack offers you *no* protection whatsoever against prosecution and that the fines doled out for these violations range up to $100,000 per incident.

Copyright Concerns

With the advent of the Internet, copyright has suffered. Students plagiarize papers, authors find their own work transcribed online so people can read it for free instead of buying their books. (Aforementioned author Harlan Ellison waged a multiyear battle with America Online because of a copyright violation in a Usenet group, which was settled in 2004.)

Michael A. Stackpole, who podcasts chapters from his novels, acknowledges that Internet piracy is a problem. "Piracy is always a threat," he says. "We see folks scanning and posting books all the time, and it's really tough to get them to stop. Some folks just don't regard copyrights as legitimate, so they violate them on purpose or out of ignorance."

When it comes to podcasting the written word, keep plagiarism and copyright in mind. You *cannot* read something that belongs to someone else on a podcast without permission. It doesn't matter if you are honoring the author, if you're convinced that it will help the sales of the book, or if you're

> **NOTE**
>
> There is the matter of "fair use," allowing you to quote a portion of a copyrighted work without permission for the purpose of commentary or criticism. The keys here are that the quote can't be a "substantial" part of the work, and you must attribute the source. The problem with this is people are often confused about exactly how much they can quote, and an author can take someone to court to challenge the use of their material. For more information, check out the following "copyright and fair use" site from Stanford University:
>
> http://fairuse.stanford.edu/Copyright_and_Fair_Use_Overview/chapter9/index.html.

just trying to be a good fan. It's not yours to podcast, and you can get into trouble if you continue to do so. Even worse, if you attempt to make money through donations or advertising while releasing copyrighted material, you could get into more trouble.

Serialized audiobooks and stories comprise a very popular section of podcasts, but this is also one of the more dangerous areas to deal with if you disregard copyright. If the stuff you're writing isn't yours, make sure it's in the public domain or published under the Creative Commons license, which we discuss in detail in Appendix B.

Does Giving Your Work Away Increase Sales?

It is not just the fear of copyright violation that causes authors to avoid posting their work online—in audio form or otherwise. Years ago, authors feared giving their work away simply because, well, it was giving their work away instead of selling it. People do not expect doctors, construction crews, and teachers to work without pay, but several people don't even blink at the thought of creative types giving away their work. This can devalue the work, causing the public to wonder the old adage about why they should buy the cow (a book in a store) when they can get the milk (stories, chapters, and so on) for free online.

One argument seemed to come up frequently, and it is the same argument that several small magazines claim when they can't afford to pay their authors: The exposure is good for you. This opinion was viewed with considerable skepticism for some time, but as the years went on, the Internet seemed to prove the adage. Whereas an independent, nonpaying print magazine might get your work in front of hundreds of eyes at best, the Internet is global and can present your work to potentially millions. Here is what Michael A. Stackpole has to say on the subject:

"A writer has to weigh the positives and negatives of posting [work for free]. To me, the positives of exposure outweigh the negatives of having stuff ripped off. Because I post stuff and include a copyright

---

CAUTION

It is *never* okay to violate copyright. We can't stress this enough. *Always* podcast work that falls under one of the following:

- **In the public domain**—A simple web search will let you know whether or not something is copyrighted.
- **Your own work**—Remember, if you've sold the work, you should check your contracts to make sure you own the rights to release it in audio format. You may not.
- **Under Creative Commons license**—See more about Creative Commons in Appendix B.
- **You have permission**—If an author or publisher gives you permission, you're home free. But be sure to get the permission in writing.

*notice, if anyone were to take a story and make a movie and make
lots of money, I'd get all of it once my lawyer was through with them.*

*"Give readers a sample on your webpage, and you can draw them into
reading your books. Is that worth it against the possible losses by
piracy? I definitely think so. In addition, posting stuff to the Net
rewards longtime readers by giving them something they've not seen
before. That's always a good thing."*

Many authors, especially mid-list authors and those just starting out, began making
their work available online after it had been printed elsewhere. Check your favorite
authors' sites; they may have free fiction listed there. Once podcasting came about,
authors began taking a chance, thinking that podcasting their fiction may increase their
fan base.

Mark Jeffries, author of *The Pocket and the Pendant*, is enthusiastic about using podcasting to widen a fan base.

*"Instead of looking at this as, 'Oh I'm losing money by giving my book
away for free,' you should look at this as, 'Oh, I'm getting millions of
dollars worth of promotion for free—I have this megaphone called
"podcasting" on the Internet, to the entire planet.' Normally, for that
kind of exposure, traditional printers haggle all kinds of deals with
Barnes and Noble, etc., for endcaps, prominent placement, etc. Now,
anyone can get the mindshare of the book audience out there without
that kind of upfront cost."*

When Scott Sigler, author of the podiobooks *Earthcore* and *Ancestor*, ended his first
podcast book (*Earthcore*), he had 10,000 listeners. Here is what he had to say about his
experience:

*"There was no print book available when I launched the podcast, so
all of those fans are due to that podcast. It definitely widened my fan
base."*

Many of these authors started out with no or little fan base and have gained one due to
podcasting. But what about the established authors? Is it worth it for established
authors to begin podcasting their work?

James Patrick Kelly firmly believes it has widened his fan base:

"Of this I am more certain. When I ego-surf Technorati and Ice Rocket, I can see that the podcast is getting some serious attention in the blogosphere. And then there are my website traffic statistics, which are crude but instructive. In the 3 months just before the podcast launch, my site was averaging 2,100 hits a day. In the 3 months since, I've been getting around 5,000 hits a day."

Concern for Production Value

We discuss in this book the pros and cons of editing and the importance of preparation, and you can learn more about the nitty-gritty details on how to beef up your production values in other fine podcasting books. We are also proponents of the opinion that if you're just starting out, you shouldn't dump a big bag of money into equipment, because if you find you don't like podcasting, it could be a waste.

But when it comes to podiobooks and other written work, the listener has some expectations above normal podcasts. If the podcast is more conversational, then the listener is usually all right with the normal issues that plague podcasters: poor sound quality, pauses, background noise, and so on. But because people are used to audiobooks having a certain professional quality, they don't want people reading fiction to them that has an amateur quality.

If you're just starting out, this can put you at a paradox: You don't want to spend too much money on your podcast at first because you want to see how you like it and how much of a splash you make on the podosphere, but it's difficult to make that splash when you're making subpar recordings.

The good news is that most people are forgiving to new podcasters. They will see how your first few are before passing judgment, because we all need a little time to get our feet under us when starting a new podcast. But if you have a novel or other large piece of written work in front of you, you might want to test out your sound quality before beginning, because although most podcasts grow in quality, you'll want the first chapter of your book to sound like your last.

Poetry, essays, and short stories live in a more forgiving world, because they are stand-alone pieces and can afford to increase in quality as you realize you like the medium enough to sink some money into better equipment. But unless you want to rerecord your early chapters after you establish a better sounding recording, you will want to start out with the best possible sound quality you can.

Think beyond the current life of your podcast. Yes, people are going to download now, but if the book or other collection of writing remains available, people will download it in the future. You want your first effort to sound as good as your last. Some undoubtedly excellent writing has simply not been listened to due to bad audio quality. You're podcasting to be heard, so don't cause your listeners pain when they hear it.

Addressing the Written Word

A brief note to end this chapter: If you are passionate about writing, you should know that several podcasts about writing (and books in general) are available. Here's a handful to check out:

- Michael A. Stackpole's The Secrets (http://www.stormwolf.com/thesecrets/podcasts/)
- Mur's I Should Be Writing (http://www.ishouldbewriting.com/)
- Tee Morris's The Survival Guide to Writing Fantasy (http://teemorris.com/blog/)
- Paula Berinstein's The Writing Show (http://www.writingshow.com/)
- Kiki Opdenberg's The Kissy Bits (http://kissybits.blogspot.com/)

If you don't think your writing is ready to be published, either in print or podcast form, then these podcasts might give the advice (or simply the confidence) you need to start.

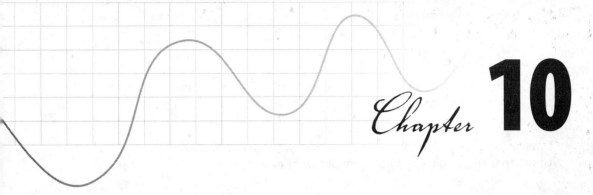

THE GREAT EDITING DEBATE

*"It would be nice if we were all instant 'personalities,' with minds enchanting our listeners no matter what the subject. Unfortunately, we're all too human. If you can imagine a toddler playing violin for the first time, consider your listeners' take on your first broadcasts. Whether or not you **want** it to be the case, you're going to need a lot of practice. But for now you can edit.*

"In times past, editing involved a metal tray, a razor, splicing tape, and tons of time. Software now allows us to shape our shows in ways tape editors never imagined, and precise edits which once took minutes or hours now take seconds. In my opinion editing audio is calligraphy. It is an art! And should be treated as one.

"Aim to preserve a natural feel, but edit copiously, especially at first. Just like the toddler, you will get better with practice and patience. Expect to make mistakes and to learn from them—your audience will appreciate your efforts."

—Paul, The PK and J Show

Why You Should Edit

Podcasting takes time. Some people have an hour-long show every day, plus day jobs, children, friends, other hobbies, and commutes. Editing often takes twice the time, or more, than it took to record the podcast. So why do it? After all, isn't podcasting supposed to be from the people, raw and unfiltered?

That concept is attractive, yes, until you listen to some of the raw and unfiltered podcasts out there. Sure, several people can do unedited shows and get away with it: Adam Curry has at least one "Senseo" burp per podcast, and no one gets on his back about editing. But for most of us, if we have excessive noise, distractions, or vocal tics, our listeners will be so distracted by the annoying noise that they won't hear anything about what our podcast is supposed to be about.

If you want your podcast to serve as more of a professional service rather than a conversational audioblog, you will definitely want to edit.

Defining "Professional" Quality

As we say again and again, you don't need $500 worth of audio equipment to produce a podcast that sounds professional. The most important reason for your podcast to sound professional is for the audience not to hear audiobooks with coughing interrupting the climactic scene or DJs leaning away from the mic to yell at their dog to get his nose out of the cat box.

Granted, some people want their podcast to be conversational and don't want to cut out the interruptions of their lives. But still, even those people can benefit from cutting out distracting noises or recording away from excessive background noises.

Easier on the Listeners' Ears

Your podcast can have vital and wonderful information, gut-busting humor, and poignant messages, but if it is painful to your listeners when they hear it, they will unsubscribe.

If your audio has sibilant *s*'s and popping *p*'s and levels that are all over the board, driving your listeners to dive for their volume control, you will lose them. Taking some time to tone down the pops and even out the levels is a small price to pay for keeping your subscribers happy.

We discuss evening out your levels via audio compression in Chapter 11, "Keeping the Podcast Consistent."

> **TIP**
>
> To fix problems with sibilance and popping, make sure your microphone is the correct distance from your mouth (do some test runs to determine what constitutes a good distance), see if speaking over the mic sounds better than directly into it, and invest in a pop filter, if necessary.
>
> In the case of the pops, though, you can also edit them out by hand. They're easy to find; they are the spikes in the file. Be careful when editing them: You can remove the spike but the word may sound truncated to the listener when you're done

Excessive "Ums"

Many of the vocal tics we have in conversation just flow past our ears, rarely noticed unless used to excess. It's, uh, pretty obvious, you know, that the vocal tics just sort of come out when, uh, they're written down, but it's surprising how much they stand out when podcasting.

Although we want to believe that many podcasts are more like conversations than sterile radio shows, the listener's ear picks up on vocal mistakes more in podcasts. Perhaps it's just that we're so used to smooth, practiced radio voices that we can catch any mistake. Whatever the reason, listeners easily notice the stray "um" and "you know." These hesitant words stand out like a mud-covered pig in a church service. They make the podcaster sound unsure and lacking of the credibility he or she hopes to build.

The good news is that, when you're editing, these words are usually very easy to catch. Just look for the solitary sound in your track. It's likely where you paused, said "um," and then continued (see Figure 10.1).

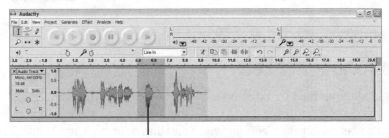

This short spike between the pauses in audio often indicates an "um"

FIGURE 10.1

When you're editing your podcast's audio track, the "ums" in your audio file usually stand out.

"When you're recording something that you know you're going to edit later, it's okay to make mistakes. Just start back a little bit and do it again. It helps to leave "markers" near your retakes so that you can easily find them again and fix them in your sound editor. You could knock on the table or tap your microphone with a pen. Anything that leaves a clear, sharp sound to get your attention.

My favorite marking device is a plastic clicker—the kind some people use for dog training. When I stumble over a word or a phrase, I just click with the clicker and start over from a couple of sentences back. This leaves a very distinct spike in the waveform on my editing software, so I can find it visually and fix my goofs without missing anything.

—Steve Eley, Escape Pod

An example of just such a peak in the audio wave form is illustrated in Figure 10.2.

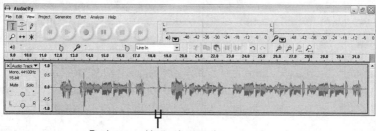

Peak caused by a sharp noise

FIGURE 10.2

You can purposely make sharp noises to create peaks to alert you to where you need to edit.

Why You Shouldn't Edit

If you haven't guessed by now, both of us are firmly on the editing side of the debate. But it wouldn't be fair if we didn't cover the other side, exploring the reasons why you shouldn't waste your time editing while creating your podcast. Many of the most popular podcasters do not edit at all, so it's clear that some people do just fine without taking the time to edit.

Keeping Away from Radio Correlation

Several podcasters have a cynical and jaded view of radio. They view it as sterile audio, corporate-driven, and dumbed down to the lowest common denominator to appeal to the most people. Podcasting gave them an outlet to listen to new and fresh material, and it gives them the outlet to present new and fresh material to other radio haters.

So why on earth would they want to polish their podcast to sound like a radio show when they were so pleased to get free from that yoke?

Enjoying the Amateur Quality

Along the same lines, there is camaraderie in podcasting that celebrates the independent status of our shows. We don't have the mega-corporations of radio behind us: We market ourselves, and some have thousands of happy listeners. We have a connection to our listeners, letting them know we are people too—just regular Joes and Janes sending out a message for whomever cares.

Editing the podcast takes away from that personable atmosphere. If you want to present yourself and your life to your listeners, then editing out your little vocal tics, your dog barking, and your kid's interruptions dilutes that version of you.

Time Constraints

New podcasters quickly learn two things about this hobby: It is fun and addictive, and it takes more time than you figured it would. If you ask people on the streets if they have several hours free in a week, most of them would say no. We already have families, friends, jobs, other hobbies, other responsibilities. Podcasting is fun, yes, but recording, compressing to MP3, and uploading takes a lot of time. Editing can more than double that time.

If your choice is don't edit or don't podcast at all, you might want to just go ahead and podcast without editing and see how well you're received.

You're Just That Good

Finally, there is the factor of skill. Some people who have a background in radio and know how to fill silences with words other than "um" and "you know" can produce a clean podcast and sound near to perfect. Adam Curry's history in broadcasting makes his Daily Source Codes seamless, for example.

If you have a similar experience, or have training from a class or organization such as Toast Masters, then podcasting without editing should be a snap. This confidence can also come with experience, as you become more comfortable with the hobby.

Listen Before You Upload

Regardless of where you stand in the editing debate, it is vital, imperative, and of utmost importance that you listen to your podcast before uploading it.

Look, we know what it's like. You record and it takes forever. Then you do post-production, editing, adding music, whatever. Compressing to MP3 takes a while, as does uploading. Do you really want to tack on another 10 minutes to an hour, depending on how long your podcast is, to listen to it? Not to mention the fact that since you just recorded it, and perhaps edited it, you're really not up for listening to it yet again.

CAUTION
Listen to your podcast before uploading it!

Yeah, you know you're entertaining, but listening to your own podcast several times gets tiring.

"*I feel like many podcasters actually get a false impression of what they are doing. I know this especially because of doing Adam's [Curry] show on Sirius [Satellite], I go through hundreds and hundreds of promos every day and I listen to way too many podcasts. I am often amazed and I think to myself, 'Did these people listen to this, did they actually think that a promo that sounds [all distorted] could be listened to?' We get promos like that where for a whole minute there is someone speaking completely distorted, and I think they sent that in and they really want Adam to play it, how is that possible? Haven't they listened to anything else beside what they just did?*

"*My feeling is that you are just so excited about what you do that you don't even hear it for what it is. That is not actually a bad thing; being excited about what you are doing is a good thing—that is what makes a lot of great creativity. You really have to learn to step back and listen objectively…. My advice to all podcasters is listen to your show before you publish it.*"

—**P.W. Fenton, Digital Flotsam, and producer**
for Adam Curry and Podshow

Still. It's worth it. Whether you want to have a professional-quality podcast or an amateur-sounding conversation, you want the podcast to be worth listening to. So take some time to listen to the final version to avoid the following pitfalls.

Sample Rate Problems

Sometimes when opening more than one track to paste in other sound files, we can mess up and mix them together. If the files are the same sample rate, that's fine, but if they are different, then you've got problems. This problem can cause your podcast to sound like half of it was done after you attended a party with too many helium balloons, or maybe like it is being played on a record player at too slow a speed. For the listeners, this is funny at best, and, at worst, annoying enough to cancel their subscription. It also makes you look like you don't know what you're doing.

It's a common mistake. Several of us have done it at the beginning. The lucky ones were those who caught it before their podcast went live; the others went blithely about their day until someone wrote them an email saying, "Uh, dude, what's up with the helium-voices in your podcast?"

Even if you know your sound program inside and out, mistakes still happen. Perhaps mistakes have a greater chance of slipping by you if you are a more experienced user of these programs, because you might think you have it all under control. So whether you're a podcasting newbie or a wily vet, you should still listen before you upload. It will benefit you and your listeners.

> **NOTE** If you want to include a file of a different sample rate into your podcast, make sure to include it on a separate track and mix the tracks together when you save to MP3.

> **NOTE** We recommend you do your final encoding with a sample rate of 44.1 kHz. This will make your podcast the most compatible with the various flash players used on the different podcast directories and websites. Do not use 48 kHz, because it will cause problems for either you or many of your listeners.

Factual Errors, Private Information, and More

Sometimes you don't know what you're saying is incorrect until you hear it. Odd as it may seem, the listening part of the brain is not in the same area as the speaking part. If you've ever said something and then wondered if you were correct—whether you messed up the date or time or something more substantial—it's a good idea to listen to your files in order to catch these potential mistakes.

Although factual problems don't come up very often, you should give your podcast an objective listen just to catch things you may not want to say at all. Things that seem just fine when you were talking could seem different when you are listening to them, so you should give yourself a chance to decide whether what you've said might alienate your listeners (or someone close to you) or make you look ill-informed.

Along the same lines, it's possible you could have been caught in the conversational tone of the podcast and ended up talking about something that perhaps you shouldn't have. Some podcasters (or their spouses) prefer to keep their family's personal information private and don't want information such as children's names, schools, or address to go over the podcast. And then you have the "didn't think it was a problem" incident of talking about Aunt Shirley's bladder surgery, where you think it's fine and your spouse disagrees with you. Listening to a podcast will let you catch personal information and give you a chance to cut it out.

To be perfectly honest, many podcasters can lose track of time and go on and on, especially if they have a co-host to chat with. They lose the topic of the podcast, and may even get sidetracked with in-jokes and discussions that have no interest to their listeners. Topics that seem hysterical or at least interesting when you are "in the moment" may not be as funny to a third person when listened to later. We're not implying that you're boring; we're just saying that when you lose track of what you are trying to say, the interest other people have in your train of thought can wane. You can catch tangents like this by listening to your podcast before you post it.

Other problems you'd never think to catch can crop up: accidentally hitting the Paste command twice while editing the file and getting identical sound bytes one after the other, assuming background noise isn't as intrusive as it actually is, or forgetting to correct errors even after combing carefully through the file during the editing process.

Although these problems can wreak havoc on your podcast by either angering your family or embarrassing yourself in one way or another, they're all easy to fix with a quick listen and some judicious editing.

Corrupted Files

Perhaps the worst nightmare of all for podcasters is the corrupted file. You work and work on your podcast, upload it, and go to bed. Then your listeners begin to download something that sounds either like 5 minutes of silence, 15 seconds of horrendous screeching, or 10 minutes of you repeating one sentence over and over. The podosphere has seen examples of all of these, which can be caught simply by listening to your show before uploading it.

If you've ever worked with computers, you've likely heard the old adage, "save early and save often." This applies to podcasting as well. Save the uncompressed file before you edit. If you want to be really careful, then save after every editing step you take. Make sure to save the final, uncompressed edited file. This ensures that if you make a mistake somewhere along the way, you should be able to go back only a few steps to fix it. Re-recording the podcast from scratch is *not* fun.

We do understand how busy life can get, and how you're lucky if you find time to podcast regularly, much less edit and then listen to the final product. But if you want your podcast to sound good to your listeners' ears (instead of making them bleed), consider editing and giving the podcast a listen before uploading. Although these steps take time, they're simple to do and worth it to avoid embarrassment and the potential of lost subscribers.

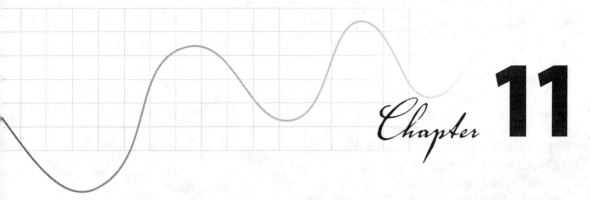

Chapter 11

KEEPING THE PODCAST CONSISTENT

"I think other podcasters need to make an effort to be unique,
be consistent, be creative, and be concise."

—Andrew, Working Podcast

Maintaining a Consistent Release Schedule

In this chapter, we talk about the importance of being consistent with your show. People, for the most part, do not like change. When it comes to keeping your core listener base, consistency in your release schedule, your format, and your sound levels are all very important.

Because with podcasting there are no set rules, technically you can release your show whenever the mood hits you. One day you could release four shows, not release another show for a month, and then release shows every other week. There is nothing to stop you from releasing on a random schedule—unless, that is, you are looking to grow your audience.

"My advice to people is to be consistent in
terms of putting up a show when you say
you are going to put up a show."

—Cat from the CatFish Show (www.catfishshow.com)

A recent survey conducted by Peter Chen from Monash University of over 300 podcasters showed that roughly 50% released a new show once a week. Given the strong TV culture in the U.S., this is not that surprising a number. Most people have been conditioned from an early age to expect their favorite shows once a week. They have also been conditioned to expect the shows they like to be available on the same day of the week and at the same time of the day. So if you are releasing a show once a week, you want to pick a day during the week to release the show on and then stick to that same day every week. During your show, you also need to communicate your schedule to your listeners.

NOTE Many prominent podcasting networks long ago realized the importance of keeping a consistent schedule. For example, the Tech podcasters require members to release on a regularly set schedule, sticking to a regular day of the week as well as a rough time of day that those shows are to be released.

"You kind of have to put some effort in if you want to get a strong, loyal audience and be consistent. We try very, very hard... to do it every week. That is one of the things. If you are going to do it every week, then [make sure you] do it every week."

—Jason, Delta Park Project (www.deltaparkproject.com)

And this is not just about weekly shows. This goes for daily shows and shows that are released a couple of times a week. If your listeners are expecting shows on Wednesdays and Saturdays, then make sure those are the days when the show will be released. According to the Monash University survey, only about 25% of podcasts are released more frequently than once a week, with about 7% releasing a new show daily. Keith from Keith and the Girl talks about doing a one hour-long show every day:

"You have to look at it sometimes like it is work. You know if you hate it then you can't do it, but it is a job... you have to make yourself do it. [But] you still have to like doing it."

If something comes up that causes you to have to skip shows, you should let the listeners know. Even if that means releasing a 1-minute show with you saying that the show will not be released as scheduled. Just let them know why and when the show will be back. In December of 2005, Chemda from Keith and the Girl was on a musical tour in the Northwest region of the U.S., and it was difficult for them to do a show every day. One week they only put out two shows. Normally, their fans are extremely vocal about such things. Keith was asked what the feedback was from their fans on not doing a show every day while Chemda was away. Here is what he said:

"I haven't gotten feedback too mean for only being able to do two shows that week. Maybe because we explained ourselves [ahead of time]. [We received] a couple 'Where's our free shows?' and 'F-you's' but that's par for the course."

Because they took the time to explain to their listeners what was going on, they received very little negative feedback for missing the shows. Yes, their listeners were disappointed that they would not get a "free show" every day, but they remained listeners.

Podcasting is about time-shifting audio and making it such that the files are downloaded to the listeners' computers and/or MP3 players in the background without any additional effort from the listener. However, podcasts cannot grab the listeners, strap headphones on them, and make them listen to your show. They still need to check their computer or their MP3 player to see what shows are available. This is where having a set schedule helps. If a listener knows your new shows are available for their drive to work on Wednesdays, they will look for it each Wednesday. As we move forward with podcasting, there will be more and more ways to listen to podcasts, but one thing that will not change is your listeners' expectation of when your show will be available. So whether they are listening to you every day, week, or month, make sure when that mental timeslot set aside by the listeners to play your show comes up that your new show is already downloaded on their computer, MP3 player, cell phone, or other new media player.

Keeping the Format Consistent

Your listeners are used to what you are doing, and oftentimes change is not accepted well, even if it is for the better. You are far better off to change your show slowly over a period of time than to one day go from doing a 15-minute show with tips from guests and product reviews to a 30-minute show with two interview segments, a news segment, and stories from listeners. Although the new format may bring you more listeners in the long run, your current listeners might object to such a sudden and drastic change to the show. You are best to spread out such changes and, most importantly, communicate those changes to your listeners. Let them know what you are planning to do and see what their response is. Change is not a bad thing, but sudden and abrupt change is likely to shock your listeners, and a certain percentage will unsubscribe.

Another aspect in keeping a consistent format involves the content of your show. If you are doing a music podcast and your focus is on death metal, switching over to a format of religious rock is not going to leave you with many or any of your old listeners. Although this example is extreme, the results will not be much different if you switch from one genre of music to any other. And it is not all about music; if you have a podcast about *Star Wars* and then you switch to talking just about *Harry Potter*, a certain percentage of your listeners will move on. You would be better off to start a second podcast focusing on the new subject matter than trying to fit both in one show if you already have an established listener base. If you feel adding a new subject is an evolutionary change, such as having a podcast about *Star Trek* but now you also want to talk about *Battlestar Galactica*, you would be best advised to ask your listeners what they think of adding discussions on the new subject.

NOTE
We are not saying not to change your show. We definitely do not recommend letting your show become stale, and we always recommend you podcast about something you have a passion for. If you are the type of person who has many passions, you just need to think through the changes you want to make. If they are drastic changes, oftentimes it is best to start up a new show, as discussed earlier.

When Rob was thinking about expanding the people he interviews from just podcasters to also those providing podcasting services, he asked his listeners for their opinions. Overall he received a collective thumbs-up on the idea from his audience. Then, after doing an interview with a service provider, he once again solicited feedback from the listeners. Overall he found the feedback to be positive; however, quite a few listeners said to make sure that the majority of the interviews were still with podcasters—advice Rob took to heart.

Overall, whenever possible, try to keep the format of your podcast consistent from show to show. Whenever you do decide some change is needed, make sure you solicit feedback from your listeners. Sometimes you will want to ask them beforehand for their opinion; other times you will want to ask them within that show what they think about the change. But no matter what, if you are going to make a change, ensure you somehow involve your listeners in that change and let them know they have some say in the podcast.

Consistent Volume Levels

Podcast consistency isn't just about release schedules and content. If you are going to be adding in clips from other people, such as music, promos, bumpers, tech tips, feedback, or even commercials, you need to keep the volume levels close so as not to cause the listeners any discomfort.

If you already have a show produced, we would like you to try this experiment: Put on a good pair of headphones and listen to your latest show. Keep track of how many times you want to adjust the volume up or down. Now think about when you are listening to broadcast radio: How often do you have to change the volume? The reason why you do not need to adjust the volume levels with broadcast radio is that they heavily compress the audio.

Audio compression in this case should not be confused with audio data compression, where you are converting the audio to a smaller format file such as MP3 or AAC. The audio compression we are talking about is peak-limiting or peak-reducing of the signal, such that you keep the output levels from getting too loud for one instance compared to the rest of the audio stream. Both Wichita Rutherford from 5 Minutes with Wichita and Derek from Skepticality stated that the number-one thing that podcasters can do to make their shows sound better is to apply audio compression and peak-limiting.

For the most part, we are trying not to get overly technical in this book. This is one area, however, where we need to get a little geeky so that you can understand why audio compression is needed and are not intimidated by it (see Figure 11.1).

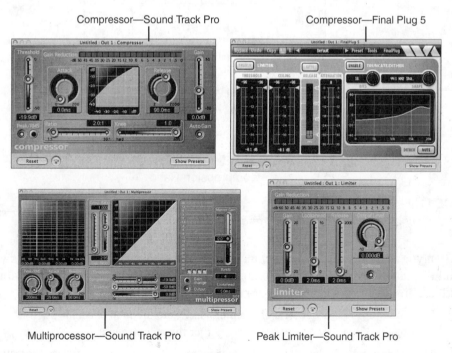

Compressor—Sound Track Pro

Compressor—Final Plug 5

Multiprocessor—Sound Track Pro

Peak Limiter—Sound Track Pro

FIGURE 11.1

Different types of software compressors and limiters.

Compression

Compression is the reduction of the audio signal above a set output level, known as the *threshold*, by a given ratio of reduction. The compression ratio typically varies between 2:1 and 8:1 for most applications. *Ratio* refers to the amount of reduction in an output signal once it passes the threshold level. With a ratio of 2:1, for each increase in signal level of 2 dB, the actual output level will only increase 1 dB.

> **NOTE**
> dB (decibel) is a measure of loudness of sound. It is not a linear measurement. Each 3 dB increase in constant noise will double the sound's power; however, the human ear will perceive a doubling of loudness for every 10 dB increase.

As an example, Figure 11.2 shows the output levels for an input signal of +10 dB and a threshold of 0 dB for various compression ratios. For a 2:1 ratio, the output would be +5 dB. For a 4:1 ratio, the output level would be +2.5 dB after compression.

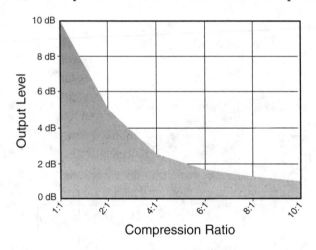

FIGURE 11.2

The net effect of various compression ratios on an input signal of 10 dB.

When you're dealing with any technical area, some special terms are commonly used, and this is definitely the case with audio compression. Here are some basic terms you will see in the audio compression arena:

- **Limiting**—A stronger form of compression where the ratio of compression is 10:1 or greater. This is done to set a hard limit for the output signal.

- **Threshold**—The level at which the compressor/limiter starts to reduce the output level. This is chosen in combination with the compression ratio to make sure there is no clipping of the signal.

- **Attack**—The length of time after the threshold is passed before the compressor will start reducing the output level. With audio presets for vocals, you will normally see an attack time of 2 ms as the default.

- **Release**—The length of time before the compressor allows the output level to return to normal after the signal drops below the threshold. Typically for vocals this is between 20 and 40 ms, as the default.

- **Gain**—The amount of boost you want to add to the overall signal. This is done to bring up the lower level of the signal closer to the threshold, thus reducing the overall difference between the upper and lower range of the audio stream.

- **Hard knee**—A form of compression where once the signal reaches the threshold level, the software immediately begins to compress at whatever ratio is set. In some cases, this makes the compression very easy to hear; consequently, the higher the compression ratio, the easier it is to hear.

- **Soft knee**—A form of compression where there is a gradual onset of the compression. The compression ratio is gradually increased as the signal level gets louder until, when it passes the threshold, the full compression ratio is achieved.

Of all these terms, the concept of gain could use an additional explanation. As an example of why gain is used, let's assume you and your co-host are talking. Typically your voice is peaking between −9 and −3 dB and your co-host, who is a little more timid, is peaking between −15 and −9 dB (see Figure 11.3).

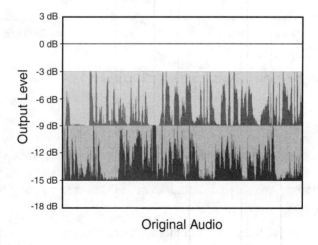

Original Audio

FIGURE 11.3

Original audio tracks for two different people.

Now let's look at what happens to this signal when gain and compression are applied (see Figure 11.4). With +6 dB of gain added to the signal, your voice is boosted to −3 dB to +3 dB and your co-host's voice is boosted to −9 dB to −3 dB. With a threshold of −3 dB set and a ratio of 6:1 for compression, your voice after compression is between −3 dB and −2 dB. Therefore, your overall recording went from a range of 12 dB (−15 dB to −3 dB) to a range of 7 dB, making the overall difference in your voices much less. And with some additional gain and compression, you can make this even tighter. Compression only lowers those sections of the audio track that are louder than the threshold level. It does not lower those sections below the threshold, nor does it raise any of the lower levels. If you want to raise any of the signal, you need to apply gain. Gain, however, raises all sections on the track, at least until the point when the signal level reaches the threshold level, and then compression kicks in also.

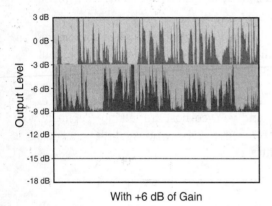
With +6 dB of Gain

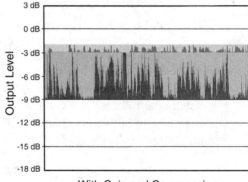
With Gain and Compression

FIGURE 11.4

Audio signals with gain and compression effects applied.

Choosing Your Target

Your job as the podcaster is to pick the threshold point, the compression ratio, the gain, and the attack and release times that result in the best overall sound while keeping the signal from clipping and having digital artifacts. This is something that you will learn only by doing.

Compression is one of the most intimidating areas for new podcasters, but there is no real reason for it to be. As with most things, there's an initial learning curve that is quickly overcome. Compression that is done well results in a level output signal that your listeners cannot even tell was compressed to begin with. Compression done poorly results in unwanted digital artifacts that are very annoying and distracting for your listeners. Figuring out the proper settings for compression is done by trial and error, as every podcaster requires slightly different settings for peak results. For most applications, compression is best done in post-production with your editing software. If you do not do any post-production, you may want to look at a hardware solution for compression (for example, dbx 160a or dbx 266XL compressors). Either way, the overall approach to compression will be the same. The goal is to equalize the output levels of the audio so that the overall audio stream stays at a consistent level and makes the listening experience a pleasure for your audience.

People sometimes equate being consistent with being boring. That is not at all the case. There is nothing exciting about allowing your volume levels to vary all over the place. Nor is there anything exciting about making your listeners guess when your next show will come out. Some key goals as a producer of your show are to present a podcast that is physically easy on the ears, mentally easy to follow, and available when your listeners expect it.

About Software Compression

If you plan on doing your audio compression on your computer, we would recommend the following process flow:

1. Record and edit your show, including adding in external clips.
2. Listen to the different clips and segments and quickly adjust the levels by hand to get them close to one another. (By doing this, you will require less gain and compression later on, which will help preserve the overall quality of the audio.)
3. Turn on the audio compression plug-in in your editing software and monitor the output levels to make sure you are not peaking above 0 dB.
4. Adjust the settings on the gain and the compression to where the overall volume levels of all the clips sound similar and look to be peaking at 0 db on the level monitor on your software.

For your first time setting up your compressor you will want to try adjusting some of the settings mentioned previously (attack and release time, soft / hard knee, compression ratio,…) until you get a sound quality you are happy with. This is not an exact science and everyone's settings will be different.

Chapter 12

YOU'RE NOTHING WITHOUT YOUR AUDIENCE

"One of the things I really enjoy about podcasting as a listener is that sense of community…. And most of the better podcasts give you that sense of community…. You get a sense that you know the podcaster, you know a little bit about their lives. You [Rob] have shared some personal things on your show from time to time. And most of the podcasters seem to do that, and I think that is really attractive to a listener."

—Jeff, a podcast listener

Although it is important to make sure you create a show that you would want to listen to, it cannot be all about you. Obviously you (and every other podcaster) are very interested in having others listen to what you create. If you truly did not care about anyone else listening to your show then 1) you would not have an RSS feed to distribute your show, 2) you would not have a website where listeners can download the show, and 3) you would not be reading this book.

A key reason we have heard from listeners about why they enjoy podcasting so much is the interactive nature of podcasting. Many podcasters go out of their way to communicate with their listeners, to include the listeners in the show and to build a community around their show. Some podcasts are actually mostly about using listener contributions on the show, such as the Working Podcast and 5 Questions.

Using Forums to Interact with Listeners

Even if you never plan on having a single minute of listener-generated content on your show, you still need to engage your audience and make them feel like they are part of your show's family. As was mentioned in the quote to start this chapter, the most popular podcasters create a community around their show. These podcasters realize that their show needs to be more than just 30 or 60 minutes of audio a week that listeners find on the podcast's RSS feed. You need to engage and involve your listeners almost every day, even if your show only comes out twice a month. One of the best ways to keep your listeners engaged with your show on a daily basis is with the use of an open Internet forum like the one shown in Figure 12.1, where listeners can go to post feedback, questions, ideas, and so on. Examples of some podcasts that do a great job in using a forum to build a community include The Dawn and Drew Show (http://dawnanddrew.podshow.com/dnds_bb/), Keith and the Girl (http://keithandthegirl.com/forums/), The Nate and Di Show (http://www.nateanddi.com/forum2/), The PK and J Show, (http://moose3d.com/vanilla/), and Digital Photography: Tips from the Top Floor (http://www.tipsfromthetopfloor.com/forum/). We recommend you check out each of these shows' forums.

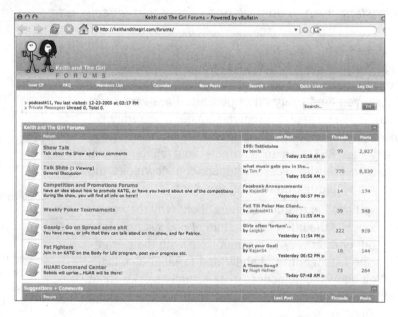

FIGURE 12.1

Keith and the Girl forums: where you go when five shows a week just doesn't give you enough of Keith and Chemda.

The Making of a Successful Forum

Chris from Tips from the Top Floor asks that listeners post questions to the forum board rather then send him the questions via email. Additionally, he has a "top-secret" area on the board that only registered users can access. (There are over 1,300 registered users on his forum.) In the "top-secret" area he posts special recordings he has made that might not fit well with his show, but he feels would be of interest to some of his listeners. These recordings are usually a little more personal and involve sound-seeing tours, where in one case Chris recorded himself driving on the Autobahn.

In addition to his forum, Chris also told us about another thing that he does to engage his listeners:

"I give out assignments, and most people really love them and they go out and they shoot pictures and they submit the assignments and then later on they can see how other photographers interpreted the same topic as opposed to their own interpretation."

One of the most original uses of a forum to engage the listeners comes from Nate and Di. They created the "Censored Word Game." Here are the instructions from their forum on how to play:

We have chosen a "dirty word" to censor on our board.

Here's how you play:

Your job is to try and guess the word.

We will give one hint per day until someone guesses correctly.

Enter your submissions below.

If you are wrong, you will see your word, but if you are right, you will see your word replaced by *'s.

As you can see from the preceding figure, Keith and the Girl has a very active forum with over 1,900 registered users. This community makes sure that the show is at the top of the Podcast Alley voting each month and does a great job in spreading the word about the show. Keith and the Girl also came up with another good way to engage their listeners: They host Friday night online poker tournaments. They even put a cash bounty on Keith's head to help liven the tournaments up a bit.

Obviously, you cannot talk about podcast community building without mentioning The Dawn and Drew Show. From basically the beginning of podcasting, this show has done an incredible job of reaching out to listeners and giving them a place where they could gather. Most of the time that has been in cyberspace. But in the Spring of 2005, a physical gathering of Dawn and Drew fans took place in Los Angels, and another fan-appreciation event was held at the Portable Media Expo in November of 2005. Many people traveled from out of state to attend these two events to see and meet Dawn and Drew and other fans of the show.

Forum Hosting Services

If you do not currently have access to set up a forum on your website, don't worry. There are sites on the Net that will host your forum for you. The following list of forum-hosting services includes a couple free options and a couple premium ones:

- **ForumUp (www.forumup.org; free)—** This is the service we used to create an open forum for this book (at http://totpm.forumup.org). Be sure to stop by and let us know what you think of the book on this forum. Note that if you build your own forum at this site, the URL will be easy to remember. It will be *yourdomain*.forumup.org.

> **NOTE**
> Both ForumUp and Armleg.com are very easy to set up because they use PHPbb for the forum, which is one of the most popular forum software packages. Of course, nothing in life is truly free—both services place Google Ads on your forum. If you are looking for one with no ads, you will need to pay for it.

- **Armleg.com (www.armleg.com; free)**—The URL for your forum on this site will not be as easy to remember as with ForumUp. With this site your URL would be http://www.armleg.com/forum/*yourdomain*.html.

> **NOTE**
> The prices listed in this section were current as of March 17, 2006, but are subject to change.

- **Ezboard (www.ezboard.com; $12 per year)**—Nice, professional-looking forum with no advertisements.

- **vBulletin (www.vbulletin.com; $85 per year)**—This is the service used by Keith and the Girl. It also has no advertisements.

Soliciting Listener Feedback

Listener feedback is one of the best rewards you will receive as a podcaster (many times it is the only reward, but we talk more about that later). However, getting that feedback may not happen as much as you would like, especially when you are first starting out. Clinton from the Comedy4Cast had this to say about a lack of feedback:

"Don't get discouraged if you ask for listener feedback and fail to get a huge response. This does not mean people are not listening. Remember that many people listen to podcasts on portable music players, a situation which does not lend itself to spontaneous email replies. Sometimes if you are getting little or no feedback, it can mean that your listeners are satisfied with your show, as people are more apt to write if there is a problem."

If you want listener feedback, you need to offer many different and easy ways for your listeners to get you that feedback. The following sections list but a few different services/methods for getting feedback.

Phone Voicemail Number

Many podcasters offer a voicemail line for listeners to call. Mur's is 206–202–1MUR, Rob's is 206–666–HELP, Dawn and Drew's is 206–666–DUCK. (Okay, they give out a letter other than *D* found on the 3 key.)

So you might be wondering why each of these phone numbers is out of Seattle (206 is the Seattle area code). Because that's the location of a free phone voicemail service called k7.net (www.k7.net), which is very popular with podcasters (see Figure 12.2). It allows you to pick a vanity phone number and set up the voicemail to be sent directly to you via email, all for free.

With many people today having unlimited long distance on their cell phone or home phone, having a long-distance phone number may not be that big of an issue. However, if you want to offer a toll-free number (at least in the U.S.), you can use the new service from Gcast (www.gcast.com). With this service, the listener calls 1–888–65–GCAST, enters a 10-digit code, and then enters a four-digit PIN. The listener records a message and then at the end hits the pound key. This submits the message as an addition to an RSS feed you create for feedback. You can then have the messages downloaded into your aggregator. You can also give out this second RSS feed to your listeners if you want to share the feedback unfiltered.

> **CAUTION**
>
> When using K7.net, it's important to remember that although it's free for you, it may not be for your listeners. Depending on their location, type of phone service, and long-distance calling plan, listeners may incur long-distance costs for calling a Seattle area code.

FIGURE 12.2

K7.net gives free voice mail to podcasters (but not free to listeners).

All this said, having listeners try and remember a toll-free number, a 10-digit code, and a four-digit PIN may be asking a wee bit too much (the debate between free versus easy is one you will need to decide), not to mention all the time it takes in the show to give out the numbers. So if you are still looking for a way for listeners to call into your podcast for free (again, from the U.S.), you might want to look at one of the pay-for 1-800 number voicemail services. Here's a very short list:

- **MailBox 800 (www.worldwidephone.com/unlimitedvoicemail. htm)**—$34.95 per month with unlimited voicemails

- **eVoice (www.evoice.com)**—$5 per month and $0.10 per minute of usage

- **VoiceNation (www.voicenation.com/ 800-voicemail.shtml)**—$5 per month and $0.07 per minute of usage.

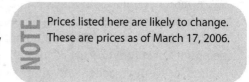

NOTE Prices listed here are likely to change. These are prices as of March 17, 2006.

Skype Voicemail

When you purchase a Skype In phone number, you also get Skype voicemail (see Figure 12.3). And some podcasters such as Nate and Di (361-288-3NAD) use this service for listener feedback. With Skype voicemail, your listeners can deliver a message via Skype directly to your Skype ID. That way, there is no charge for a phone call and the audio quality is better than a standard POTS call. You can also just sign up for Skype voicemail directly for an additional fee per month.

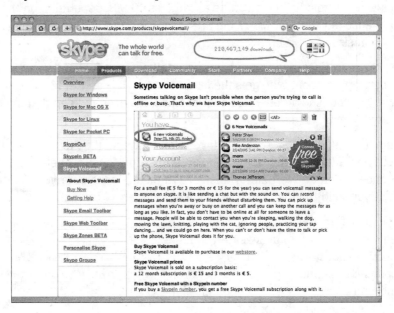

FIGURE 12.3
Skype offers more than just VoIP services; you can also receive voicemail.

Gizmo Project Voicemail

With Gizmo Project, you can also sign up for a "Call In" number. But unlike with Skype, you can choose from 50 different U.S. cities' area codes or a national number in the U.K. This is nice if you are doing a local/regional-oriented podcast. Additionally, with Gizmo Project you get free voicemail with the free service, which allows anyone else with Gizmo Project to leave you a message, and the messages can be set up to be sent to you directly via email.

For more information on Skype and Gizmo Project, **see** "Using Skype and other VoIP Services," **p. 137** (Chapter 7, "The Art of the Interview").

Email

The easiest way for someone to send you feedback is via email. Most podcasters set up a special email account for their show, with most using Google's service, gmail (www.gmail.com). The one feature with gmail that makes it so popular with podcasters is the very large inbox (2 GB at the beginning of 2006). This means people can send you audio feedback they record on their end and not fill up your inbox. Some audio feedback you get from listeners can be as large as 10 MB, depending on the length and how they encoded the file. Many email systems will not allow emails that are larger than 2 MB in size.

Another key reason for setting up a special gmail account for your show is so you don't have to be worried about who gets the email address. It is almost like a P.O. box for snail mail. Lastly, if your show generates a lot of email, it's good to keep that mail away from your everyday mail.

Speaking of email, don't let it pile up. If your fans can find time to listen to you and then send you their adoration, the least you can do is send them a brief "thanks" in return. If you honestly don't have time to answer the email, make sure you mention on your show that you read them all but don't have time to answer them.

Once you do set up a way for people to send you feedback, you need to make sure you let them know about it each and every show. We recommend mentioning it at the beginning and end of each show. Additionally, if you have a call-in number for your listeners to leave voicemail, you should include that number in your name tag for ID3 tags and your title tag from the item section in your RSS feed. (More information can be found at www.podcast411.com/id3tags.html.) This allows a listener on an iPod to easily find your number to leave feedback.

> **NOTE**
> If you want to get in touch with us, Mur's gmail address is mightymur@gmail.com and Rob's is podcast411@gmail.com

> **TIP**
> The other free web-based emails, such as Hotmail and Yahoo! Mail, are also good ways to go, but their storage and message limitations are not up to gmail's capabilities. If you want your listeners to send you audio comments, then gmail is our recommendation.

Remember, chances are if your listeners are using an MP3 device to hear your show, they do not have immediate access to email. However, most will have access to a cell phone. So while they are thinking of giving you feedback, putting your call-in number where they can easily find it should help increase the amount of listener feedback you receive.

> **CAUTION**
>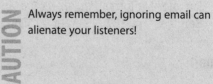
> Always remember, ignoring email can alienate your listeners!

Incorporating Your Audience

The amount of listener-generated content varies quite a bit from podcast to podcast. Some shows have no listener-generated content, whereas others, such as 5 Questions, rely almost completely on it. Remember, the more work you can "outsource" to your listeners, the more time you will have to sleep.

Steve Eley at Escape Pod uses different podcasters/listeners to narrate the stories. Mur has read several stories for Escape Pod, including one she collaborated with Rob on (Episode 28). By passing the heavy lifting off to others, Steve has been able to concentrate more on reviewing new stories for future shows. Plus, the different narrators bring different styles and personalities to each recording, which has helped make this one of the most popular podcasts.

One show that uses both email feedback and audio feedback from listeners is 5 Questions. In fact, a majority of the content on the show is from listeners. But listeners of this show also contribute in other ways. Greg, the host of 5 Questions, had this to say:

"The show is very interactive, not only from a show perspective, meaning that the audience is providing the content for it, but our audience is really good at telling us what they like and what they don't like. About half of the features that exist on the show now are because our listeners have asked for them. And I really tend to think about this show not so much as my show, as it is everybody else's show.

This is the podcast show for the person that doesn't have the ability to podcast. They can call a 206 number, record their answers, and be on a show. And the beauty of this is that this show really can reach everybody and you can be a star of a podcast. All you have to do is just call us up and tell us what you think."

If you are willing to listen to your audience, you may find that not only can they contribute greatly to the content of your show, but they can also contribute to the format of your show.

If you are doing an interview show, your audience can be a great source for unique questions for your guests. Because podcasting is time-shifted, you will need to let your listeners know ahead of time who it is you will be interviewing and instruct them to send in questions via email or in audio format. This helps bring in questions you might not otherwise have thought of asking.

The most common use of listener content on a podcast is playing listener feedback. As we mentioned earlier, there are many different ways to get this feedback, and there are even more ways to use it in your show. Shows such as The Dawn and Drew Show, The Nate and Di Show, and The PK and J Show all play listener feedback. Nate and Di play voicemail messages at the end of each show. Some of these are very strange, but they are always entertaining. PK and J, however, mix in listener feedback throughout their show.

Of course, we can't forget to mention simply reading listeners' email on your show. Tim Henson does this quite a bit on Distorted View Daily, along with playing audio clips sent in to him by listeners. In addition, many of the strange stories Tim reads on his show were submitted from listeners. The more listener-generated content you use on your show, the more listeners will submit content. If they know your show is also their show, they will go out of their way to make sure others know about the show. Getting listener feedback starts with you asking for their help and then giving listeners an easy way to get that content to you.

Your Show Notes Are Your Podcast's Map

"In the time it takes me to listen to one podcast, I could have scanned through 30 or 40 blogs." This is the biggest complaint about podcasting from those who read a lot of blogs. This is why having show notes is so important. It gives potential listeners the chance to quickly scan what is going to be on your show before they decide to download it.

Remember, not all your listeners will be subscribed to your feed (Rob averages about 25% of his listeners coming through direct downloads rather than RSS subscription). Many podcasters use blogging software to post their show notes, and this allows for another way to get listener feedback through the Comments feature. If you are going to put up show notes, we highly recommend that you allow your listeners a way to leave feedback.

Earlier we discussed using a forum as a way to build a community. Some podcasters also use their forums as a place to post their show notes. This offers an easy way for your audience to leave feedback, and it also allows you to see how many times the show notes for that episode were accessed. What's more, it is another way to let people know about your forum and to get them more involved in the show's community.

Detailed Notes

Some show notes are extremely detailed, with breakdowns on what was being talked about at exact times within the show. An example of some very detailed show notes would look like this.

00:00: Introduction.

00:41: Song by The Reverse Engineers.

04:37: News—New computer arrived and will be setting up.

05:28: News—Wife not happy about new purchase. Need to buy something. Call out to listeners for gift ideas.

06:41: Tech tip—Talked about how to edit out buzz from background.

09:12: Listener feedback—Played clip from Bruce at the Zedcast.

11:40: Promo—Played promo for SG Show.

13:10: More listener feedback—Played clip from listener named Steve, complaining that the show is not released often enough.

14:20: Asked listeners to let me know how often they would like to see the show released.

15:02: Gave feedback number and email address and wished all a happy new year. Next show will be on Friday.

16:00: Song by Cruisebox. End of show.

When notes are done to this level of detail, they almost always have links to external references. In this example, there could be links to the two songs mentioned, the Zedcast and the SG Show, plus one to the computer purchased and maybe one more to a picture of the angry wife.

If you are looking to put together the most detailed show notes possible, you should investigate doing what Adam Curry does with the Daily Source Code (along with at least 50 other podcasters), and that is to use WikiNotes (http://www.shownotes.info). WikiNotes allows you to engage your audience by helping you fill in the show notes (see Figure 12.4). This program uses a wiki—a program or website that allows users other than the owner to edit and add information. This allows the users to add comments, links, and other information to your show notes. This collaborative effort makes your listeners a part of the podcast beyond passive listening. Looking at the different podcasts listed at this site, you can see varying degrees of success. You can see that Adam Curry gets a very detailed breakdown of his shows from listeners, whereas others get basically no interaction from their audience.

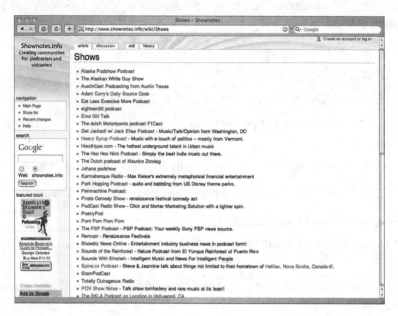

FIGURE 12.4

Shownotes.info gives wiki technology to people who want more interactive show notes.

We suggest that if you go this route, you put in your show notes to start and allow your listeners to make additions and changes. Do not expect them to do all the heavy lifting for you.

Bare-Bones Notes

Sometimes all you really need for show notes is just a quick outline of the show and couple of links to some items mentioned during the show. This is typically what you would choose for an interview show. You really do not want to give away too much about the interview, but you would want to point out who you interviewed and give a link to that person's website if he or she has one. This allows your listeners to find out more about the person before or after listening to the show.

Mur's podcast, Geek Fu Action Grip, uses bare-bones notes. She tries to keep track of the main topics covered in the podcast and links she referenced, but that's about it. The show notes for show #47 illustrate this:

Geek Fu #47 — Things That Should Be Funny
November 13th, 2005

- My rant on Christmas decorations
- Lessons of the Geek Fu Master podiobook
- I'm writing a book with Rob from Podcast411!
- I have too many podcasts to listen to.
- My rant on "Happy Holidays"
- Essay: Things That Should Be Funny, But Aren't (Pt 1)
- Posted in General || 12 Comments »

We would also recommend with bare-bones show notes to have a place for listeners' comments. Again, using blogging software or a forum will work fine in this situation. In the example shown here, listeners can give feedback at Mur's blog, run by WordPress. However, in this case, a Wiki approach would be overkill.

When Notes Aren't Necessary

One option is not to have any show notes at all. Because many podcasters come out of the blogging world, they feel they need to have some show notes. But certain podcasts just don't need them, such as comedy podcasts. After all, do your listeners really need to know at the 2:14 mark there is a joke about a rhesus monkey and a flamethrower? Some podcasters want their entire show to be spontaneous and do not want to give away anything about what is going to happen. If you do not need show notes, then do not post them. If your listeners disagree, they will let you know.

 "If we are really honest with ourselves, attention is what we all seek. That's certainly true of us podcasters who want nothing more than an audience, the bigger the better! But it is also generally true of all human beings. When we are little kids, it's 'Mommy, look at me! Mommy, look at what I can do.' As we grow up, we learn to seek attention in subtler ways but the hunger for it never goes away."

—Dr. David Van Nuys, Shrink Rap Radio

Dr. Van Nuys' quote is so important to remember. Make sure you give your listeners the attention *they* are looking for. It does not have to be just from you. It can come from other listeners of the show. Again, this is why it is so important to try and build a community around your show.

Part **III**

MARKETING AND PROMOTION

Chapter **13**

USING YOUR SITE AS A MARKETING TOOL

"You've got a megaphone to the whole planet and it costs you nothing."
—Mark Jeffrey, The Pocket and The Pendant

A podcast is an audio file that exists on its own, tethered only by an RSS feed. That's all well and good, but most people prefer to have a web log (blog) to go with the podcast. A blog allows podcasters to post show notes, list contact info, and give the podcast a tie to the visual world. Importantly, the blog is where people who do not quite get podcasting yet can go to manually download your show. Some podcasters prefer to expand their site to include a great deal more content, supporting the podcast with a full website.

Your Choices

The majority of podcasts have a simple blog to post their show notes and links to the podcast. Blogger, WordPress, and Libsyn all offer this basic service. However, some of the bigger shows are going beyond the simple blog to house their podcast and are instead building a full-fledged website around it. A website adds supplemental material to the podcast. Just as a podcast can give an established site more content and therefore more worth, a website can give an established podcast the same.

The Blog

Thousands of podcasters can't be wrong, right? The content we create is aural, not visual, so for most of us, a blog does all the work we need. It gives us a place to post our show notes, links, and contact info. Also, many blog services automatically generate our RSS feeds for us.

Some use their blog as a place to dump show notes; others use it as an actual blog, writing about things related to the podcast as the days pass. It can be a place that ties your users to your podcast and keeps them interested in the podcast and you.

Jim Van Verth of The Vintage Gamer podcast (http://www.thevintagegamer.net) uses a WordPress blog as his podcast's home. He prefers a blog because he doesn't feel his podcast needs a full website.

"I was already using WordPress for another blog, and I was familiar with the way it worked. I don't need a full site because this is a hobby. I might think about [making a site] if I were doing this professionally."

—Jim Van Verth, The Vintage Gamer

The pitfalls to a blog are simple: that's all there is. You can add links to friends or podcasts, some buttons for PayPal or Google Adsense, but as for actual website content, the site is pretty flat.

The Website

Some shows, especially the bigger ones, find that having a full-fledged website to support their podcast is the way to go. Sure, you still have a blog area to post show notes, and you have to have an RSS feed, but there's also much more you can do.

The award-winning podcast Eat Feed has an extensive website at http://www.eat-feed.com. The site offers a weekly "featured listener," book reviews, bios of guests, and extensive "about the podcast and contact" information. Host Anne Bramley spends about an hour a week updating the site.

"It never actually occurred to me to do a blog rather than a full site. But I'm glad I started off this way because of the control I have—especially for things like creating the recipe index and using affiliates to sell books featured on the show. Plus, I feel it helps both in presenting

ourselves as a professional business to our potential sponsors and
being able to offer them a customized presence that a blog might not
allow for."

—Anne Bramley, Eat Feed

The downsides of a website are few, but significant, which is why most podcasts, like The Vintage Gamer, simply don't need them. They take up considerable time (and possibly money) to create and maintain—time you could be spending on podcasting. So before you start building a grand site for your podcast, question whether you need it and if you have the time to keep it updated to be of use.

Hosting Services

You have many choices when it comes to your blog, and many free choices can be found online. But your podcast needs to have a place to live, and the bandwidth with which to serve it to your listeners generally remains static. Once upon a time this did not come cheap, but like with most things, the podcasting landscape is always changing, and today you have plenty of options.

Free Services

You can't get cheaper than free. Although a lot of free things seem too good to be true, some modest free podcasting services are available that can serve your needs quite well. Although they're not buff enough to take care of the kind of bandwidth the TWiT podcast needs, they are enough for beginning podcasters or people who just want to get their feet wet without worrying about a blog or website. This section details some of the free services available.

Internet Archive

The Internet Archive (http://www.archive.org) is a nonprofit organization that was founded to build a library of sorts. Its purpose was to give permanent access for scholars to digital historical collections. It has expanded with the times, currently holding collections of texts, audio, moving images, and software as well as archived web pages. This also means, of course, podcasts.

Pros: Internet Archive can handle any amount of traffic you throw at it. You can upload both audio and video.

Cons: It will stream slow and there is no stat package. This site is only for hosting your MP3 file, you will still need to get a separate blog account to handle the RSS feed.

Openpodcast.org

The oldest podcast service out there, Openpodcast.org was up and running in October of 2004. It's the brain child of Ben Tucker, and it serves as a distributor for anyone with a short (5 minutes or less) podcast. All you need to do is record your podcast and email it to the submission address, submit@openpodcast.org. If you don't have a recording setup, or you happen to be out and about and dying to podcast, call Openpodcast's number 206-350-OPEN and podcast through the phone.

All the podcasts go out on the same feed. It's a popular feed for people wanting to hear lots of short, interesting, and sometimes strange things, but it's also a good place to send promos.

Openpodcast has three rules:

- No copyrighted material.
- Be creative.
- Have fun.

The first of these rules is probably the most important, but if you don't follow the other two, then it's pointless.

Pros: Fun and free, and you have a guaranteed listener base of at least 1,500 people (as of this writing) for your very first podcast.

Cons: Your time podcasting is limited, and you will be included in a feed with so many other podcasts you might get lost in the shuffle of a mass-delete.

Gcast.com

New as of December 2005, Gcast is the creation of the Garageband.com group (see Figure 13.1). Gcast offers phone-in (with a toll-free number) or upload technology, with the added bonus of allowing you to manipulate your files before saving to MP3 and publishing. Besides the free hosting, Gcast offers perks such as an imbedded player to put on a website and emailing the users a direct link to the podcast.

Pros: Tons of extras. No limit to size. Podsafe music connection with Garageband.com. The ability to record and add new shows directly from a cell phone to your RSS feed. Free 1-800 number to call into service, which can also be used as a listener feedback line.

Cons: Too new for any glaring problems to make themselves known. No stats package in terms of its listener base. If you use this service, you will also want to use

Feedburner to get an idea of how many subscribers you have (plus, you will want to use Feedburner so that you are not locked into using the Gcast feed URL as your public feed).

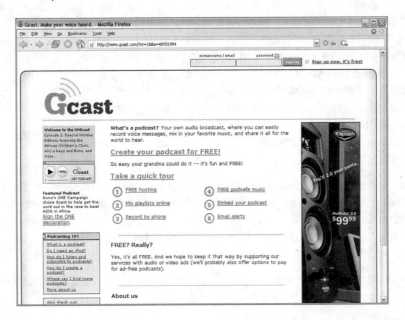

FIGURE 13.1

Gcast: so easy my grandma can use it. I think I'll ask her if she wants to.

Odeo.com

In December 2005, Odeo took its podcast recording software out of beta and made it available to everyone. It became a one-stop shop for subscribing to and recording podcats. You can read more about Odeo in Chapter 1, "A Brief History of Podcasting."

Pros: Ease of use and recording capability make Odeo a site where anyone wanting to do pretty much anything with podcasts can go. The bonus with this site is that you can record directly on the site with a simple Flash player—no mucking about with a separate program, no uploading, no fuss.

Cons: Minimal capability in audio manipulation. You can only record 3 minutes on the site, and it may crash on some browsers.

Traditional Services

If you are just starting out and you already have a website with a traditional Internet service provider, there's nothing wrong with hosting your files there. You already have a relationship with the company and know its rules, its perks, and you're already paying a price for the service. Most people don't use their entire allocation of storage and bandwidth that they purchase from their provider, so you will be assured of getting your money's worth.

> **NOTE**
>
> Most Internet users with generic websites pay no attention to their bandwidth allocations. After all, most of these sites just have some pictures and some email and only marginal traffic. It's not until you start distributing files of several megabytes to hundreds or thousands of people that you start to realize that it's pretty easy to eat up that monthly allotment of 20GB or so that many ISPs allow.

The only issue with the traditional ISP, of course, is keeping track of your bandwidth to make sure you don't exceed its limitations. Before that comes up, you can contact your ISP and make sure you find out two things: what the penalty is for going over your bandwidth, and how much it costs to get the next level of service. Also, see if you can find out whether your ISP will warn you when you are nearing your bandwidth limit.

When your podcast gets popular enough, you may want to look into the podcast-only services to avoid large bandwidth bills.

Pros: If you already have hosting, you don't need to worry about getting new hosting.

Cons: Bandwidth worries.

Podcast-specific Services

Podcast-specific services came into being in late 2004 and early 2005 as bandwidth problems started to plague some of the more successful podcasters. The classic problem with the Internet is that when you become popular, your bandwidth usage goes up, and therefore your cost to your ISP goes up. It's more expensive to be popular than to be unknown.

The podcast-specific services focus more on storage space than bandwidth prices, charging their users for a certain amount of space and giving them bandwidth for free. This type of hosting service has proved to be incredibly popular.

Libsyn.com

The big player in the podcast-specific service is Liberated Syndication (Libsyn), which offers four packages, starting with the Podcasting Basic package at $5 a month and

100MB of storage and peaking at Podcasting Professional at $30 a month and 800MB of storage. Libsyn requires no contract and has no hidden bandwidth fees.

Pros: What can we say? It's not the most popular podcasting host for nothing—it's cheap and has free bandwidth. It has very good statistics for reporting the number of unique downloads. It allows you to redirect a domain name so that your blog/site will appear as www.*yourdomain*.com, instead of with Libsyn in the URL, which is nice if you ever decided you want to change services.

Cons: Its popularity caused some server crashing issues in 2005. With over 2,500 shows sitting on its servers, when Libsyn goes down, everyone knows. (By late 2005, Libsyn did appear to have most issues resolved.)

Podlot.com

As the lesser-known "dark horse," Podlot has grown quietly, doing little advertising and allowing word-of-mouth to do its work. It has experienced few of the growing pains that Libsyn has gone through, and remains cautious with its services. Although the pricing is similar to Libsyn, Podlot also offers more storage for each type of account.

Pros: As of March of 2006, Podlot has never been down. It's also affordable to just about anyone who wants a podcast.

Cons: It's not the best choice for fledgling podcasters, because it doesn't offer as many services (blog, RSS help, and so on) as Libsyn offers.

You, the Producer

Although people may go to your website to get your podcast, they're also going to want to know something about you—the producer, the host, the star of the show. Some podcasters want to be totally anonymous; others want every aspect of their life on their site. We recommend a happy medium of information.

Using Your Full Name

Many podcasters use their full name in their podcast, which is fine. However, several use pseudonyms, for a variety of reasons. The first is simple privacy. There was a saying when the Internet first became popular: "On the Internet, no one knows you're a dog," meaning you could say you were anyone and people wouldn't know whether you were lying. People began using Internet handles instead of their own names because they wanted anonymity to say whatever they pleased.

There could be a simple reason for this, too, such as wanting to keep an Internet persona you've had for a while or feeling that if your name is too common it will be difficult to search for your podcast.

That desire for freedom has stayed with many people, and with it comes the desire for privacy. Some podcasters do not want people in their real lives to know about their podcast for professional or personal reasons. Now that a lot of schools and businesses are prohibiting their students and employees from blogging or podcasting, anonymity is important to many.

Personal safety is another reason to keep yourself anonymous, and it's sometimes a concern for some women, a topic we cover in the "Concerns for Women" section, later in this chapter.

On the other hand, there are several reasons to keep your name. Some people prefer to connect their podcast to their professional life, which would require them to use the same name they use in their profession. Mur is a freelance writer and wants her name connected to her podcast, I Should Be Writing.

It is a personal choice for everyone, but remember that it's difficult to change your mind once you go one way.

Setting Limits on Personal Information

Many podcasts are like that old Dr. Seuss book *My Book About Me*. Your podcast is about you, your life, your likes and dislikes. You. Because it's about you, you put more information on your site about you—email address, personal site (if you have one), Flickr.com account, Livejournal account, voicemail number, all your instant messaging nicknames, and even phone number or address (more on this later).

However, you should keep your personal information limits in mind when creating your website. This goes along with the point about giving out your information in your podcast. Once you put something on the Web, it could be there forever, even if you take it down.

There are some important things to consider: Do you want thousands of people to know that you're going away from your house on vacation? Do you want your fans to see pictures of your child? There's a sense of safety on the Internet, that no one can find you from your computer, but it's a false sense of security. Many people on the Internet can easily find out a lot of information about you (including your home address) from just a little clue. Therefore, you should think twice before you provide information such as your child's name and/or picture or mention his or her school. Don't think of your listeners as your friends. Many of them could become your friends, but remember they're all strangers to begin with. You wouldn't give your personal information and family vacation plans to a stranger on the street, would you?

Contact Me!

It is honestly tragic to see how many podcasters forget to put contact information on their site. They remember to update the blog, have excellent show notes, flawless RSS, and yet there is no obvious way to email, call, or IM the host on the home page.

As we've mentioned, it is vitally important to be available to your listeners to give feedback. Podcasting has evolved into nearly an interactive medium with listeners' feedback adding to the content of most shows, or even driving the show's topics. People get frustrated when they try to find a host's email address and it's not readily available on the site. (And no, it doesn't count if it's in the RSS feed because not enough listeners will know to look there.)

Providing contact information is not hard. At the minimum, post your email address, or you could go as far as putting all your IM handles (AIM, Skype, Gizmo Project, ICQ, MSN Messenger, and so on), your voicemail number, and, if you're comfortable, a physical address. Whatever you do, give your listeners some way to get in touch with you. Otherwise, you might as well be podcasting in a vacuum.

Michael R. Mennenga of the various Dragon Page podcasts has his address on the website, and he and his co-host get frequent visitors to the studio when they record their free-form variety show Wingin' It. On one Tuesday, a fan showed up at Mike's door to give him some beer and chocolate for the podcast, which surprised him, but he welcomed the fan.

"[Putting my address on the site] gives me pause because we're getting more and more popular.... I'm rethinking this open-door policy about letting people into the studio because it is my house. However, if someone [is determined] to find me and be a stalker, they can pretty much find me and do it if they're determined."

—Michael R. Mennenga, Dragon Page

In contrast, Michael's co-host, Evo Terra, has nearly no personal web presence. His personal home address isn't on the site, and he even podcasts under a pseudonym. Michael points out that Evo is nearly as easy to reach as he is because of email, Skype, and the fact that they podcast at Mike's house, which is not in a secret location.

We discussed the options open to you for connecting with your listeners in Chapter 12, "You're Nothing Without Your Audience."

Your Privacy

Privacy? Why should you need privacy? There's a certain ego behind all podcasters that does not jibe with the thought of hiding one's light under a bushel.

That said, podcasting generates fans. The word *fan* is based on the word *fanatic*—which sounds far less attractive. And when you attract fans, there might be some people who want more from you than a podcast.

Something about podcasting makes it intimate, even more so than blogs. When people hear someone else's voice and their earnest thoughts, passionate opinions, or hysterical observations, they begin to get the feeling the speaker is their friend. Some will take that feeling to an extreme.

Concerns for Women

In a perfect world, we wouldn't need this section, as women would have no more privacy worries than men, but we're not in a perfect world. We live in a world where a woman can attract a stalker by merely walking down the street. Mur once got her very own stalker by serving coffee. The intimate feeling behind podcasting can attract the wrong kind of fan. This is sad, but true.

The precautions female podcasters should take are common sense. Make sure your email address is a free one that's difficult to track (gmail is a good choice), only use voicemail services, and never use your home or cell phone. And, of course, never put your home address on your site. If you are single, doing a podcast of an adult nature, or

TIP

If you're worried about bots harvesting your email address and throwing a lot of "Via.gra" and "Low Mor.tgage Rate$" spam at you, throw a garbled email address into your "mailto" link. Either put NOSPAM in your address or spell out "at" or "dot." Your listener will have to fix it manually in their email program, but it's a small price to pay.

NOTE

We both would like to point out that the concerns we bring up here are not discussed because of personal experience. We have had nothing but good experience with the people who listen to our podcasts, and we greatly appreciate their feedback and kindness.

And as for the fans feeling like you're their friend, well, Mur is convinced that the essayist and NPR commentator Sarah Vowell would be her best friend if she would just take the time to sit down with her. So it's a common occurrence.

Fans are awesome 99% of the time. But that doesn't mean it doesn't pay to be careful.

live alone, you might think about podcasting under just your first name or a pseudonym, or you could keep your personal status (that is, that you're single and living alone) under wraps.

Some may say these are common-sense guidelines and good advice for anyone, but they still need to be said. These are not precautions that will lessen your enjoyment of life; they're not designed to cover you in bubble wrap. They are just some guidelines every woman podcaster should follow.

Getting a P.O. Box

Something that surprised us when we started getting listeners was that people wrote in saying they wanted to send us things—for free! That is both awesome and at the same time somewhat troubling. Did we want to send out personal information to strangers?

Mur did, taking a risk (and as of today there have been no crazy stalkers at her door), but that brings up a question: Is there a point in your podcasting career that you should consider getting a P.O. box?

The problem with the P.O. box, of course, is that it costs money. And if you're getting on average three or four things per year, you're essentially wasting money. But if you're doing a music podcast and artists want to send you CDs or promotional material (the same for a book review podcast or anything similar), it might be worth it to price an anonymous box at a packaging store or your local post office. This is especially true if you have a podcast about sex. Soccergirl has a P.O. box, as do Dawn and Drew (see Figure 13.2).

So when you podcast, you're putting yourself in the spotlight, which usually means you

> **TIP**
>
> If you don't want to pay for the P.O. box and you're cautious about sending out your address to strangers, you have other options.
>
> Link to your Amazon.com wish list, which hides your address from the buyer. (This only works for people whose listeners want to send them presents and not promotional materials.)
>
> Send your listeners your work address instead of your home address. (This only works if you get mail at work and don't work in, say, food service or a retail outlet.) This is not 100% safe, though, because someone could show up there and follow you home.
>
> If you live in an apartment, ask your main office if they can accept mail for you, and give that address to your listener.

want attention. But the bad thing about attention is that you may not always want all the kinds of attention you get. So keep alert, and if you ever feel uncomfortable with a listener's attention, read your email program's instructions on how to use a killfile, which deposits emails directly into the trashcan without landing in your inbox.

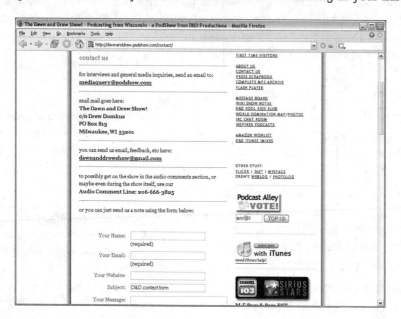

FIGURE 13.2

Dawn and Drew list their P.O. box right alongside their email and comment line information.

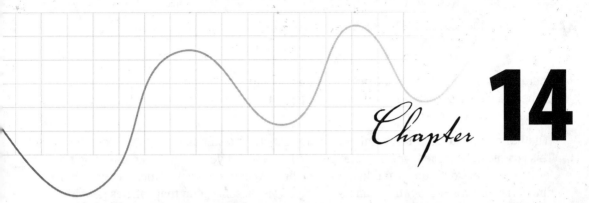

Chapter 14

USING PROMOS TO HYPE YOUR PODCAST

"Patrick McLean here with another installment of 'Interview with a Zombie.'
Say hello to the folks, Bob."

"Aaaaauuuuuggggghhhh."

"I tell you, folks, Bob here just won't shut up about The Seanachai podcast. He's
crazy about this unique, innovative approach to storytelling."

"Nnnnnuurrrrrrr."

"Good point, Bob."

—Patrick McLean, promo for The Seanachai

If you listen to podcasts, no doubt you've heard a promo. A short, 30-second to 2-minute sound clip in the middle of someone else's podcast promoting another podcast. Podcasters commonly put them in breaks in their own podcast, like little commercials. Done well, they can amuse the listener and hook them onto your podcast. Done poorly, they can annoy and alienate the listener.

Why Promos Are Necessary

Promos have multiple roles in the podcasting world. They're part mutual back-scratching service, part honoring podcasts you like, and part shameless self-promotion.

If podcasters believe that the audience of another podcast might like them too, they can suggest exchanging promos, offering their audience to the other podcaster as well.

There are also times when podcasters, just launching a new podcast, will play promos of their favorite podcasts as a sort of homage, but also to give their growing audience an idea of what they enjoy.

Whether it's about back-scratching or paying tribute, it's still all about self-promotion. This is a given because if you don't let people know about your podcast, no one is going to listen. Sure, you'll get a random listener here and there from iTunes or the other directories (maybe more if the name of your podcast is something that catches people's attention), but overall no one is going to notice you.

The fact is, you need a promo. It is your advertising. It is cheaper than banner ads (and likely more effective), and when done well it is one of your best marketing tactics.

When to Promote

The overzealous podcaster will put out a promo even before show number 1 is uploaded onto the server. The problem here is that podcasts are often growing entities, taking a couple of tries before they find their footing. Promoting before the first show is like claiming your kid will be valedictorian on the first day of high school. Even if you end up being right, who's going to believe you at the time?

Be patient. Get a few shows under your belt before promoting. After a couple of shows, you know how long it's going to average, you know better how often you'll be able to do a show, and you'll be able to make promises about your show with more confidence.

There are other times in your podcast's lifespan that you'll want to promote. We'll talk about those times later in the chapter, and more on promoting as a whole in Chapter 15, "Getting the Word Out."

Creating the Promo

Some people who find sitting in front of a mic and talking for an hour easy actually have problems when it comes to making a short, concise promo for their podcast. The promo must be entertaining, or at least engaging enough to catch the listener's attention, but it must still be true to your show; if your podcast isn't light hearted, don't make a funny promo.

People in the movie or publishing industry would call the promo your "elevator pitch." The concept is what you would say if you were in an elevator with a producer or publisher and you had 30 seconds to give a good representation of what your creative work is all about. Promos are the same. You can't go too long, yet you need to give a sense of what the podcast is about.

Considering how many podcasts exist currently, there's one more challenge: making your podcast entertaining. You can give a perfect representation about what the podcast is, but if that's boring, people are going to assume your podcast is also boring. On the other hand, if your promo is entertaining as well as informative, as Patrick McLean's Bob the Zombie promos are (refer to the opening page of the chapter), it will really stick in people's heads. After the initial Bob the Zombie promos, Patrick's podcast not only got more listeners (because podcasters *wanted* to play his hysterical promo), but Bob became a desired commodity as people asked Patrick to create Bob promos for their podcasts. Bob the Zombie (and therefore Patrick's voice and podcast) has been featured on Skepticality, TSFPN.com ads, and Geek Fu Action Grip.

What to Put in a Promo

A promo is essentially telling someone that your podcast is worth their time. This is a delicate balance to strike, because it's a pretty egotistical claim to make. However, there are some ways to get around simply stating that your podcast is the coolest thing to happen to podcasting since iTunes 4.9:

- **Have someone else do it.** Simple. It always sounds better to have someone speak for you when championing your skills. Contact a podcast you like and offer to trade promos, or simply ask politely if they'd be willing to record your promo as a courtesy. Some podcasters with particularly good voices (such as Scott Fletcher from Podcheck Review) will do a promo for you for a fee.

- **Let your show speak for itself.** Create the promo from clips of previous podcasts (another reason to wait a couple podcasts before recording a promo) that you're particularly proud of.

- **Let others speak for your show.** This doesn't involve asking other people to make your promo, but rather capturing sound bites from other podcasts that mention you and your podcast. If people are saying good things about you, use this in your promos. Out of courtesy's sake, though, you should ask permission to cut their remarks out of their podcast to use it.

Another common sense warning: Don't get so wrapped up in making your promo entertaining, fun, and compelling that you forget the most important information—your podcast's name and URL!

You would be surprised to hear how many podcasters forget this information in their promo. It's worse when they actually do their job and grab interested listeners who can't get to their podcast because they don't know where it is located.

> **TIP**
>
> When creating a promo, state who you are, announce your podcast's name, and provide your URL. Do so slowly and clearly so the people who are listening don't miss this information!

The real key to making a promo is for people to enjoy it. When Skepticality began its promo push with a spoof on the beer commercial "Real American Heroes," people played it on their podcasts simply because it was funny. The same thing happened with Patrick McLean's "Interview with a Zombie" series of ads he did for his own podcast, The Seanachai, and for The Sci-Fi Podcast Network.

Patrick paraphrases the classic advertiser Howard Gossage's quote:

"People do not listen to advertising. They listen to what interests them and, sometimes, it's an ad."

Getting Outside Voice Talent

There are still websites you can go to for voice talent for little or no money. Madtown Aces (http://madtownaces.com/), for example, offers voiceover talent for openings, closings, bumpers, and promos. You can purchase services a la carte or as a package. You can get all the mentioned services for under $40.

If that's too much for you, try out RadioDaddy. People swap talents for free at http://www.radiodaddy.com, so you can easily get a promo, bumper, music and phrases, or anything else there. It's a popular site with many talented people available to help you out.

> **TIP**
>
> The rules for RadioDaddy are fairly strict: If you're not paying for the talent, you don't have a right to demand things, insist on a rush job, and so on. It's free, but you need to go through the correct motions. You will also need to be specific with what you want, the script, and so on. As the site says, the rules boil down to this:
>
> "Be POLITE. Be COURTEOUS. Be PATIENT. Be APPRECIATIVE. PARTICIPATE yourself; even if only to comment. This is the only way RadioDaddy will be here for the long term."

What to Do with a Finished Promo

Once you have your promo finished and polished, you need to do a couple things before you email anyone. First, put it out on your feed. Any listeners you have who are podcasters might play it—and these are people you might not have thought to contact personally. If you manually edit your feed, keep the promo as the first thing on the feed; iTunes has a feature where it plays the first item in a feed if you click a podcast. (This will not work, of course, if you rely on your blog software to update your feed.)

Second, place the promo on your site, welcoming anyone to grab it. Also, put it anywhere that allows you or your podcast to present audio in a profile. For instance,

Podcast Pickle allows users to link to a promo (see Figure 14.1), and the blogging tool Blogger allows you to put an audio clip into your profile. If you have a MySpace page, add your promo to it.

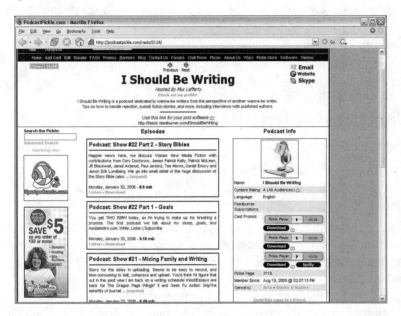

FIGURE 14.1

Podcast Pickle allows for easy access to promos.

Keeping the Promo Up to Date

In some ways, creating promos for a new podcast is relatively easy. In fact, it can get harder the longer you stick with podcasting. After all, after 20 or 40 shows, you're going to realize that the "Hey, listen to my new podcast!" promo sounds a little odd coming from a veteran podcaster. You're also going to run out of podcasts to send your promo to, and people aren't going to want to play it on their podcast week after week.

After several months, consider making a new promo to reflect how your podcast has evolved. You'll have a better chance now of getting a podcasting colleague to make the promo for you, you'll have lots of shows to pull clips from, and you'll generally have a better idea of what you want to get across to people.

Send the new promo the same places you sent the old one—sites that host promos, podcasters you think appeal to the same kind of people you would appeal to, and so on.

Be cautious, however, when deciding when to update your promo. Don't do it too often, or you'll overwhelm those you want to help you. Make a new podcast after a milestone episode (10 podcasts is not a milestone, by the way) or at the 6-month or 1-year mark. Make one to advertise a change in the podcast.

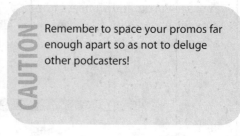

CAUTION

Remember to space your promos far enough apart so as not to deluge other podcasters!

Constructing a Promo Distribution List

Now that you have your promo, where do you send it? Here are but a handful of examples.

Other Podcasts

The obvious answer for where to send your promo is other podcasts. You want podcast listeners; who better to get to listen to your podcast than people who already listen to other podcasts? The first place to start is podcasts that you enjoy listening to. Many podcast listeners like similar podcasts, so identify the podcasts you listen to that are at least tangentially related to your show. Send the podcaster a polite note and ask if he or she would play your promo. It's more polite, by the way, to send a link to the promo instead of just attaching it to the email.

Are you part of a network? Do you think you would fit into one? Several networks exist to bring together similar podcasts, such as The Science Fiction Podcast Network (http://www.tsfpn.com) and The Tech Podcast Network (http://www.techpodcasts.com). Networks are a great way to cross-promote. If, for example, you have a tech podcast, then the podcasts in a tech podcast network would be good places to submit your promo. Some networks require their members to cross-promote other network podcasts by playing each others' promos.

If a network doesn't quite fit for you, consider just going to your area of Podcast Alley or another directory and seeing what podcasts are listed in your genre. Send a polite email and ask if they would play your promo.

Another way of going about this is getting in touch with popular podcasts and asking for "air" time for your promo. The feeling here is that if they have 10,000 or more listeners, there's a good chance that a handful of those people might be interested in hearing what you have to say.

Before you go firing off emails, get at least a little familiar with the podcast you're asking to host your promo. Some podcasts expressly state that they don't play promos for anyone, so if you send them yours, it will show that a) you don't listen to their show, or b) you assume they will make an exception for you. The first is rude and the second is egotistical, and this could backfire if the podcaster decides to let his listeners know about the "idiot" who sent him a promo.

Promo-Hosting Sites

Lucky for us, some people go sniffing out promos to find new podcasts to listen to. This is why it's important to list your promos on these sites:

■ **Openpodcast.org**—We've already mentioned this site as a quick hosting opportunity, but it's also a popular place to throw a promo at around 1,500 walls and see if it sticks anywhere (see Figure 14.2).

FIGURE 14.2
Openpodcast.org's deluge of podcasts can help you get your promo heard.

■ **Podcastpromos.com**—The podcaster Trucker Tom (http://www.truckerphoto.com/) launched this forum as a place for people to post their promos. You can submit up to three promos of 30, 60, and 120 seconds, respectively.

■ **Directories**—As mentioned earlier, many of the directories will allow you to link a promo to your show information (or will host it for you), which is an excellent way to hook listeners who are casually browsing the directory sites. If you register for a directory and the site allows a promo link, by all means put your promo there.

The Brass Rings: Podshow and The Daily Source Code

Of course, the promotion everyone wants is for Adam Curry to play their promo on The Daily Source Code. His many thousands of listeners subscribe to a lot of new podcasts based on promos that air during his show, and having him put a kind word behind your promo is an extra bonus.

To get onto The Daily Source Code, which is part of Podshow, you have to jump through a couple more hoops than with most podcasters. First, make sure it's short. Adam doesn't like super-long promos. You must put detailed ID3 tags into your promo and then email it to submit@podshow.com. P.W. Fenton will receive this, and he decides which promo goes where on Podshow (it may be DSC; it may not). Most of the shows on Podshow have massive followings, so if you're played on any of the podcasts, you're likely to have a boost in listeners.

With Adam Curry, it also helps if you customize your promo for his show. If your promo plays off one of his current hot topics, it will usually get played. This is true with any podcaster; if you go through the trouble of putting together a custom promo for a show, the person who does that show will be much more inclined to play it.

As an example, in early 2006, The Daily Source Code had a recurring bit—The Metrosexual Moment. It even had a cute little jingle. If you wanted your promo played, you could send in some comments about your "metrosexual moments" from your show. Or you could create a spoof promo for "The Heterosexual Moment," where you talk about your show, NASCAR, rugby, pulling one's finger, or something completely 180 degrees from the "Metrosexual" skit. If done in good nature and with some thought, it would definitely get played.

Chances are by the time this book is published someone else will have actually done something very similar. The point is, if you spend a little time listening to the most popular shows and then create custom targeted promos for those shows, you stand a far better chance of getting your promos played.

Finally, Podshow has created a web page where podcasters can exchange promos:

http://promos.podshow.com

Although this site is not nearly as functional as Podcastpromos.com, it is still a good place to post your latest promo and to find other promos to play on your show.

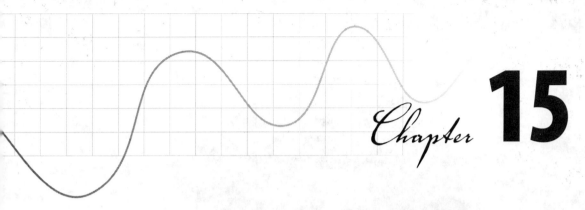

Chapter 15

GETTING THE WORD OUT

"Just because you made a great podcast does not mean you are done. Now you need people to listen to it. Getting listeners is the final step. There are so many free advertising resources on the Internet like forums, chat rooms, and such. If people don't find out about your show, it is nobody's fault but your own."

—Gary Leland, PodcastPickle.com

When it comes to potential listeners of your podcast, you will be going after four distinct groups (see Figure 15.1):

- Your friends and family
- Other podcasters
- Current podcast listeners
- The rest of the world

The illustration shown here is obviously not to scale. If it were, the first three groups combined when compared to the rest of the world would be smaller than the period at the end of this sentence. In this chapter, we talk about promoting to the first three groups; then in Chapter 16, "How to Find Newbie Listeners," we talk more about promoting to the rest of the world.

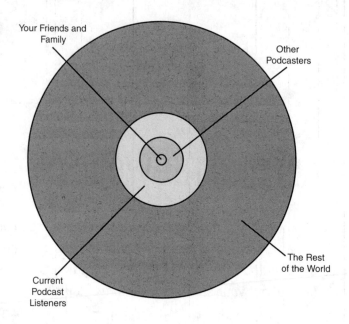

Your Friends and Family

Other Podcasters

Current Podcast Listeners

The Rest of the World

FIGURE 15.1

Groups of potential listeners of your podcast.

When to Promote

When you finally have your first show done and uploaded to the Net and have validated your RSS feed, it is so tempting to want to go out and tell everyone. Before you do, take a step back and read carefully: *Don't do it!* Wait until about your fifth show before you really start to promote.

"Why wait?" you ask. Simple: Your first show is going to stink, but your second show will stink less than your first show, and your third show will stink less than the second show. By the time you get to show five, the majority of the foul odors will be behind you.

Like everything new in life, there is a learning curve. Most podcasters agree their first few shows were horrible. Some even joke about taking them off their site and feed shortly after they were initially released. If

> **TIP**
>
> When you add your feed to all the different podcast directories, many will have a section that reads "New Shows." A number of people like to listen to new shows. If you wait until show five before adding your feed, then listeners of new shows will be comparing your new show to that from someone who released a typical first show, and yours will seem that much better.

you have never done audio recordings before or you were not on a college radio station, you will probably find it does take some time to get your podcasting legs under you. You only get one shot to make a good first impression.

Granted, if you only release one show a month, you may not want to wait five months before promoting. Also, if you are releasing a show on a subject that is time sensitive (such as coverage of the Olympics), you may not want to wait. But for most shows, we highly recommend you get past the point where you are still trying to figure out how to work with your recording setup. When you reach a point where you are able to concentrate on the content of your show, where you feel more comfortable talking into a microphone, that's when it's time to consider promoting your podcast.

What we suggest you do when your first few shows are released is to tell just your friends and family and ask for their feedback on your show. Tell them to be honest, brutal even. When Rob first started podcasting, he had a good friend who was constantly giving feedback, and it was very good and constructive criticism. You need to find a few people whose opinions you value and who are willing to tell it to you straight. And there is nothing that says your first few shows even need to be on an RSS feed. Simply upload them to a server and send the links to friends to check out. This is exactly what PK and J did before they created their RSS feed.

Voting Sites

People are fascinated with lists. There are Top-10, Top-20, Top-40, Top-100 lists everywhere you look. How many people remember listening to Casey Kasem's *American Top 40* show? (Answer: lots.) David Letterman has his Top-10 lists. There is the Top-25 Coaches poll for football, which of course causes controversy every year. Podcasting is no different. Many different podcast directories have some sort of "Top" list where they rank podcasts. In early 2006, the top five directories, as listed by Alexa Rankings, were as follows:

- podcasts.yahoo.com
- iTunes
- Odeo
- Podcast Alley
- Podcast Pickle

With Yahoo!, iTunes, and Odeo, listeners subscribe through those services to your podcast. Yahoo! and Odeo then rank podcasts

NOTE

Alexa (www.alexa.com) ranks websites based on traffic to each site. The lower the number, the better the traffic. Yahoo! usually has a rank of 1, which means it is the most popular site on the Internet. A rank of 10,000 for a site means that 9,999 other sites have more traffic than that site. Alexa goes back to 1996 and is considered one of the best ranking systems for website traffic.

by total number of current subscribers. iTunes' Top-100 lists are based on a secret formula that Apple has never publicly acknowledged. However, Apple did have an issue with the list back in July of 2005, where people could just keep hitting the Subscribe button and each click would be counted. Some bored podcasters and listeners did just that and pushed some of their favorite shows to the top. They also did experiments to see how long it took for shows to drop out of the Top-100 list. Based on those experiments, it appears to be a weighted average of new subscribers over the past 96 to 120 hours, with a higher weight toward those in the past 24 hours, or so the rumor goes.

With Podcast Pickle, listeners register on the site and then pick their favorite podcasts. The lists are wiped clean twice a year. Because you have to register, like with Odeo, the favorite votes are less susceptible to spamming. If someone stays in the number-one spot for 12 consecutive weeks, they are moved to the Podcast Pickle Hall of Fame and taken off the main list to give others a chance for popularity.

Podcast Alley listeners vote once a month for their favorite podcasts. In the podcasting world, this has given a new meaning to the phrase, "That time of the month," with podcasters at the beginning of each month pining for votes and complaining about having to do so or worse yet trying to justify having to do so.

Many other sites offer voting for podcasts, but the five listed here currently have the most influence on listeners and are the ones you are most likely to see small banners for on podcasters' websites.

Why Voting Sites Are Important

Early on in the life of podcasting (before the launch of iTunes), Podcast Alley was clearly the most important directory to be in and to be at the top of the voting list. Hordes of new potential listeners used the Top-10 and Top-50 lists to find new podcasts to which they wanted to subscribe. The mainstream news media frequently used the Top-10 list to find podcasters to interview for articles about podcasting. The press still looks at the top sites mentioned earlier to find podcasters to interview for articles on podcasting.

Times change, however. And by early 2006, iTunes and Yahoo! had more pull than Podcast Alley. Obviously, getting mentioned in any newspaper or online article about podcasting is great, but getting mentioned in a major print publication like *Parade Magazine*, *Reader's Digest*, or the *Wall Street Journal* can get your podcast far more attention than other forms of promotion.

Voting sites also help feed the ego. When you see your podcast moving up in the ranks, it makes you feel good about what you are doing. Conversely, if you spend a lot of time asking for votes and you see yourself falling down in the ranks, it really can be a huge blow to your psyche. For many podcasters, the only reward they have for doing their show is feedback from listeners. When a listener is willing to spend a few minutes to vote for your show, it means a lot.

In early 2006, iTunes was clearly the most important directory to be in. As an example of how important iTunes is for increasing subscriber numbers, in late January of 2006, Escape Pod was featured on the top of the front page of iTunes. In less than one week, Escape Pod's Feedburner subscriber numbers increased from 2,500 people to over 4,500 people.

Unfortunately, getting featured on the iTunes most popular list is not something you can influence, outside of producing a high-quality show. These spots are definitely not for sale, despite conspiracy theories to the contrary. As you can see from Figure 15.2, we do have first-hand knowledge on this.

FIGURE 15.2

The iTunes Podcast website features individual podcasts at the top of its page. It also lists its most popular podcasts along the right side of the page.

Although you cannot really influence getting featured, you can still get yourself into the top 25 of iTunes, and this also generates many additional new listeners. However, it is a little bit like the chicken and the egg scenario. Fortunately, the iTunes Top-100 list is about the number of new listeners and not total listener numbers. If you can make a splash by promoting your podcast in some other manner, that spurt of new listeners might move you into the top 25 of iTunes, and from there additional new listeners from iTunes can move you further up the rankings. This is what happened with Skepticality. They promoted hard in the skeptic forum boards, which then moved them into the top 25 in iTunes. From there the iTunes listeners moved them up into the number-one spot for a couple weeks. In September of 2005, Steve Jobs showed a list of the top-nine most-subscribed-to podcasts and Skepticality was on that list.

Finally, there is the respect of your peers. Getting into the top 10 of any of these lists lets other podcasters learn about you. From there, you have many new opportunities to cross-promote and further build your listener base. Granted, some may wonder how legitimate the numbers are if you come out of nowhere. When "Keith and the Girl" first burst on the scene in the Spring of 2005, many wondered if they were spamming the vote at Podcast Alley, but once people started listening to their show they realized they were the real deal. Their cast has been in the top 10 on Podcast Alley ever since.

Why Voting Sites Can Be Overrated

Two words: Joe Vitale. In January 2006, after just one episode, this show was number 1 on Podcast Alley. It vaulted its way into the number 1 spot by apparently spamming the vote using preexisting marketing email lists to solicit votes. This is not the first time he spammed like this; in April 2005 he did the same thing to get his book to be number 1 on Amazon. This is not the first marketing hype podcast to spam the vote, and it will not be the last. But each time this happens, it lessens the validity of the voting sites.

Some might ask, if the spamming strategy works, why not go for it? Well, as we detail in the next two sections, there are good reasons for that, too.

Negligible Bump in Listeners

Getting in to the top 50 at Podcast Alley just does not mean as much as it did in 2005. It does not take many votes to get there. During a typical month at Podcast Alley, a mere 120 votes is more than enough to ensure a Top-50 spot. Considering at least 2.5 million people are listening, this is a very small percentage of the listeners. The reality is, outside of making it into the top 25 on iTunes or the top 10 of the other four sites, you really are not going to see any noticeable increase in traffic to your podcast directly from these lists.

Plain and simple, people will continue to listen to your show because they like it. They are not going to continue listening because you were in the top 40 at Odeo, or top 10 at Podcast Pickle, or because you purchased a marketing list and spammed the vote.

There are Too Many Directories

Well over 100 different directories (www.podcast411/com/page2.html) have been created just for podcasts, and almost half of them have some sort of "voting" method to rank podcasts. With just the five we focused on earlier, that feels like too many. If you asked for listeners to subscribe and vote to just these five sites, here is basically what you would have to say on your podcast:

> *"Hey, folks, it is that time of the month again to go over to Podcast Alley and vote for the Selling Your Soul podcast. Just do a search for us in the alley and vote. Also, if you have not picked us as a favorite at Podcast Pickle, make sure you go over there and register and pick show number 75 as one of your favorites. Of course, don't forget to go into iTunes and subscribe to us. Simply search for 'Selling Your Soul'— that is o-u-l and not o-l-e—and then click the Subscribe button. The same goes for Odeo and podcasts.yahoo.com. Please make sure you subscribe there also. As always, buttons are available on our home page to each of these sites."*

That takes about 45 seconds to read out loud, and that is just for five sites. Imagine what happens as others become popular or if you wanted to cover every site. You could spend 5 minutes begging for votes in each show you produce. At some point, you need to ask yourself, "Is this the best use of my listeners' time?"

Both of us stopped asking for votes on our shows in November 2005. Rob even put out a skit at the end of his show going over all the different sites and asking the audience, "Is that so much to ask of you?" It was all very tongue in cheek.

But while plugging voting sites in your podcast may be a waste of your listeners' time, it can't really hurt to have links to them from your podcast's home page. Rob, for example, still has links on his front page to iTunes, Odeo, and Yahoo!, as well as links in the show notes for Podcast Alley and Podcast Pickle.

Podcast Networks

There are many different podcasting networks out there; the first one was the GodCast network. Many others have popped up recently. Some networks were created to be purely social (such as The 138 and The Teen Podcasters Network), where the different podcasters joined together to help out each other on their shows, to cross-promote each other, and to vote for each other on the different directories. Others, such as the GodCast

Network, TSFPN, and the Podcast Outlaws, were created to give listeners a place to go to find new shows to listen to. Then there are networks such as Podshow and Tech Podcast Network that were created to generate revenue for the podcasters in the network and, of course, for the creators of the network. We will talk more about that issue in Chapter 18, "Generating Revenue."

The following list is just a sampling of some of the podcast networks available:

- **The 138 (www.the138.com)**—One of the first social podcast networks. This group was started by Bibb, from Bibb and Yaz, in early 2005 to help individual podcasters cross-promote on the other members' shows. Podcasters in the group help out other members with show material and technical support when needed.

- **AMP (Association of Music Podcasters; www.musicpodcasting.org)**—This is the first network of music podcasters. AMP was originally formed as a way for music podcasters to share information about what indie musicians and songs they were playing on their podcasts to keep everyone from just playing the same few songs. With over 60 podcasts, AMP has a lot of combined experience with issues facing music podcasters. If you are a music podcaster starting out, it is highly recommended you make friends with at least a couple of members of AMP.

- **The GodCast Network (www.godcast.org)**—The original podcast network started by podcast pioneer Craig Patchett. This network was started to bring together quality religious-based and family-friendly podcasts (see Figure 15.3).

- **The Podcast Outlaws (www.podcastoutlaws.com)**—A small group of podcasters who pick good-quality indie podcasts to highlight on their RSS feed.

- **Podshow (www.podshow.com)**—Make no mistake about it: Podshow was created to make money for the people who started it. Podshow was the first network to bring in a large venture capital (VC) round of funding (over $8 million in June of 2005). All that said, they have worked very hard to bring in advertisers for the shows they have under contract. (We will talk more about Podshow in Chapter 18.) Podshow brought in a $100,000 contract from Dixie paper for the MommyCast in late 2005. This network is by invite only.

- **TSFPN (The Sci-Fi Podcasters Network; www.tsfpn.com)**—Once you get past the really bad color scheme on the website, you will find a wealth of sci-fi podcasts listed here, including Mur's Geek Fu Action Grip, along with over 50 other great podcasts. TSFPN even makes it easy for potential listeners to find shows they might like by breaking them up into different content ratings. If you have a sci-fi podcast, this is definitely a place you want to have your show listed.

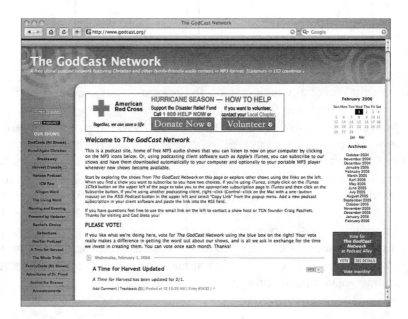

FIGURE 15.3

The GodCast Network is the original podcast network.

■ **Tech Podcasts Network (www.techpodcasts.com)**—This is a network of over 50 G-rated tech podcasts. Criteria to join are numerous and sometimes mysterious. The network is definitely commercially focused and inked early advertising deals with GoDaddy.com and Goto Meeting. If you do not want advertising on your podcast, you are best to look for a more social network. But if you are looking for revenue for your podcast, this network has lots of experience in that area—just remember, no bad words allowed.

■ **The Teen Podcasters Network (www.teenpodcasters.com)**—Founded in July of 2005, this network was started to help bring teen podcasters together, where they can communicate with each other and help one another. This is more of a social network, and there is even a voting page for the different shows. If you are teenager and a podcaster, you should check out this network.

Networks can be a great way to get added exposure for your podcast, but you need to make sure you know what you want out of a network before you join that network. Here are some questions to ask yourself:

■ Are you just looking for exposure or do you also want to get some revenue from your show?

- Are you looking to find like-minded podcasters who will help you develop your show?

- Are you just looking for a group of people to give you more votes at Podcast Alley?

Talk to the members of any network you are looking to join. Ask them off the record to tell you what they like and dislike about the network. Find out who has recently left the network and go and ask them why they left. Many different networks are out there, and more will pop up every month. You as a podcaster need to make sure you are careful before joining any network and weigh the costs of joining. Some networks put restrictions on the content of your shows; others force you to play promos for the network or advertisements from sponsors of the network, and they even force you to play those ads at the beginning of your podcast. Even worse, some lock you into long-term one-sided agreements. It is crazy (in our humble opinion) at this early stage in podcasting for someone to lock themselves into a multiyear contract—unless, of course, there is a huge signing bonus. If you are looking at joining a network and you are required to sign a contract, *please* have a lawyer review it for you.

Community Building

"Talking people into listening to their first podcast is one way to get new listeners. However, I think it is much easier to get people who already listen to podcasts to check your show out. They already understand podcasting. I feel that podcast forum boards are a great place to find new listeners. First of all, you know the forum members are involved with podcasting and enjoy them. It is just a matter of promoting your show. Don't be afraid to promote your show, or yourself on every podcasting forum you can find. No one knows more about you and your podcast than you do."

—Gary Leland, PodcastPickle.com

Beyond the networks, there are communities—and podcasting started very much as one big community. However, when any community gets large enough, it starts to splinter into smaller subgroups and cliques. With most online communities, forums are the local watering holes. Using the forums at popular podcast directories and podcasting sites is a great way to meet other podcasters. Some of the more active message boards include the following:

- Yahoo! Podcasting Message board (http://groups.yahoo.com/group/podcasters/)
- Podcast Alley (http://podcastalley.com/forum/)
- Podcast Pickle (http://www.podcastpickle.com/forums/)
- Apple Forum: Producing Podcasts (http://discussions.apple.com/forum.jspa?forumID=1107)
- Podcasting News (http://podcastingnews.com/forum/)
- Podcasting Rigs (http://podcastrigs.net/forum/)
- PodCast411 (http://podcast411.com/forums/)
- Podfeed.net (http://www.podfeed.net/forum/)

At each of these sites, you should be able to find people who will answer your questions. You will also find lively debate on a few of these forum boards that you can join in on. Remember, flame wars (fights between various posters) do not equal community building; they equal community trashing. Most importantly at these forums, you are likely to find like-minded people and some you may even come to call friends. Additionally, some podcasts have very large and active message boards, such as the following:

- Dawn and Drew (http://dawnanddrew.podshow.com/dnds_bb/)
- Keith and the Girl (http://keithandthegirl.com/forums/)
- Digital Photography Tips From the Top Floor (http://www.tipsfromthetopfloor.com/forum/)

As far as promoting your show goes, many of the forums mentioned here have a place where you can pimp your latest show. By all means, take advantage of this. Like any forum, spamming will not be tolerated. So promote in moderation and only where allowed.

One of the best ways to build listeners is to cross-promote with other podcasters. Just shooting emails to podcasts you like and contributing to their shows is a great way to start community building. Reach out to other podcasts similar to yours. Come "bearing fruit," and you will be received much better than if you come looking for others to do something for you.

Once you build up a relationship with specific podcasters, you will find most will go out of their way to help promote your show. And if one of those podcasters is part of a social network, there is a good chance you will be invited into that network. With The 138 network, the only real requirement for entry is that a potential member is already contributing to and promoting two or more current members.

Online is not the only place to build communities; you can actually build a podcasting community of friends in person. Podcaster "meetups" (http://podcasting.meetup.com/) are a great way to do this (see Figure 15.4). There are over 20 different podcaster meetup groups, with membership ranging from 3 to over 200 people. If you do not have a local group, start your own. It is really easy, and it gives you a reason to contact your local paper to talk about podcasting and your podcast (more on that in the next chapter). Talking to someone via Skype is one thing, but when you actually get to hang out in person with someone and commiserate over drinks about your lack of sleep since you started podcasting, that is where great friendships are made.

FIGURE 15.4

The Podcasting Meetup Page lets podcasters build an in-person network with their colleagues.

Another way to community-build is by going to podcast conventions. Portable Media Expo (PME) and PodcasterCon were the two biggest conventions for podcasters over the past 2 years. Yes, these can be very cliquish. But it is really a great experience to meet fellow podcasters and get a face to put with each voice.

> **NOTE**
>
> Rob cannot count the number of times when he met people at PME and PodcasterCon and they said, "Wow, you look nothing like what I expected." Granted, he is still not sure what to make of those comments, but the optimist in him thinks it was a compliment.

Being able to break bread with fellow podcasters and share ideas about podcasting is an unforgettable experience. Additionally, it gives you a great opportunity to promote yourself and your show to those who can help spread the word.

Podcasting Directories

We mentioned earlier that there are five key directories when it comes to voting, and that there are over 100 different podcast directories out there. So which ones do you want to be in?

"A podcast directory is like a phone book. If you opened a store, you would want to be in every phone book in town. If you start a podcast, you should try and get in every podcast directory on the Internet."

—Gary Leland, PodcastPickle.com

If you are doing a podcast focused on law issues, you will probably find that the blawg directory (www.blawg.org) helps bring you more listeners than an entry in Odeo or Podcast Alley. If you find a genre-specific directory that matches the topic of your show, do everything you can to become friends with the person who runs that directory. Offer to help out and contribute articles. Ask to interview the person for your show, so that you can talk about his or her site and, of course, so you can bond with that person. Many of the directories have a list of new entries; this is a great way for potential listeners to find out about your show (given that you wait until you have at least five shows done before submitting).

When building up your listener base, you want to start at your core and work out (refer back to Figure 15.1). That means starting with friends and family. When your family and friends start complaining that all you talk about is podcasting, you know you have reached your goal with that group. Next you want to court other podcasters. Who better to spread the word about your show than those who already have an audience to spread that word to. At the same time, you want to start courting other podcast listeners through forum boards and directories. Once you have done this, you should have a good fan base from which to push out toward the rest of the world—or at least be ready for the next chapter.

> **TIP**
>
> Like Gary, we recommend you add yourself to every general podcast directory and every genre- or topic-specific directory that fits your show. You can find what is considered one of the most, if not *the* most, complete list of directories for podcasts at www.podcast411.com/page2.html.
>
> From there, you will have links directly to the submit page at the different directories.

Chapter **16**

HOW TO FIND NEWBIE LISTENERS

I promote Projekt Podcast on music boards and lifestyle boards for people who migrate to gothic culture and its various incarnations. It seems like a no-brainer, but as you know, in the early stages of podcasting most of the podcasters were mostly just there for one another, listening to each others' shows. They promoted their shows on the boards of directories like Podcast Alley and the Podcast Pickle, but not in a lot of other places.

—Swoopy, Skepticality and Projekt Podcast

I n previous chapters, we covered how to produce and distribute your promo and get your word out to other podcasters, your friends and family, and established podcast listeners. But those are small numbers, relatively. Now we discuss how to get the word out to the rest of the world—where the real numbers lie.

- Contacting Local Media
- Press Releases
- Online Message Boards and Forums
- craigslist and Other Boards
- Guerilla Marketing Tricks

Contacting Local Media

They say charity and self-promotion begin at home. (Okay, the self-promotion thing hasn't caught on as a saying yet, but it'll catch on any day.) Regardless, don't shoot as high as the *New York Times* or *Fox News* when you're trying to get the attention of the media: aim for your local hometown media.

Don't knock your local newspapers, television, and even radio (yes, radio!) stations as good tools to promote your podcast. They love community stories, and a popular podcaster among them is something they would want to hear about.

Newspapers

Local newspapers are always looking for someone who makes a splash, someone to put on their features page. Most papers nowadays give email addresses for their different departments; even the individual writers usually give out their own email address.

In contacting local media, be polite and mention that you haven't seen the paper cover local podcasters, and offer your site and podcast for their perusal. Don't be pushy: Reporters are busy people; it may take them a while to get back to you. Wait a few weeks before following up with them. Don't follow up more than a few times though—the more annoyed you make them, the less likely you are to get a story.

> **NOTE**
>
> When pitching yourself to any local media, be sure to promote yourself as someone they can talk to about podcasting as a whole. When they talk to you, they will of course mention your show(s), as this is why you're an expert, after all. You will get your coverage.
>
> Do not, however, say, "I have this awesome podcast and you should interview me about it!" Be humble and present it as you doing them a favor: "I've noticed your local coverage hadn't addressed topic X, which is something I talk about weekly on my podcast, and I think I can help offer some perspective."

If you want to go through the snail mail, you can send a combo audio/data CD of your podcasts to the newspaper itself (this can work for TV and radio, too). The audio CD will allow them to play your podcast in a CD player, which will help you get past people who are paranoid about viruses. But make sure, if you go this route, to still include a letter stating who you are, what you do, and why you think it would make for an interesting story. Don't make it too long; just get your point across and let your podcast speak for itself.

Television

Local news also enjoys covering area residents who are doing something new and exciting. Unless a nationwide tragedy has struck, there's little bad news that will stop the local news from doing their amusing features just after the sports.

Like the newspapers, the email addresses and phone numbers of the local TV stations should be easily found on their websites. Your pitch should be similar to the newspaper's: You hadn't seen podcasting coverage on their news and you wondered if they would like to learn more about it from you.

Even if your interview takes a long time and they shoot you doing your entire show, remember it's likely going to be cut down to a 2-to-3-minute spot (in which you may be seen speaking for 45 seconds). But those 2–3 minutes will be seen by thousands, even millions, depending on your area. That can only do good things in your quest for podcast fame.

Radio

Ah, radio. This one is tricky. Most podcasters proudly say that they got into podcasting—either listening or producing—because they couldn't stand what the radio was putting over the airwaves. After these inflammatory (whether true or not) statements, it seems odd to go after the local radio stations to see if they would like to cover you.

There are options, however. First, check and see if your radio station has a podcast. Many are starting to podcast their morning shows with limited or no ads, giving people only the content. National Pubic Radio releases over 100 of its most popular shows via podcast (see Figure 16.1). If the station is open to the idea of podcasting already, it might be safe to contact them for coverage. You can, like for the newspaper, send them a CD of your highest quality (recording-wise) material and mention that you're available to discuss podcasting if they ever do a story on it.

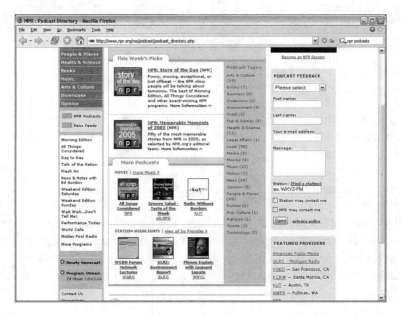

FIGURE 16.1

NPR is not afraid of the mighty podcast.

You can submit your show to KYOU in San Francisco (www.kyouradio.com). This is a radio station that plays only podcasts. Once on KYOU, you should then contact your local radio stations and see if they might have an open timeslot to play your podcast. Robert Keeme, from the KeemeCast, now has his show podcast on his local radio station. Many smaller local radio stations will be open to free content.

> **CAUTION**
>
> If you get a local radio station to agree to air your podcast, make sure you do not sign over any rights to your show. You only want to give them a license to use your material, and you want to retain all copyright ownership and full distribution rights.

Is There No Such Thing as Bad Publicity?

So what if you give an hour of eloquent interview and they boil it down to a sound byte and a photograph, misquote you, and make you look like an adorable kid with a hobby instead of the serious podcaster you are. Is it worth it to argue?

It's all in how you see it. If you're merely disappointed with your coverage, your picture is small and below the fold on page 14, and they treat you like someone with a cute hobby, that's annoying, but there's not much you can do about it. Be grateful for the coverage and use the story as a launching pad for the next media opportunity. After all, you can still say you were featured in said publication. The new target doesn't need to know you only got 2 inches at the end of the Local section in the paper. The truth is you got the coverage, and now you're trying to get more.

There are times when you'll want to contact the media outlet, however, as actor and stay-at-home dad Dan Klass of the Bitterest Pill discovered when the *New York Times* incorrectly called him a "self-identified addict." He politely wrote them and mentioned that he was not and had never been an addict, and his show's title was a reference to the saying that something is a "bitter pill to swallow." He was worried about the impact the *Times* article would have on his career (not to mention what people would wonder about his fathering abilities), as he didn't want potential employers or clients to see him as something negative that he clearly wasn't. He finally received his retraction, but the reporter worded it to imply no fault on the *Times'* shoulders: "…he said that the description was intended as a humorous reference likening himself to fans of his podcast who call themselves addicts, and that he is not really an addict."

Dan has this to say about the incident:

> "*At the time I was crushed. If it had been* **The New York Post**, *I would have laughed it off, but* **The New York Times**? *As far as I know, people believe what they read in the* **New York Times**, *or at least they used to. Holy cow! I was worried that their characterization of me would hurt my family and career. (Only famous addicts get acting jobs. The non-famous ones are not worth insuring.) It's also a touchy subject with me, as I've lost friends and family members to drugs and alcohol, and live a very clean-and-sober life myself. I was angry that they got me and my show so wrong, and I was angry to learn the hard way that the old adage is true: You can't believe everything you read.*

> "*Of course, there is the other old adage, this one about press, good and bad: Just spell my name right. Now that so much time has passed, it's easier for me to be objective and see that there were no negative ramifications (as far as I know) from what was printed. The only lasting result is that I now have a great quote or two about The Bitterest Pill from The Old Gray Lady, and that is the most important thing in the long run. They made me seem like a drug-addled negligent father for a moment, but my future promotional pieces will read that* **The New York Times** *said I'm 'intelligent' and 'endearing' for years. In the end, I win.*"

> **—Dan Klass, The Bitterest Pill**

So if you don't like the coverage you get, determine whether it's merely irritating or downright damaging to your person and your podcast.

Press Releases

Formerly the tool of corporate PR officials, the press release is now something that anyone can come out with to announce something new and exciting that has to do with his or her company or other enterprise. Authors, musicians, and, yes, podcasters have sent out press releases.

So the first question is, how do you write it?

The good thing about press releases is that they are incredibly formulaic. Look at any press release and you'll see the same things:

- **FOR IMMEDIATE RELEASE**—This text always appears in capital letters, you can also use EMBARGOED FOR RELEASE UNTIL....

- **Contact information**—This includes your name, phone number, email address.

- **Headline**—One descriptive sentence with the first letter of each word capitalized. Be creative and avoid exclamation marks.

- **First Paragraph**—Should start with "*CITY, STATE, Date*" followed by two dashes (—) surrounded by single spaces. The paragraph should be a strong fact-based summary of the newsworthy nature of the release. Make the reader care.

- **Second Paragraph**—Contains supporting information and relevant quotes cleared for media use. Correct spelling and grammar are imperative throughout the press release.

- **Final Paragraph**—This contains a summary of the facts and a call to action, usually urging the reader to visit a relevant website (say, your podcast's site) for more information.

- **Boilerplate info**—Starting with "About *you/your company*:", write a paragraph describing you and your podcast (with URL), the date you began podcasting, how frequent your podcast comes out, and so on. Write about your podcast as if it were your business, and use this same paragraph at the end of every press release, only changing it when something big happens to your podcast (you double your listeners, for example).

- **End**—Press Enter twice and place three pound signs (###) centered on the line to indicate the end of the press release.

- **Misc.**—The press release should be kept to 500 words and printed on company/podcast letterhead if mailed or faxed.

Don't be coy with the text: This is a one-page "Just the facts ma'am" info-dump. Remember everything you learned from essay and newspaper writing in school and tell who, what, when, where, and why. It's there for people to put out information if they feel like it, but it's also designed to entice people to contact you for an interview, and that's when you get clever. Tell what you want to say in the first sentence. Did you win an award? Did you get an interview with someone who's been in hiding for 4 years? Did you land a million-dollar advertising deal for your podcast? Say it up front. Include quotes from yourself. It's here where you can get witty and clever and sell yourself and your podcast.

And now we're to the second question: To whom do you send it?

They're not called "press releases" for nothing. Send them to the press. Local, statewide, maybe even national if you think the news is big enough (hint: it has to be *really* big). But also send it to websites that might be more likely to pick up web-related news, as well as other podcasts that might enjoy hearing about podcasting news.

Another option is to use a service that sends out press releases to a preset group of media agents. Most of these services will also write the press release for you. These services aren't cheap, though. Many cost from $99 for the writing to $400 for the release. (But hey, if you've landed that million-dollar ad deal, you can afford a $400 media blitz, right? The rest of us, however, have to do the grunt work and gather email addresses of media outlets.)

"Like in any press release, keep it brief, avoid the over-techie jargon (such as aggregator, podosphere, podcasting client, and so on), and then focus on telling your media resources what your podcast is all about. Once the press release is done, email, or print-and-fax, that release to as many local contacts as you can."

—Tee Morris, author of the podiobook *Morevi*

Some press release service sites you may want to check out are listed here:

- PRNewswire (www.prnewswire.com)
- PRWeb.com (www.prweb.com)
- PR Free (www.prfree.com)
- SBWire (www.sbwire.com)

PRNewswire is the one that seems to be used the most by podcasters and is one that Rob has used with a decent amount of success.

Online Message Boards and Forums

These days there's a message board for everything under the sun. Knitting, MINI Cooper enthusiasts, fans of a computer game, people who think the Southern United States should secede again—there are more niche forums than there are niche podcasts. Therefore, it should be easy for you to Google your podcast topic and find at least one, and probably several, message boards of potential listeners.

There is, however, a huge catch-22 when it comes to self-promotion on the Net. People who spend a great deal of time on the Internet are always looking for "something else cool" to find and tell their friends about. So if you let them know about your podcast, they're going to jump all over it. But—and this is a huge but—if you appear like you're spamming the forums to just run in and say, "Hey, take a listen at my awesome new podcast that is focused on tomato gardening!" then no one is going to care. You are a stranger and you're not there to make the community better; you're there to try to get their attention, and many net-savvy people resent that.

So how do you walk the line? Become a part of the community. Yes, this will be a time-sink, but hundreds of new listeners are worth a little research. Begin contributing to the forum community. If the forum software allows you to create a signature (a signoff message that appears at the end of each of your posts), put your podcast name and URL there. If Mur were to try to promote her podcast on a writers' forum, she would put the following in her signature:

~ ~ ~

Mur Lafferty

mightymur@gmail.com

I Should Be Writing – The podcast for wanna-be writers by a wanna-be writer. http://www.ishouldbewriting.com

~ ~ ~

Taking this example further, if someone asks Mur about the signature, she would answer them simply and invite them to check out the site. If this doesn't happen, but she does become a more recognized person in the forum, she might answer a general writing question and follow it up with, "...and I talked about this in more depth in my podcast, I Should Be Writing, show 52. If you have some time, here's the link: http://www...."

People will react more positively to you and your podcast on the Net if you're already one of them. Breezing into an established community to post your podcast is like trespassing.

Derek and Swoopy from Skepticality already spent time on skeptical message boards, so when it came time to promote, the path was obvious. Swoopy describes how they did it:

*"Our Skepticality audience was largely built by spreading the word about our podcast on message boards and forum communities devoted to skepticism, humanism, and critical thinking. We did online chats at places like Skeptic Friends Network, and reached out to publications like **Skeptic Magazine**, **Reason**, and **Free Inquiry**. That's where our contacts are, that's where we get our interview subjects from, and they in turn help build our listening audience.*

"Many science podcasts could benefit from this kind of exposure. Find your niche, and then go find your people where they live and show them you are speaking to them specifically. They'll appreciate it, and support you."

—Swoopy (of Derek and Swoopy), Skepticality

craigslist and Other Boards

craigslist (http://www.craigslist.org) is an 11-year-old community board that started in San Francisco and by 2006 had reached over 150 cities worldwide (see Figure 16.2). It's a simple concept: The board takes the public community bulletin board hanging in popular places and puts it online to great popularity and effect.

Anything can be posted on craigslist. Anything. Seriously. Homeless men seeking love, people wanting to sell their furniture, and people advertising "services" only scratch the surface of what can be found there.

Podcasters have gotten on the bandwagon as well, mostly music podcasts looking for new music to play. But it's a good place to advertise your podcast. craigslist does not charge for most postings; it makes money only from charging for employment positions. These and other community boards are excellent (affordable) places to advertise your podcast.

craigslist also has forums, so you can post about your podcast there as well. If you do this, however, be sure to follow the instructions we gave you in the previous section regarding posting in forums.

FIGURE 16.2

craigslist.org is all about function over form.

Guerilla Marketing Tricks

Many people, even marketers, don't believe marketing works. Well, of course it works for Britney Spears and Coke and the NFL, but for the little guy? We just can't compete. Either we don't have the money, or if we do have the money, we don't have the name recognition that will make people care. So we have to do other things to get the attention of the world—hence the term *guerilla marketing*.

"Good to meet you. Here's my card."

Everyone has business cards nowadays. Even if you don't use your corner copy store, your computer probably has a simple paint program. Business cards are easy to create and print.

"Print up some business cards with your show's logo or title, the location of the show's blog, and the network. Offer to talk about podcasting whenever and wherever you can (SF/F conventions, tech expos, etc.) or talk about podcasting at venues that cater to your podcasting

topic.... Word-of-mouth and old-fashioned networking is one of the
most sound ways of reaching out to the outside world and generating
interest in your podcasts."

—Tee Morris

In addition, most computers have CD-burning
capability. So why not mix the two? You
could burn a podcast or a promo on the large
CDs, but they're a little large to casually
carry 10 with you. Ideally, see if you can find
the tiny 3.5-inch writable mini CDs (see Figure

> **TIP**
>
> If you do print your own business
> cards, be sure to use a heavy card-
> stock that's already perforated for you.

16.3). Slip them into a plastic sheath along with your business card and always have a
handful on you for when you meet someone new.

FIGURE 16.3

The mini CD (right) is a perfect mate to your business card, and easily slips into a pocket
or wallet.

You can also drop a stack at the counter of your local record store, comic book store, or
grocery store—anywhere local where you know they won't mind helping to promote
homegrown artists. But always ask before leaving a stack of something on the counter!
If you don't, the proprietors of those establishments will almost certainly just throw
them in the trash.

Droplift.org

Now let's go 180 degrees from the last section. Droplift.org is a fascinating site that encourages people to subvert what they consider strangling copyright law and the recording industry's hold on music distribution.

Taking the opposite of "shoplift," the site encourages people to download the free music from their website, print out the liner notes, burn CDs, and carry them into music stores. Instead of taking something out of the store, the people are to leave the CDs there for unsuspecting shoppers to find and take home.

So who says you can't do this with podcasts? Burn a handful of podcasts to a CD and droplift them into the Spoken Word or Music Compilation section of your favorite music store. You might get a listener or two out of that, but better than that, it's a subversive way to get your point across.

Check out droplift.org to find out more about their guerilla tactics.

Some podcasters have taken this a step further and started burning CDs of their show and then putting them in the thin plastic or paper sleeves. On the back of the sleeve they

> **CAUTION**
>
> ## More Trouble Than They're Worth?
>
> Mini CDs, although useful and just downright adorable, have created some problems during their lifespan. Many desktop computers have a smaller groove in the CD tray in which to put the little CDs for burning or reading, but many laptops (namely those from Apple) have only a slit to put the disk in (called a slot-based loading mechanism).
>
> If you have one of these types of CD drives, find out if it can handle mini CDs. If you can't find it on the Web, call your computer support center. We're serious; you don't want to get a mini CD stuck in your disk drive with no way of retrieving it. Only use mini CDs if you're sure they're compatible with your computer!
>
> For that matter, make sure the people you're giving it to can read it. It would be bad if you give people a disc that is going to screw up their computer. Granted, they should know what kind of disc their computer can take, but they're not going to be mad at themselves when they call support, they're going to be mad at you.
>
> This will not help you get listeners.

put double-sided tape. On the back of the CD they place a label that says "Bonus CD." Next, they look up in Amazon what books are hot sellers in the category that best matches their show. (If you have a podcast on food, then maybe you want to target Rachel Ray.) Then they go to their local bookstore and find that book and droplift the CD into the back of it, removing the backing on the double-sided tape, thus making it look like the CD belongs with the book. Of course, we ourselves would never condone such actions (wink, wink).

Colleges, Conventions, and Other Groupings of Radical-Minded People

College campuses are a great place to hang flyers. Granted, everyone else will be hanging flyers there to promote their band, to get a roommate or ride to Chicago, or to advertise for a medical study. But these boards are places people do go to so they can check out the latest happenings (see Figure 16.4).

FIGURE 16.4

Briefly removing "The Cube"—the bulletin board for the University of North Carolina at Chapel Hill—for construction hasn't stopped students from making their announcements seen.

Along the same lines, conventions and expos are often good places to dump business cards or flyers. Take a stack to put in strategic places. Any expo, convention, or conference that remotely refers to the topic of your podcast would be a good place to put your card or flyer. And you don't even have to wait for conferences. Keep an eye out for community areas that allow flyers or cards. Coffee shops with wi-fi hotspots are also a great place to leave flyers, because you know a certain percentage of the clientele are going to be tech savvy. The packaging store near Mur prides itself on being a community area, and it has a business card rack near the counter where area entrepreneurs post their cards. You can find accountants, real estate agents, and marital-aid home party distributors.

Andy Affleck, host of Take Control of Podcasting on the Mac (http://www.takecontrol-books.com/mac-podcasting/) says this may not work for all podcasts, however.

"If you are doing a show that would be of special use or interest to a given community, certainly. But Joe's Podcast about Tropical Fish isn't one I'd bother advertising [locally]. Joe's Today in the Town Council, however, is."

—Andy Affleck, Take Control of Podcasting on the Mac

Your Listeners: Stealth Marketing Tools

Stealth marketing is a term advertisers use to market to people who don't know they're being marketed to. They might send models to bars to drink a new beer, for example.

Using your listeners like this is more honest, because they already listen to—and presumably enjoy—your podcast. Put the word out to your listeners to not be shy in telling people about your podcast. If someone looks at them quizzically while they're listening to your podcast and laughing on the bus, have them tell the person why. At parties have them discuss podcasts (notably yours) in conversation.

You could even have a contest and give a prize to whichever listener brings you the most new listeners. Have the new listeners send you an email telling you who got them to listen, and the person with the most emails gets a t-shirt or CD or something.

If the listeners are uncomfortable talking to strangers and evangelizing your podcast, there are other, simple things they can do, such as linking to your podcast from their home page, mentioning you in their blog, or simply telling a friend.

One caveat: Don't lay it on too thick. As we learned during the "Vote for me!" fury in 2005, you can turn listeners off if you ask them to be part of your popularity party every podcast. Mention it once or twice a month that you'd like their help, but don't make it their duty, don't make it seem like you're desperate, and, above all, don't make it the focus of your show!

Chapter 17

BUSINESS PLANNING

The best way to make money off of podcasting is to get a large audience. Without an audience, no one is going to pay you to podcast. The best way to get a large audience is to produce a quality show, with interesting and informative content that you are passionate about. If you are not passionate about the subject of your podcast, you will never build a large audience.

—Rob, podCast411

This was part of Rob's response to an email he received from Anisha, a 13-year-old girl interested in whether or not it was possible to make money off of podcasting. Rob gets this question almost every day, often multiple times per day.

The bottom line is that you need to think of podcasting as a hobby—very few people will ever make money from their hobbies, and very few people will ever break even with podcasting. Probably greater than 90% of those who podcast will not break even, and less than 1% will ever make enough to compare with a day job.

The current rush into podcasting is very similar to the gold rushes of the past. In this case, the podcasters are the ones panning for gold. A very small number will hit it big, a modest amount will just cover their costs, but most will lose money doing it. Hopefully, those people who lose money will have taken the time to enjoy the fresh air, the outdoors, and the companionship of fellow 49'ers. History shows us that the people supplying equipment and services to the 49'ers were the only ones who really made any money during those gold rushes. And the same will likely be true in podcasting. However, addressing how to make money from those services is well beyond the scope of this book. This book is meant to be a guide to the 49'ers to point out the best ways and locations to pan for gold, so to speak.

In this chapter, we go over the different equipment options and the reasons for picking those pieces of equipment. We break down how much it costs to equip yourself, what it takes to break even, and we even look at the mythical goal of quitting your day job. In this chapter, "gold" is going to be advertising revenue. In Chapter 18, "Generating Revenue," we will expand into looking for silver, copper, and other forms of revenue.

If your podcast is a part of a business, we will look at the issues of using a podcast to promote a product, service, or brand name. Remember, for the most part what we are looking at is uncharted wilderness, and the risk/reward at this time is just not known.

Enough with the cheesy metaphors, and on to the business of making podcasting a business.

Balancing the Costs

Podcasting started out as a hobby, and as with any hobby you can spend a little or a lot of money, depending on how crazy you get. In this section, we are going to break down how much it will cost for you to get your recording setup based on four different types of recording needs and three different levels of investment—basic, intermediate, and semi-pro. We are not going to get into the pro-level setups for two simple reasons: 1) pro-level equipment is crazy expensive, and 2) to at least 99.9% of the public you will sound just as good with a semi-pro setup as you would if you had a pro-level setup.

Here are the four different type of recording needs, as summarized in Table 17.1:

- One person, in studio
- Two people, in studio
- In studio and VoIP
- In studio, VoIP and remote recording

For more information on VoIP, **see** "Using Skype and Other VoIP Services" **p. 137** (Chapter 7).

Our selection of equipment is based on our own experience, the experience of podcasters interviewed on podCast411, and other podcasters we have talked with. Costs are based on 1 year of hosting service. All prices were current as of March 2006.

Table 17.1   Recording Needs vs. Levels of Investment

Need	Type of Investment		
	Basic	Intermediate	Semi-Pro
One person	$25	$300 to $410	$665 to $785
Two people	$25	$450 to $590	$780 to $990
In studio with VoIP	$40	$430 to $557	$1,020 to $1,560
In studio, VoIP and remote recording	$110	$610 to $737	$1,760 to $1,930

The costs listed here assume you already have an Internet-connected PC that is capable of everyday tasks, such as audio compression.

We realize that in many cases you are going to need to present to a boss or a very demanding spouse or parent a detailed list of equipment you will need to get your podcast up and running. In Table 17.1, we broke down how much it will cost based on the type of recording you will be doing and the level investment you wanted to make. In the following sections, we break down in detail what equipment is needed for each type of recording.

One Person

This is the easiest setup in all of podcasting. This is when you are just going to be recording your own voice and possibly add in other sound clips.

Basic Setup

If you are doing just an audioblog of a "sound-seeing" tour, or are going to be reading a prepared script, the "basic setup" will be fine. You can get started for a mere $25. For editing software, Audacity is the best and cheapest option; it is free. For your mic, a simple USB mic is best ($25). You can find generic USB mics at any retail electronics store. For free hosting services, you have a few options. Internet Archive is one option, but it requires some level of technical skill, and you will need to also create a free blogger account to handle the RSS end of things. The easiest free option is Gcast (www. gcast.com), where even most "flashing 12's" will be able to set up an account with very little mental angst. This is a great and easy way to get into podcasting. You can even call in your shows from a phone and add the recording to your RSS feed all while being out on the road. You also have the option of recording at home on your computer, editing the recording, and then uploading to Gcast.

This setup is not recommended for anyone who is looking at generating revenue from the podcast. However, if you are just looking to get some experience podcasting, this setup is fine.

Total cost: $25

Intermediate Setup

For the intermediate setup, we are looking at podcasts that need multiple tracks to mix in many different sound clips or that are recorded live and need to mix in other sound files. Now your total cost for a setup has jumped to between $300 and $410 (this includes 1 year of hosting).

With the editing software, you may want to move away from Audacity and to something with a few more features (although you can still use Audacity at this point for many applications). On the Mac side, Garageband is clearly the number 1 piece of software when it comes to recording a podcast. If your Mac does not have Garageband 3, it will cost you $80 for iLife 06. On the PC side, two of the more popular podcast-specific programs are Castblaster and Propaganda; both cost $50. Garageband 3, Castblaster, and Propaganda all have features specifically designed for podcasters, such as auto-ducking and sound effects. Both Propaganda and Castblaster let you test-drive their programs before buying, so check both out before making a choice.

For the mic, the Samson USB mic is one of the cheapest ways to move to a condenser mic because no preamp is required to supply phantom power. Cost of the mic is $80. With

NOTE If you have an older version of GarageBand you will still be able to create a podcast with it, however, some of the newer features in Garageband 3 make it easier to produce a podcast. Specifically, if you have a .Mac account or if you are looking to create an enhanced podcast Garageband 3 comes in especially handy.

Condenser Microphones vs. Dynamic Microphones

Without getting into the technical details, the primary difference between these types of microphones, from the user's perspective, is that condenser mics require a power source (known as *phantom power*) and dynamic mics don't.

Because of how the condenser mic is designed, and with the aid of the power source, condenser mics are more sensitive than dynamic mics. This results in a warmer and more natural sound recording with the condenser mic. However, this design also makes them much more fragile.

For remote recordings, the dynamic mic is usually the best choice, especially if you will be doing the "man on the street" type of interview.

The microphone used in a studio or laboratory to record vocals will be a condenser mic. The microphone used by the local rock band onstage, which will likely be dropped often, have beer spilled on it, and carried into the mosh pit, will be a dynamic mic.

any condenser mic, you will need a mic stand and a pop filter. Condenser mics are very sensitive to movement and also to the popping *p*'s in your speech. Both a mic stand and a pop filter will help greatly improve the sound of your recording, and each cost about $25 (see Figure 17.1).

On the hosting side, if you use Garageband 3 on a Mac, the easiest solution is to upload to a .Mac account. You will want to upgrade your account to the 250GB transfer limit per month (total cost is $200). However, if you think you will have more than 250GB's worth of transfers, this is not the best solution for you.

NOTE
Phantom power is typically a +48 DC voltage that is supplied from an external source to the microphone to electrify part of the audio-sensing element. This voltage typically is supplied from a preamp, mixer, or digital recorder, but can also come from converting the voltage on a USB line from a computer (as is the case with the Samson C01U USB mic).

FIGURE 17.1

Rob's setup for his condenser mic with mic stand and pop filter.

Also note that using Garageband 3 to transfer directly to .Mac means your files will be encoded as AAC format rather than MP3 format. This means your listeners will need iTunes or Quicktime to listen to your show on their computer, and only an iPod will allow them to listen to your podcast on a portable player. Additionally, there is no real stats package with .Mac for you to know the exact number of full and unique downloads.

For a podcast you want to make money with, you really want to look at a hosting solution that offers you a good stats package and unlimited downloads. For podcasters, that usually means Libsyn. Based on a package where you need 250MB (approx 500 minutes spoken word, 250 minutes of music, or 50 minutes of video) of uploads a month, your cost will be $120 a year with Libsyn. Again, there is no limit on the downloads.

> **TIP**
>
> For a 250GB transfer limit, if your show is spoken word and 20 minutes long, the file size will likely be about 10MB. If you release your show once a week, you would reach your monthly limit with 6,250 listeners. However, with an hour-long show five times a week, you would max out at 416 listeners. Both numbers are theoretical and do not account for multiple download attempts—in the real world, you should cut those subscriber numbers in half to be safe.

Some shows hosted with Libsyn have over 250,000 downloads a month, which equals well over 3TB (terabytes, or 1,000 gigabytes) bandwidth, and podcasters using this service pay just $10 a month for that.

Total cost: Between $300 and $410

Semi-pro Setup

With a semi-pro setup, you are looking for the ability to finely edit your recordings. Plus, you want as good a sound for your voice as possible. You want to use audio-level compression to give your podcast a nice polished sound. As with the intermediate level, you will also likely have multiple tracks to mix together. On the editing software side for a Mac, Soundtrack Pro ($300) is highly regarded (See Figure 17.2). On the PC side, most everyone who uses Adobe Audition ($350) loves it. Both programs offer many different editing tools, including very good compressors and sound clean-up tools.

For mics, you will want a condenser mic to get a good clean sound. Condenser mics can run you anywhere from $50 (MXL-990) to $100 (Audio Technica AT2020) to $120 (Apex 415). Yes, you can spend much more, but for the extra money most of your listeners will not notice much if any difference.

In addition to the condenser mic, you will need a preamp to supply the phantom power needed to operate the mic. The M-Audio Mobile-Pre USB preamp ($130) is a very good investment and offers some nice features. It is completely USB powered, making it nice if you will be taking your studio

> **NOTE**
>
> **Preamp:** Also known as a *preamplifier*, a preamp is an amplifier that precedes another amplifier, which will further amplify the signal. Basically the job of the preamp is to amplify the low-level, high-impedance signal from the microphone to make it useable by the computer's audio-recording software, where the signal can again be amplified and processed.

on the road. It has two mic inputs with two on-board microphone preamps. And of course it supplies +48 VDC phantom power.

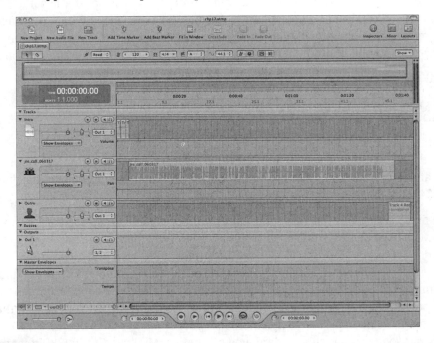

FIGURE 17.2

Soundtrack Pro in use with multiple tracks.

With a condenser mic, you will need a mic stand ($25) and pop filter ($25). In addition, you will need an XLR-to-XLR cable ($15) to connect the mic to the preamp. (No, these cables do not come with the mic or the preamp.) For hosting services, again we would recommend Libsyn ($120).

Total cost: Between $665 and $785

Two People

This is when you are recording yourself and one co-host and possibly adding in some sound clips. The recording can be done in your studio (office, bedroom, kitchen, wherever you can have privacy), and there will be relatively little background noise.

> **NOTE**
>
> **XLR:** Most people say that XLR = eXternal Left Right or eXternal Live Return. But in reality the name came from ITT Cannon, the maker of the connector. It started out as the X series, and then *L* was added for "Latch" and then *R* was added for "Rubber Gasket" (hence, XLR). It is a three-wire connector found on basically all professional and semi-pro sound equipment. It is so widely used because of the relative noise-free pickup of the cables.

Basic Setup

Essentially you can just duplicate the setup from the one-person basic setup we listed previously ($25). You and your guest just share the mic. This is what Dawn and Drew did for the first 9 months of their show. As we said before, we only recommend this as a way to start out, and not for a show with any intentions of generating revenue.

Total cost: $25

Intermediate Setup

For the intermediate setup, we are looking at podcasts where you and your co-host would need multiple tracks to mix in many different sound clips, or you are recording live and need to mix in other sound files. Now your total cost for a setup has jumped to the $450 to $590 range.

The differences between this setup and the intermediate setup for one person is that you will have two condenser mics ($100 total), two pop filters ($50 total), two mic stands ($50 total), two sets of XLR-to-XLR cables ($30 total) and a mixer ($50). For the condenser mics, we recommend the MXL-990s ($50 each), and for the mixer the Behringer UB-802. This is one of the cheapest mixers that also supplies the +48V phantom power needed for the two condenser mics. You would then come out of the mixer and into the Line In jack of your computer. If your computer does not have a Line In jack or if your sound card is substandard, you can get an iMic from Griffin ($30) that will plug into your USB port.

Total cost: Between $450 and $590

Semi-pro Setup

With a semi-pro setup, the key differences between a one-person setup and a two-person setup are the use of the mixer and the additional mic, pop filter, mic stand, and XLR cable. We recommend stepping up to the Yamaha MG102 Mixer and an iMic ($100 + $30) or the Alesis Multimix 8 USB ($150). Both mixers can supply phantom power for up to four different condenser mics at one time—compared to only two for the UB-802. This gives you some added flexibility if you

> **NOTE**
>
> **Mixer:** A mixer is a device that takes two or more audio signals and combines them into a single audio stream. Think of the mixer like the soft-serve ice-cream dispenser at your local frozen custard stand. On one side is vanilla, on the other chocolate, and in the middle is a place where you can get both mixed together. Essentially that is what a mixer is doing electronically with two audio signals.

ever want to have a third person drop in as a guest. The iMic is recommended so that you can feed the mixer output into your USB port via the iMic. The Yamaha is not set up for USB, whereas the Alesis has a USB port.

For the mics, you can choose between the MXL-990 ($50 each), the Audio Technica AT2020 ($100 each), or the Apex 415 ($120 each). It is important when buying two mics to try and get the same make and model. This will make matching up levels between you and your co-host much easier.

Total cost: Between $780 and $990

In Studio with VoIP

This is when you are recording yourself and a guest or co-host who will be talking to you via Skype, Gizmo Project, or some other VoIP software. The recording will be done in your studio and there will be relatively little background noise on your end, but the guest's side may have less of a controlled environment.

Basic Setup

As with the previous basic setups, we are going to stick with Audacity for the editing software. However, you will also need another piece of free software, Gizmo Project, for your VoIP calls. This allows you to talk to another person, computer to computer, for free. Plus, Gizmo Project has a built-in recorder that records both sides of the conversation pretty well.

For a mic, you will need a basic USB mic, but you will also need a headset because you need to make sure the person you are talking to does not hear his or her voice from your speakers back on your mic. This will cause stammering and stuttering when that person is talking.

For situations where you need to interview someone over the phone, you can use the Gizmo Call-Out feature to call and record phone conversations. If the person you will be interviewing needs to call you, you can set up a Gizmo Call-In number, or better yet you can use FreeConferenceCall.com to set up a free conference call number. For hosting services, we will stick with either Internet Archive and Blogger or Gcast.

Total cost: $40 (plus $0.02 per minute for Gizmo Call-Out calls)

Intermediate Setup

The main difference between this setup and a setup for just a single person is the addition of software to record VoIP calls—Audio Hijack Pro ($32) for the Mac; Hot Recorder ($15) for the PC. Both programs allow you to record VoIP calls from Skype, Gizmo Project, Google Talk, and iChat. We also recommend a program called Sound Soap 2 from Bias ($100) for cleaning up the audio of your recordings. This will be especially helpful if you record Skype Out or Gizmo Call-Out calls. Other than that, all the other recommendations from a one-person intermediate setup would apply.

TIP Anytime you are recording and you think you may need to clean up the background noise, it is best to record about 5 seconds of "silence" at the beginning and end of the recording. This allows your audio-cleanup software to identify the background noise and remove it from the track in post-production.

Total cost: Between $430 and $557

Semi-pro Setup

As with the semi-pro setups we previously covered, we continue to recommend Sound Track Pro or Adobe Audition. We also recommend Sound Soap 2 ($100) to help clean up background noise and any Skype Out or Gizmo Call-Out calls. Back in Chapter 7, "The Art of the Interview," we talked about the different ways to record a VoIP call. For the semi-pro setup, we recommend the method where the audio is taken out of the computer and recorded on a digital recorder. To do this, you need a mixer ($100 to $150), a preamp ($130), a condenser mic, and a digital recorder. For the digital recorder, you can use the iRiver IFP-899 ($130). If you want something with 24-bit recording capability, you can go with the Edirol R1 with a 2GB CF card ($500). It's unlikely, though, you'll notice much difference between the iRiver at its best setting and the Edirol R1. You also need a mic stand, pop filter, cables, and a headset ($90 total). Libsyn remains the ideal choice for hosting this setup.

Total cost: Between $1,020 and $1,560

In Studio with VoIP and Remote Recording

This is where you are recording yourself and a guest whom you will be talking to via Skype, Gizmo Project, or some other VoIP software. It also includes guests you will be doing telephone interviews with. You may also be doing man-on-the-street-type recordings or other type recordings outside of your studio. Background noise outside of the studio will be a question mark.

Basic Setup

The key difference between this setup and that of the VoIP basic setup is the addition of the iRiver IFP-890 digital recorder ($70). This is what you will use to record interviews with the proverbial "man on the street." The IFP-890 has a built-in mic so you will not need an additional mic at this level. With this model, you will get about 3 1/2 hours of record time at the highest mono level setting.

Total cost: $110

Intermediate Setup

The key difference between this setup and that of the VoIP intermediate setup is the addition of the iRiver IFP-899 digital recorder ($130), the RadioShack unidirectional mic ($40), and the XLR-to-1/8" cable for the mic ($10). With the IFP-899 vs. the IFP-890, you will get about 14 hours total recording time at the max setting for mono. Additionally, with the RadioShack mic you will cut down on a lot of the background noise compared to the internal mic of the IFP-899.

Total cost: Between $610 and $737

Semi-pro Setup

The key difference between this setup and that of the VoIP semi-pro setup is the addition of the PMD-660 digital recorder ($560), two Shure SM-58 mics ($100 each), and cables ($30). We recommend you get the PMD-660 from www.oade.com with the basic MOD. The reason for this is the standard PMD-660 has a widely reported issue with its preamp, and Oade makes changes to the unit that greatly lower the noise floor of the preamps. The Shure SM-58 mics will give you good audio quality and greatly cut down on the amount of background noise. The SM-58 was designed for intoxicated musicians and can take a tremendous amount of abuse.

Total cost: Between $1,760 and $1,930

Equipment Summary

The following is a complete list of equipment, software, and services mentioned in this chapter:

Mics:

$25	Logitech USB desktop mic
$40	RadioShack unidirectional mic
$100	Shure SM-58

Condenser Mics:

$50	MXL-990
$80	Samson CO1U USB
$100	Audio Technica AT2020
$120	Apex 415

Mixers:

$50	Behringer UB-802
$100	Yamaha MG102
$150	Alesis Multimix 8 USB

Preamps:

$130	M-Audio MobilePre USB

Digital Recorders:

$70	iRiver IFP-890 (256MB model)
$130	iRiver IFP-899 (1GB model)
$500	Edirol R1 ($420) + 2GB CF Card ($80)
$640	Marantz PMD 660 with basic mod from Oade.com ($560) + 2GB CF card ($80)

Mac Recording and Editing Software:

Free	Audacity
$80	Garageband 3 (Part of iLife 06; $80 or free with a new Mac)
$300	Soundtrack Pro
$100	Sound Soap 2

PC Recording and Editing Software:

Free	Audacity
$50	Castblaster
$50	Propaganda

| $350 | Adobe Audition |
| $100 | Sound Soap 2 |

Accessories:

$30	Griffin iMic
$25	Mic stands
$25	Pop filter
$15	XLR-to-XLR cable
$10	1/4"-to-1/4" cable

Podcast Hosting Services:

Free	Internet Archive. No forced advertisements.
Free	Gcast. No current requirements to add in advertisements.
$120	Libsyn ($5 to $20 a month depending on upload needs). Great stats package.
$200	.Mac ($99 year + $99 for 250GB monthly bandwidth)

NOTE We realize many other solutions are available that will give results equal to those we recommend in this chapter. So before you send us an email telling us we should have recommend XYZ mic instead of the MXL-990, please realize for space issues we needed to narrow down our recommendations to those pieces of equipment most used and recommended by those we talked to and the equipment we use ourselves. We made all recommendations without any *quid pro quo* from any of the companies mentioned. (Although now that the book is completed, we would be more than happy to receive free stuff to review for the next edition….)

Personal Podcasts

For personal podcasts, we assume that the podcast itself is going to be your revenue stream. This means you are not using it to shill a book or sell some other product or service (see the next section for that situation). For this section, we look at the amount of money you need to generate from your podcast to get a good return on investment (ROI) or even to get you to where you can quit your day job. In the next chapter, we will look at many different ways to generate revenue from your podcast and website, but for now we will concentrate on ad-generated revenue from the podcast only.

The first phrase you need to know about is cost per thousand (CPM). You will hear this phrase tossed around a lot when talking to the different advertising networks.

The CPM you can get for your show means how much advertisers are willing to pay per

NOTE So if CPM stands for cost per thousand, why isn't the acronym CPT? This expression is actually based on roman numerology, in which M equals 1,000.

1,000 downloads of your show with their ad inserted into your podcast. The CPM you will be able to get for your show depends greatly on the niche your show addresses. If your show is a tech show or a comedy show, sadly you are going to be in the "dime a dozen" category and will be on the lower end of the scale (before you flame, Rob wrote this and he has a tech podcast) and will be lucky to get even close to a $50 CPM. However, if you have a really niche-type show such as White Roof Radio (a show about MINI Coopers), a company that does conversion kits for MINI Coopers will more than likely be willing to pay a much higher CPM to get an ad to its targeted market. We talked with Jonathan Cobb, CEO of Kiptronic, about what a good CPM is for podcasting.

> **TotPM:** *We noticed on your site you had a recommended CPM of $50, and you even said that could go as high as $200. What has been the feedback at this point and time from advertisers about those ad rates?*
>
> **Jonathan Cobb:** *So far they have been very positive. I don't think we have really had any trouble getting desirable rates. As Mark [McCrery, CEO] from Podtrac noted, it can go way up depending on the niche-ness…. I think it is going to run the gamut, though. I think that $50 is a good kind of middle-of-the-road number; it might be higher, it might be lower. That is where we recommend people start.*

For our calculations, we assume an advertiser is willing to pay a CPM of $50, and because many podcasters will likely find this advertiser through a network, there is a split to be accounted for. Most of the podcasting networks we believe will settle on a 70/30, 75/25, or 80/20 split with the majority going to the podcasters. So after the split, we assume for our calculations you get a net of $35 per 1,000 downloads.

If we go back to our chart of type of need vs. investment (Table 17.1) and try and figure out how many subscribers (not downloads) you would need to just break even in the next 12 months, Table 17.2 is what we find for a show produced weekly.

CAUTION

Some networks will offer much worse splits, with some less than even 50/50. Usually these networks try and explain this by stating they can bring you better deals. Be very careful of these used-car salesmen. If someone makes you sign a nondisclosure agreement (NDA) to see their T's and C's (terms and conditions) and then their T's and C's suck, they had you sign the NDA because they don't want people to know they are out to take advantage of you and other podcasters. Look for networks that openly state what their T's and C's are. As an example, both Podtrac and Kiptronic have been very open about their T's and C's and both offer very good splits, with the podcasters getting at least 70% of the revenue.

Table 17.2 Number of Subscribers to a Weekly Show Needed to Break Even

	Type of Investment		
Need	Basic	Intermediate	Semi-Pro
One person	14	165 to 226	366 to 432
Two people	14	248 to 325	429 to 544
In studio, with VoIP	22	237 to 307	560 to 879
In studio, with VoIP and remote recording	61	336 to 405	990 to 1,083

From this table, you can see that you only need 14 subscribers for each show over a 52-week period to break even for the basic setup for a one- and two-person show. However, the highest-end setup requires an average of 1,083 subscribers per show over a 52-week period to just break even. To put that into perspective, only about 50 podcasts out of 20,000 using Feedburner (that allowed the public to view their stats) had more than 1,083 subscribers at the end of January 2006.

Not everyone does a weekly, show so in Table 17.3 we also charted the break-even numbers by total needed downloads in the thousands.

Table 17.3 Number of Total Downloads Needed to Break Even

	Type of Investment		
Need	Basic	Intermediate	Semi-Pro
One person	710	8,570 to 11,720	19,000 to 22,430
Two people	710	12,860 to 16,860	22,290 to 28,290
In studio, with VoIP	1,140	12,290 to 15,910	29,140 to 45,710
In studio, with VoIP and remote recording	3,140	17,430 to 21,060	51,430 to 56,290

Based on this table, it takes 710 downloads to break even for the one-person basic setup and over 56,000 downloads for the highest-end setup. This means for a show with 500 subscribers released each weekday, it would take over 22 weeks before you reached 56,000 downloads.

Now let's look at that whole "quit your day job" thing and what it would take to do so. If we look at the real median income in the U.S., for 2004 it was $44,389. So lets assume that is the number you need to get to quit your day job. Table 17.4 lists the yearly revenue generated for shows that are released one, two, three, and five times a week and have 1,000, 5,000, and 10,000 subscribers per show.

Table 17.4   How Much Yearly Revenue You Can Generate Based on the Number of Shows per Week vs. Downloads per Show

	Number of Subscribers		
Frequency	**1,000**	**5,000**	**10,000**
Weekly	$1,820	$ 9,100	$18,200
Two times a week	$3,640	$18,200	$36,400
Three times a week	$5,640	$27,300	$54,600
Five times a week	$9,100	$45,500	$91,000

From this chart we can see the following:

- If you release your show five times a week, you would need about 5,000 subscribers to quit your day job. According to Feedburner, there are about 12 shows with that many subscribers, and only one show is released five times a week.

- If you released your show three times a week, you would need about 8,000 subscribers. About eight shows would qualify according to Feedburner and again only one show is released three or more times a week.

- If you released your show twice a week, you would need almost 13,000 subscribers. We are now down to about four shows according to Feedburner, and again only one show is released two or more times a week.

- If you released your show once a week, you would need about 25,000 subscribers. That would leave only two shows according to Feedburner, and unfortunately both those shows have multiple hosts. So, splitting the take, technically the hosts could not quit their day jobs.

What does this all mean? Well, first, don't type up that resignation letter just yet. And second, it is going to take other revenue streams besides ad revenue for you to quit your day job. In Chapter 18, we will get into those other revenue streams.

Granted the number of people who were subscribing to podcasts in January of 2006 is a far smaller number than those who will be subscribing in January of 2007 and so on. As more and more people learn about podcasts and start subscribing, a few shows will break free and reach subscriber numbers where their hosts can make podcasting a full-time gig. But the overall percentage of podcasters who will be able to do this will always be very small. Probably less than 5% of podcasters will make enough money to simply cover their overall costs. And less than 1% will make enough money to even consider quitting their day job.

If you are getting into podcasting just to make money, you are most likely going to fall short on reaching that goal, or at least the odds are stacked against you. Remember, podcasting is really a hobby at its heart, and just like you do not expect to make money flying RC airplanes, you should also not expect to make money podcasting. If it happens, great. Let us be the first to say job well done. But if it does not, we hope you entered into podcasting because it was something you wanted to do and you are having fun doing it.

Corporate and Small Business Podcasts

Earlier we mentioned the cost of the equipment needed to get into podcasting, but there is also the labor cost to account for. When calculating the cost of doing the podcast, you also need to figure out how long it takes and add in the hourly cost of producing the show. A good rule of thumb is that most shows will involve at least two people and take about 5 hours of time from each to do the prep work, show recording, editing, and posting (this would be for a 20-to-25-minute show released once a week). Based on that and the employees' time and benefits, you are looking at about a $500 cost in labor to produce the show each week.

There is also the issue with how your podcast sounds; this will reflect well or poorly on your company. Many companies prefer to contact experienced podcasters who can produce the show for them. You can expect to spend between $300 and $3,500 per week, depending on the workload you unload on this third party. If all you want them to do is edit up the sound, edit the ID3 tags, and upload the file, your costs will be on the lower end. However, if you want them to conduct interviews and edit those interviews, provide voice talent, and do all the other production work, the cost can move up quickly toward that $3,500 mark or even higher.

Just like with the company newsletter, it is often very possible to find someone in the company who will volunteer to do the podcast. Obviously the larger the company, the more likely you are to find a willing participant to take on this job in his or her spare time (that is, off the clock).

There are many different reasons why a business would want to podcast. The following is a list of some of the more common business goals for a podcast:

- Brand building
- Promoting a service

- Promoting a book, movie, CD, or DVD
- Promoting a newspaper or magazine
- Promoting an event, conference, or expo

Let's look at each of these in a little more detail.

Brand Building

Obviously anything you can do to build up the brand image of your company is going to be a good thing. Countless numbers of books have been written about the importance of brand building. Podcasting offers a new way to help build your brand. You can use this new medium to go out and advertise or sponsor podcasts. Or you can create your own podcast that talks about the market you serve and use the podcast as a way to show people your company is a solid player in that market. How many people really think Dr. Phil is the best or even one of the best psychiatrists? But because of his show, it now costs a lot more to lie on his couch than it did when he first started practicing. How many people have heard of Dr. Matthew? Now how many have heard of Dr. Ruth? They both do the same thing; the big difference is that Dr. Ruth had a nationally syndicated radio talk show and has written books. Thanks to podcasting, anyone or any company can have their own worldwide distributed show.

Promoting a Service

Let's say your company offers tax-preparation services. You could use a podcast to talk to different tax accountants from your company about common mistakes people make and other tax issues. If you make the show entertaining and informative, you could use the podcast as an infomercial for your company. (Of course, if you can make a show about tax issues entertaining, you need to pack your bags and head to LA; there are a few shows on the WB that need some help.)

There is nothing that will limit you on the type of service you could promote. You could do a show on electrical wiring, massage therapy, dog grooming…whatever. Do not think just national; think local too. As more and more podcasts come out, there will be more and more regional directories. Check with the folks at your local paper about having them add a section on their website for local podcasts.

When you do the show, offer up coupon codes to those who listen or simply say, "Mention that you listen to our podcast when you call and you will receive X% off." This is one of the best ways to measure if your podcast is generating revenue. Additionally, by doing a podcast on a specific subject, you are presenting yourself as an expert on that subject. Whether you state that or not, that is the impression people will get. This goes back to brand building; in this case, the brand can be you.

Promoting a Book, Movie, DVD, or CD

If you are a book author and you do not have a podcast about that book, shame on you. How well a book sells is highly dependent on how well the author promotes the book, and here is a way for you to get personal with potential readers of your book. If you have previous books, especially out-of-print books, you could possibly podcast a previous book as a way to promote a new book (check with your publisher on audio rights first, though). Tee Morris did this very successfully with *Morevi: The Chronicles of Rafe and Askana*, to help promote the upcoming print release of *Legacy of Morevi*.

With a movie release today, success seems to be all about the initial weekend for the big movies and viral marketing for the smaller releases. Podcasting can help both groups. With a major release, you can generate good buzz for the movie by creating a podcast series where you interview all the major stars in the podcast. Then a month or so before the release you start releasing episodes, helping bring hype to the release date. One of the first movies to attempt using a podcast to help the movie was *House of Wax*. Unfortunately, they chose Paris Hilton to do the podcast, and the podcast was dismal—and that's putting it nicely.

Other movies have decided to start promoting during the actual filming by releasing podcasts from the set. Small-budget films that engage with a potential audience from the point when they start filming can potentially increase ticket sales by over a million dollars.

Let's say you have a small-budget film. You create a podcast series about the making of the film. Each week you release a podcast about what happened on the set that week—what surprised you, what pleased you, and what made you mad. You then take it through post-production work and on to promoting of the movie, all along mixing in interviews with cast members. This takes a small amount of time and very little editing. You then get an intern to post the shows and promote the podcast on the message boards and other podcasts. By the time the movie is released, you have built up a listener base of 1,000 people, half of which have podcasts of their own. Each of those podcasters then promotes the movie to their audience (average size of 250), and a third of them actually go to the movie. Of course, no

> **TIP**
> Just because you record some audio, link it to an RSS feed, release it upon the world, and hype that you have a podcast does not mean it will automatically help you. The podcast still needs to be something of value to the listener for it to be of value to you.

one goes alone to a movie, so on average each person brings two friends. This means your podcast generated about $1.28 million in ticket sales.

The numbers are very theoretical, but at $1.28 million, that would at the end of January, 2006 alone put you in 19th place for the past week's ticket sales.

Promoting the release of a DVD of a movie is really no different from promoting the release of the movie in a theater. However, many DVDs that are released are for training, self-help, and exercise. Podcasting offers you a way to promote those types of DVDs. You can create a podcast series where you play some clips in your show from the DVD, but the key is not to make your podcast all about selling the DVD. You need to format the show such that your audience gets added value from listening to the podcast.

Interestingly enough, the new *Battlestar Galactica* TV series not only released a podcast to coincide with the release of each episode, offering listeners behind-the-scenes commentary from producer Ronald Moore, it also repackaged that commentary as part of the DVD release. This is probably the first time content created for a podcast was then included with a DVD release for a major TV show or movie. If you are a fan of *Battlestar Galactica*, you really need to subscribe to the podcast from Ronald Moore.

If you are part of a band and you have a CD coming out, podcasting is a great tool to promote it. By creating a podcast series around the album, you can let people know what you were thinking when you wrote and performed each song. You can use it as a way to promote when and where you will be performing. We highly recommend you check out the podcast from The Reverse Engineers (www.thereverseengineers.com/) as an example of what bands should be doing to promote a new album. In addition to music, there are also instructional and self-help CDs you can promote. Brain Sync: Theatre of the Mind (www.kellyhowell.com) is an example of a podcast that is used to help promote a series of self-help CDs.

Promoting a Newspaper or Magazine

Many newspapers are now using podcasting as a way to reach out to new customers. The *Roanoke Times*, *San Francisco Gate*, and *The Denver Post* were some of the earliest newspapers to embrace podcasting.

> **TotPM:** *What is it that you are trying to present with the format of your show?*
>
> **Roanoke Times:** *I think the key thing that we want to show people, and this was sort of the guiding principle for the publication before there was even thought of a podcast, was that we want to show*

*people that there is stuff to do in our region of the country that they
may have not known about.*

*TotPM: Do you see podcasting as something that all newspapers will
be moving towards?*

***Roanoke Times:** We see it as a thing that some newspapers will be
moving towards. We think that some newspapers do not have the foresight to see that, we think the editor here has the foresight to see the
future as in what online can do for a newspaper. Declining readership
is happening to all newspapers around the country. People are turning
towards the Internet for all their news.*

Newspapers are in a unique position in their community to become the one-stop source
for news and entertainment. To offer audio content costs a newspaper as little as $300
to get set up, yet it will cost millions upon millions of dollars for the local radio station
to get the equipment needed to print a newspaper. With podcasting, the barrier to entry
into audio and video broadcasting is basically nonexistent.

With magazines, podcasts can be used to complement the material in the latest issues
and also as a reminder for people to go out and buy the latest issue. With both newspapers and magazines, you already have an established advertising base to pull from to
help generate revenue to not only offset the cost of the podcast but to also help bring
in some positive cash flow while at the same time building the brand of your journal.

Promoting an Event, Conference, or Expo

Leading up to a conference, you can have interviews with speakers that will be at the
conference. At the event, you can record and later podcast different sessions and interviews with guests. After the event, you can have roundtable discussions to talk about
the successes and failures of the conference and start planning for the next year. You
can even release different sessions recording throughout the year leading up to the next
event. You can talk with exhibitors prior to the event and have them discuss any special promotions at their booth and why they are attending. This gives you another way
to get sponsorship for the event.

The Balticon Podcast (www.balticonpodcast.org/wordpress/) is a podcast created
specifically to promote a sci-fi convention in Baltimore (see Figure 17.3). Paul Fischer,
the new media ninja warrior for the convention, mentioned they were getting listeners
from all around the world. Essentially, they are helping build the brand of the event
with their podcast, while also letting everyone know what will be happening at the

con. If you have a comic con, sci-fi con, or knitting con, you should be using a podcast as a way to interact with your potential attendees year round.

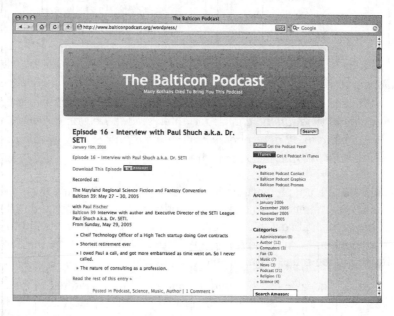

FIGURE 17.3

The website for the Balticon Podcast helps promote the Balticon sci-fi convention in Baltimore.

There are other uses of podcasting in business applications. You can use them to train internal associates or an external sales force. You can use podcasts for a multimedia press release, or as a way to get news out to a specific group of customers.

Podcasting on its own is not going to take a company that is headed for bankruptcy and turn it around so that everyone's 401k gets a big boost. But if used correctly, a podcast can improve and expand the brand of your company, and it can also help generate new customers. The immediate impact to the bottom line will likely be minimal if at all for large corporations, but for a small business looking to sell a book or service, the podcast can give a nice boost to sales. For any business where the promotion of your product or service highly influences your total amount of sales, the podcast is a new promotional tool that can make a significant impact when used correctly.

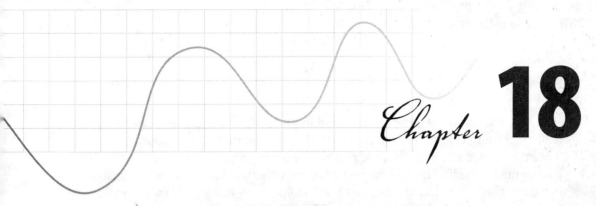

Chapter 18

GENERATING REVENUE

"The smaller advertisers are still trying to understand podcasting. The more sophisticated media buyers are all very intrigued [about podcasting]. One of the big challenges is getting them to work with independent brands, which is essentially what podcasters are. When you deal with the larger advertisers, it is often about reach."

—Gregory Galant, CEO of Radio Tail

When it comes to generating revenue from your podcast, you as the producer of that show have many different methods to choose from. In this chapter, we explain some of the more obvious methods, along with some of the more unique methods podcasters use to generate revenue. Although there is no one method or combination of methods that is universally accepted as "best," everyone pretty much agrees that without an established audience, all methods to generate revenue will fail.

Sponsors and advertisers are attracted to audiences; audiences are not attracted to sponsors and advertisers. So if you do not already have an established audience, and you picked up this book and jumped right to this chapter, STOP! Go back and read the rest of the book. Your first question should not be, How do I make money from podcasting? Your first question should be, How do I make a podcast that is of value to my listeners? There is a reason this chapter is at the back of the book. In fact, if making a horde of cash from podcasting is your ultimate goal, I suggest you immediately refer to the various tables in the "Personal Podcasts" section of Chapter 17, "Business Planning." Call it a reality check.

With that disclaimer out of the way, two of the most obvious methods to generate revenue from your podcast involve sponsorships and advertising. But before you approach a business to sponsor your show or pay for advertising on your show, it is important to put together a media kit that explains what your show is about and who is listening. However, before you can do that, you need to figure out how many people are listening to your show, who they are (demographic data), and where they are located (geographic data).

Tracking Stats and Getting Listener Info

"If the answer [to the question on how do you track stats] is you have to install something else that enables the playback [and stat collection] which only benefits the advertiser and the publisher and not the listeners, I do not think that works."

—Rick Klau, VP of Business Development, Feedburner

When it comes to your stats, the number-one question that needs to be answered is, How many people are listening to your show? Although the question is pretty straight forward, the results are often a bit fuzzy. What you are really looking for is the number of unique downloads of your show. By "unique" we mean the number of *unique listeners* who have *complete downloads* of the show. This is different from a show's "total downloads," which is always higher because some listeners download multiple copies and many don't complete the full download. Additionally, many people just getting into podcasting make the mistake of counting the number of times their XML file is hit each day and think this is the number of subscribers. Nothing could be further from the truth, because your listeners' podcatchers are likely to hit your feed once an hour. Plus, you will also have the different podcasting directories pinging your feed. So you can pretty much ignore the number of hits to your RSS feed as it appears in your raw log stats unless you have a tool to parse those logs.

> **TIP**
>
> One tool that analyzes your raw logs is Podalyzer at http://hexten.net/podalyzer. This is not a tool for the "flashing 12's" or even those of moderate techie skills. This is a tool only for the über geeks. It is a Perl script that analyzes raw server logs and produces reports on MP3 downloads.

Feedburner

Luckily for those of us less geeky there is Feedburner, a service that over 45,000 different podcasters have used. Traditionally, the service was used to track the number of subscribers to a blogs RSS feed. Thus, with the arrival of podcasting, Feedburner became a very widely accepted service when looking at tracking the number of subscribers to a show. Feedburner is useful because it looks at the number of *unique* requests for your RSS feed in a 24-hour period. It is not just counting the raw number of hits to the RSS feed.

Up until early 2006, Feedburner only looked at the number of subscribers to a show, so this meant if you had 20% to 30% of your downloads as direct downloads, they would go unreported. That changed in early 2006. Rick Klau with Feedburner had this to say about its new offerings:

"We now have the ability to track downloads in addition to tracking subscribers. We are trying to more accurately represent how many people did your content actually reach for each episode for each day. We are not getting into the business of hosting MP3 files. That is not the business we are in and not one we want to get in."

When asked if Feedburner would be offering a way for podcasters to generate revenue, Rick had this to say:

"Feedburner, who took the lead in providing monetization opportunities for bloggers and publishers on the text-feed side, has every intention of doing the same for podcasters. As of this writing, it was still very much an open question of which approach would be the right one."

Rick did state that by the time this book was published the specifics on how Feedburner could help podcasters generate revenue would be much better defined. Therefore, be sure to go to www.feedburner.com to see the latest offerings for podcasters and how it compares with those mentioned later in this chapter.

Libsyn

Liberated Syndication (Libsyn) is the biggest player on the hosting side of podcasting, with well over 3,000 podcasters using this service. One of the reasons for the popularity of Libsyn is the stats package it offers (see Figure 18.1). One thing Libsyn does is to break out the downloads by those subscribed to your show and those that do a direct download. Rob spent over 10 months tracking the results from Libsyn and comparing them to those from Feedburner, and he found that the number of downloads from subscribers after 7 days was very close to the peak subscriber number given by Feedburner during that 7-day period. And by close he means less than a 5% difference, and typically less than a 2% difference. Rob has also talked to other podcasters who use both Feedburner and Libsyn and found that many other podcasters had similar results.

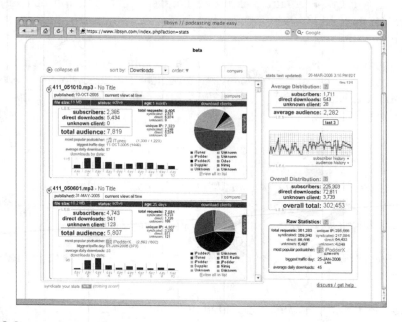

FIGURE 18.1

Libsyn stats showing the number of subscribers via RSS and direct downloads for a single show, the overall downloads for all shows combined, and the average audience size for the last three shows.

Both Libsyn and Feeburner look at unique downloads and have separate algorithms to calculate that number. Because the numbers are very close, it is unlikely that both services are in error the same amount and in the same direction. What this means is that you should feel comfortable reporting stats from either service to a potential advertiser.

Determining Your Demographics

Once you get an idea on the size of your audience, you need to figure out who that

NOTE Some in the podcasting community have reported issues with either Libsyn stats or Feedburner stats. However, based on our own observations and those that other podcasters allowed us to review, we feel confident that the stats from both services are reliable. We do realize that no stats are 100% accurate, and we do not mean to imply these services are. They are just much more accurate than simply looking at the raw log files.

audience is. You can choose from a few different ways and services to try and figure this out.

Audible.com offers the service Wordcast Pro, which provides some very nice information.

"With Wordcast Pro, if you are making the content freely available and you just want to use it for the accurate audience measurement, [then] you as the producer receive first name, last name, and email address [for each listener].... They are not our customers, they are your listeners, and as such there is some metadata that you rightfully should receive as part of that transaction.

"Similarly, if you decide to sell your content, we would give you all those things we just discussed [first name, last name, and email address] plus city, state and ZIP Code so that you could do some more geographic segmentation on your audience.

"Now we will also have the ability to create surveys.... You can make those surveys either optional or required. And then you can use that data to build a demographic description or you can target ads with it."

—John Frederico, Audible.com

In addition to Audible, both Kiptronic and Podtrac have surveys that you can add to your site to have your listeners fill out. You probably have seen one or both of these surveys' buttons on the sites of some of your favorite podcasts. With Kiptronic, you get access to a single-page summary of information after just 10 surveys have been completed. For Podtrac, the data is available after 50 surveys have been completed, but it also includes a full eight-page summary. That said, listeners can also fill out the Kiptronic survey more quickly, making them more likely to do so. Figure 18.2 shows the summary slide from the Podtrac survey for Escape Pod.

Remember, if you are having a hard time getting listeners to vote for you, you will likely have a hard time getting them to fill out a survey. You could always make up your own survey. If you have your show notes on your forum, you could put a new poll question up with the release of each show. Start simple: male or female? Then ask for age range, income range, educational background, and so on.

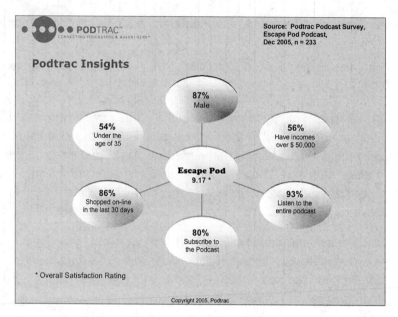

FIGURE 18.2

Summary slide from a Podtrac survey for Escape Pod.

If you do not place your show notes on your forum, you can simply link to the forum and have a different question with the release of each show. Or you could email out surveys to those listeners who have sent you emails, asking them to fill out the survey. You might offer up a prize, such as an iPod Nano or a $25 iTunes gift card, to one random person from all those who fill out the survey. This is a lot more work on your part, but it may result in more feedback if you are not getting results from simply asking people to fill out your survey.

> **TIP**
>
> If you're looking for a good way to find out where your listeners live, you may want to make use of the Frappr map tool (www.frappr.com). Many podcasters use this as a way to build a community around their podcast, but it also provides valuable information about where your listeners are located.

Creating a Media Kit

Once you have gathered together all the information about how many people are listening to your show and who those people are, you are then ready to start putting together a media kit. When a potential advertiser is looking for a show to advertise on, he is usually going to have to justify spending that money to someone above him.

The information you give him in your media kit is often used to make his case about why he decided to advertise on your show.

Some advertising networks offer a generic media kit; however, you should still put together a detailed kit yourself. Something to remember about the advertising networks is that the best publicly known advertising deal in podcasting was not brokered by an ad network, it was brokered between a podcaster and an advertiser with no middleman. Having a good media kit gives you the opportunity to at least see if you can broker your own deal. Even if you already decided to use a network because you do not have the time to look for advertisers, having your own detailed media kit makes your podcast stand out in the eyes of potential advertisers when comparing you to others in your network.

We realize that not everyone has created a media kit before, so we are going to take you through the different items you need to address in a media kit and show you, step by step, how to create one. Here is the basic outline of what should be in your media kit:

- What your podcast is about
- When and how often you release shows
- What podcasting is
- Why they should advertise on a podcast
- Who is listening to your show (demographics)
- Where the listeners are from (city, state, country)
- Who you are
- Where you have been mentioned in the press
- Why people are listening to your show
- Sponsorship and advertising opportunities
- How much it will cost to advertise with you
- Contact information

The following sections break down in detail each section of the media kit. The page numbers are for reference only; based on your specific information you may be a couple pages shorter or longer.

Page 1: The Cover Page

We are back to the issue of first impressions—but this time it is not about listening, it is about viewing. You need to make the cover page look professional and visually appealing. In the top half of the page, place a picture/image of your show logo and name (see

Figure 18.3). The bottom half of the page covers what your podcast is about and when you release shows.

FIGURE 18.3

The cover page for the Skepticality media kit demands your attention.

Here's an example of a cover page that addresses these questions:

Sample Cover Page Text

What is the XYZ Show?

The XYZ Show is part of the new wave of talk shows on the Internet known as *podcasts*. Our shows are listened to all around the world.

The XYZ Show covers the controversial subject of Sleeveless Vests (SVs) and how they are affecting today's youth. We have interviews with world-renowned experts in the field of SVs and talk with celebrities that SVs have touched personally. Some past guests include Michael J. Fox, Bob Denver, and Captain Kangaroo, to name just a few.

The XYZ Show is produced twice a week (Wednesday and Saturday) and is made available for download directly from thexyzshow.com via RSS subscription and from the iTunes podcast directory.

> The podcast is recorded in a talk show format and has three main segments. The first segment lasts about 5 minutes and covers the latest news, notes, and advice on SVs. The second segment is an interview with someone from the SV community and lasts 10 to 15 minutes. The last segment runs 5 to 10 minutes, and it is where we play feedback from listeners, read email sent in, and comment on that feedback.

The formatting and spacing of the text on the cover page should be consistent with the format of the text on your website. This will help reinforce the brand image of your show. We are not saying to use a funky sideways stencil font; the text still needs to be readable. If you do not have a font on your site that easily transitions to print, then choose a standard font such as Times New Roman font size 12, with 1.5 line spacing.

Now after you have introduced the potential advertisers to your podcast, many are going to wonder what a podcast is and why they should care.

Page 2: What Podcasting Is

The second page of your media kit is where you should explain what podcasting is in a manner that someone who is not very technical can understand and why it is they would want to advertise on a podcast. The following is our example. Feel free to use all or part of this explanation in your media kit.

> ### Sample Page 2 Text
> What is podcasting?
>
> Podcasts are basically radio shows on the Internet (like Howard Stern, Rush Limbaugh, and Dr. Ruth), but what makes them special is how the shows are delivered to the user. Podcasts are like magazine subscriptions, in that the listeners have to subscribe to the show. The shows are then automatically delivered to the listener. Because the shows are time-shifted (recorded at one point in time and then downloaded and listened to at a later point in time), the audience has the opportunity to listen at their leisure. They can also listen multiple times to a single episode, offering repeated exposure to your advertisement.
>
> Podcasting has seen phenomenal growth. In early 2005, it was estimated about 200,000 people were subscribed to podcasts. By early 2006, the number of people subscribed to podcasts was estimated to be close to 10 million, and many are estimating that by 2008 there will be over 100 million people subscribed to podcasts. In 2005, because of its meteoric rise in popularity, *podcast* was declared Word of the Year by the New Oxford American Dictionary.
>
> Another key area where podcasts differentiate themselves from traditional radio is that you can get hard metrics on the number of times a show is downloaded (whereas radio estimates listeners based

on people filling out a journal). This helps when trying to accurately calculate your ROI from advertising on a podcast. Podcasting provides you the accuracy in metrics of magazine advertising with the intimacy of a spoken-word advertisement offered from traditional radio.

Finally, you do not need an iPod to listen to a podcast. Podcasts can be listened to on any portable MP3 player, any computer, any cell phone that can play MP3s, and most PDAs. There are well over 750 million devices worldwide that can be used to listen to a podcast.

It is important that you let people know that you do not need an iPod to listen to a podcast and that any computer can be used to listen to a podcast. This lets those who are not very technical understand that the potential audience for your podcast is very large.

Page 3: Who Is Listening to Your Show

Now that you've introduced your podcast and educated your potential advertiser on the nature of podcasting, it's time to go over the demographics of the listeners.

There are four key metrics any advertiser wants to know:

- Gender
- Age
- Household income
- Where your listeners live (break this down by city, state, and country)

If you really want to show that you've done your homework, you could also include the following information:

- What percentage of your listeners subscribe to your podcast versus those who opt to get it via a direct download
- What type of device they listen to your show on
- What type of operating system they use (Windows, Mac OS, and so on)

You may also want to include topic-specific data geared to your type of show. If you have a show on parenting, maybe you want to break down the number of kids your listeners have. Figure 18.4 shows an example of what the demographics page could look like. If you gather enough information on your listeners, this section could be three or four pages long.

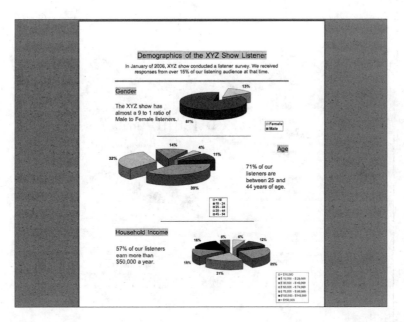

FIGURE 18.4

Age, gender, and household income demographics for listeners of the XYZ Show.

Page 4: Who You Are and Who Likes You

Advertisers do in fact care a great deal about the type of person they associate with their products and services. It's not purely about the size of your audience. So this page of your media kit needs to give them some background information on yourself and, if you have any, your co-hosts. Some fun facts are always good here. You want to try and connect with your potential advertisers. They need to understand what type of person is going to be hawking their wares.

This page is also a good place to list where your podcast has been mentioned in the press or on other podcasts. It's always better to have other respected individuals and publications espouse the virtues of your podcasts so that it's not just you saying, "Hey, I'm great. Take my word for it." If you have some good quotes from the press or other podcasts about your show, you should share them here. (See Figure 18.5.)

FIGURE 18.5

Skepticality in the news. This shows some great examples of using news quotes in your media kit.

Page 5: Why People Are Listening

This might sound like a hard question to answer, but chances are you already have the answers in the form of feedback from your listeners. This is a good place to have quotes from your listeners. Let them state in their own words what they think of your show and why they listen. If you can convey to your potential advertisers that you have a loyal fan base, they will feel much better about advertising with you. If you have the data and it is positive, this is a good place to add in trend lines for your subscriber stats and/or total download stats (see Figure 18.6).

Page 6: Sponsorship and Advertising Opportunities

Potential sections for this page include the following:

- **In-show advertising**—This is where you let potential advertisers know what type of advertising or sponsorship you are willing to accept on your show. Will you accept pre-produced ads, or do you only want to do host-read ads? When will the ads be played in the show? In the "Page 1: The Cover Page" example, we used three distinct sections for the fictitious XYZ Show podcast. You can let potential advertisers know there is an opportunity for an ad between the first and second section and the second and third section. If you have a limit on the length of the ads, let them know that also. Obviously, the more rules you have, the more advertisers you will alienate. But at the end of the day, it is still all about building an audience. Placement of commercials and the types of commercials you choose can both greatly affect your ability to not just grow your audience but also to maintain your current audience.

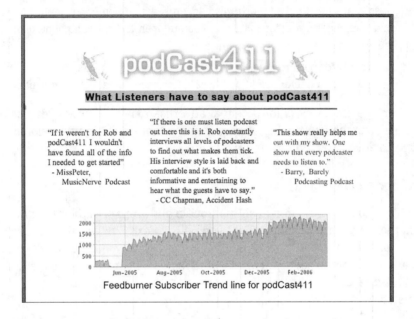

FIGURE 18.6

Quotes from listeners and subscriber stats for podCast411.

- **Website advertising**—If you are willing to have website advertising to go along with in-show advertisements, you should state that here. Let potential advertisers know the size of the banner ads you can accept and where those banners will be displayed. If you have stats on website hits, include that information.

- **Show note advertising**—If you have detailed show notes, let advertisers know about the opportunity to advertise here also. This would include advertising on your RSS feed.

- **Promotional giveaways**—If you are willing to have in-show giveaways of products, mention that also. This would include giving out coupon codes for the listeners.

- **Pricing**—Regardless of how many options you give advertisers with regard to how they could integrate their message into your show, one of their primary concerns will, of course, be the cost to them. If you will consider taking sponsorships, let them know the minimum length of time you are willing to sign a sponsorship deal for and at what price level. If you have price breaks for longer periods of times, list those also. If you are looking for more of an advertising model, let them know what your asking price is for CPM (that is, cost per thousand). If you have no idea how to determine how much you should be charging an advertiser, stay tuned. We tackle that issue in "Determining a Fair Price," later in this chapter.

Also, you should tell all prospective advertisers that you understand that all advertising campaigns are unique and that you are open to discussing additional options for sponsorship and advertising with them.

■ **Contact information**—Finally, end with your full set of contact information, including email, phone number, fax (if you have a fax machine), and a snail mail address.

Remember, the media kit is for potential advertisers, not for your audience. Don't use slang from your show in the kit without defining that slang. Be professional and do not assume the advertisers understand podcasting.

Where to Send the Media Kit

Now that you have gone through all the trouble and work of putting together the media kit, you probably want to know what to do with it next. First, you can link to it from the website for your podcast, or at a minimum you can let potential advertisers know it exists and ask them to send you an email to request a copy of the media kit. The latter is suggested if you are giving out information in the media kit such as your real name or home address.

We have heard many podcasters say, "Because my show is X-rated, no one will want to advertise on it." This is absolutely *not* true. Go and pick up a copy of the latest *Playboy* or *Penthouse* magazine. Both are filled with advertisers that would be a good fit for an X-rated or even R-rated podcast. If you have a podcast about paintball, then get a couple magazines on paintball and see what companies are advertising. Google those companies, find a contact, and then email or snail mail your media kit. Also, go to blogs and websites that talk about a subject related to your podcast. Look and see who is advertising in the banner ads for those sites.

Finally, if other podcasts out there are similar to yours, listen to find out who is advertising on them. These advertisers will likely be interested in advertising on your show. In some cases, advertisers will approach you, but for the most part you will need to be the one knocking on doors and selling your show. Your media kit is one of the most important tools you will have when you are trying to get advertisers to hand over their cash.

Advertising and Sponsorship

There is a difference between sponsorship and advertising. With a sponsorship, the sponsor is usually mentioned around the beginning or end of the show (maybe both, depending on how much the company is offering), and it is usually a very brief mention by the host. Many times, this might just be a trade of its product for a sponsorship of a show. Other times, the company may pay the podcaster a set amount regardless of downloads.

With advertising, a commercial of 10 to 30 seconds in length is placed in the show or read by the host. A commercial provides a hard sell of a specific product or service. Many of the advertising networks are going to offer just commercials for your podcast rather than sponsor it.

Here are examples of the type of content commonly found in a sponsorship plug and in a paid advertisement:

- **Sponsorship**—"Today's show was made possible by Acme Crowbars. Check them out at acmecrowbars.com."

- **Advertising**—"Your parents making love, Dick Cheney naked, and Chevy Chase hosting a talk show. Folks, the next time you have a mental image you need pried out of your head, think about Acme crowbars. Did you know that Acme crowbars come in five different sizes and six different colors? They are crafted from the highest quality steel and made in the U.S. Go to acmecrowbars.com and order your crowbar today. And don't forget to enter the code 'xyz podcast' to get 10% off your purchase."

As you can probably tell, sponsorships are what you would hear on NPR at the beginning or end of a show. Advertisements are what you see during every commercial break of your favorite primetime network TV shows. Besides content, the other difference is with how the price of the deal is calculated. With a sponsorship, your show and website are often sponsored for a period of time. An example would be your show being sponsored by Acme Crowbars for 1 month, during which time you will have an Acme Crowbars banner ad on your site. Regardless of traffic to your site or the number of downloads to your show, you are paid a flat fee for the month.

With advertising, it is usually a per-download deal with no additional expectations for advertising on your website or in your show notes. So if you have a CPM rate of $40 agreed to, and your show is downloaded 2,000 times, you would be paid $80.

How Advertising Networks Work

Advertising networks are created to aggregate talent and bring a more attractive group of vehicles upon which potential advertisers can use to get their message out to their target customers. The advertising network works as the go-between for many podcasters and the advertiser, thus making the life of potential advertisers easier because they only have to deal with one entity rather than 100. The advertising networks are able to create a relationship with large advertisers (such as Podshow with Earthlink) that would not be possible for the small independent podcasters.

Two different types of advertising networks appear in podcasting: the open network, where anyone is free to join, and the private network, which usually only adds members by invite or by a vote of the current members. We are going to look at some examples of both groups in this section. This is by no means a complete list, but we think the information given here should provide you with the basis of what is a good deal for you, the podcaster.

In the following lists, we look at each network, the splits, and the commitment lock-in by those networks, plus other information we think is important when making a decision on whom to go with when picking an advertising network.

Open Networks

One of the key advantages podcasters have in joining an open network is that the network has to compete to get you, the talent, signed up (see Figure 18.7). This means it has to offer you a better split if it wants to sign anyone with any type of following. It also means the network has to offer other services to keep you long term. Additionally, the network likely has shorter lock-in periods so as to encourage more podcasters to sign up. These open networks require lots of talent to get their business model to work.

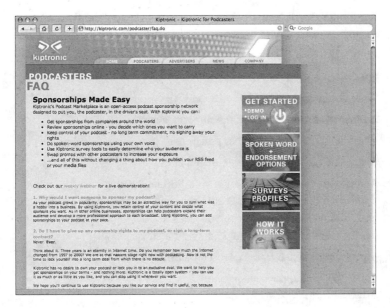

FIGURE 18.7

Kiptronic Podcasters FAQ page.

The following list, which is sorted alphabetically, consists of nine open podcast networks and their stated terms of service or information obtained from current members as of March 2006. Be sure to check over any contract they offer you to see what their current terms of service are before signing.

- **ClickCaster (www.clickcaster.com)**

  Split: Varies between 25% and 75% to the podcaster.

  Time commitment: To be determined.

  Ad insertion: To be determined.

  When ad plays: To be determined.

  Stats: The network supplies stats. You host MP3s on its service.

  Additional: The site has tools to record and edit your podcast from the browser.

- **Fresh Media Works (www.freshmediaworks.com)**

  Split: Varies between 33% and 70% to the podcaster.

  Time commitment: None.

  Ad insertion: Several methods to choose from.

  When ad plays: Decided between the podcaster and the advertiser.

  Stats: None. Up to the podcaster to track.

Additional: Fresh Media Works claims its biggest differentiator is that it allows podcasters an easy way to become owners in the network.

FruitCast (www.fruitcast.com)

Split: 50% to podcaster.

Time commitment: None.

Ad insertion: Automatic by the network's server.

When ad plays: Beginning or end.

Stats: The network provides detailed stats.

Additional: You have to change your RSS feed URL to use the network's service. It claims that if you are using Feedburner and giving out the Feedburner URL for your feed, then you are okay. But if your feed is from another service or you are not giving out the Feedburner feed URL, this will be an issue.

Kiptronic/Libsyn (www.kiptronic.com)

Split: 70% to the podcaster.

Time commitment: None.

Ad insertion: Automatic by the network's server.

When ad plays: Beginning, middle, or end.

Stats: Provided by Libsyn.

Additional: Ability to have ads inserted based on location of where the download is requested from and also based on date. If you are one of the more than 3,000 customers of Libsyn, this is a good service to use because it will not require you to change the way you do anything.

Podbridge (www.podbridge.com)

Split: Varies. In general Podbridge expects the split to be similar to Google AdSense (it has been widely reported that the split is about 78.5% for the publisher).

Time commitment: None.

Ad insertion: Automatic by Podbridge.

When ad plays: The podcaster determines the location and number of advertisements by placing a special tone in the show.

Stats: The network supplies stats.

Additional: Requires listeners to register and download a plug-in for iTunes to track what shows were played and how much of the shows were played. Podbridge is also able to target advertisements to specific demographics. This service is available for both audio and video podcasts.

- **PodcasterAds (www.podcasterads.com)**

  Split: 75% to the podcaster.

  Time commitment: None.

  Ad insertion: Podcaster reads and records the ad within the show.

  When ad plays: Determined by the podcaster.

  Stats: No indication of stats that would be available.

- **Podshow (www.podshow.com)**

  Split: 40% to the podcaster.

  Time commitment: 1 to 3 years (1 year to start, with an option on the network's end to lock you into an additional 2 years).

  Ad insertion: Preproduced ads manually inserted by the podcaster.

  When ad plays: As agreed between the podcaster and advertiser.

  Stats: The network track stats.

  Additional: The network offers podcasters another way to make money by getting the podcasters to sign up their listeners as "registered listeners" on the Podshow network.

- **Podtrac (www.podtrac.com)**

  Split: 75% to the podcaster.

  Time commitment: 3 months.

  Ad insertion: Manually by podcaster.

  When ad plays: As agreed between the podcaster and advertiser.

  Stats: Provided by Podtrac using a redirect you put in your feed.

  Additional: The network provides a detailed survey to help gather data on your listeners. It also has a nice flash player you can put on your site.

- **RadioTail (www.radiotail.com)**

  Split: 75% to the podcaster.

  Time commitment: None.

  Ad insertion: Automatic by the network's server.

> **CAUTION**
>
> When looking at an advertising network, do not use any service that requires you to change the URL to the RSS feed you give to the public. Enough networks are available that do not require this change, so use one of them instead.
>
> Trying to make a change to your feed is a huge issue, and you will lose listeners. Plus, getting that change in the major directories is often very difficult, if not impossible. Keep in mind that if you do make the change, down the line if a better opportunity comes up or if that service shuts down, you will have to make changes all over again.

When ad plays: Any time specified by the podcaster.

Stats: The network tracks the stats on its server.

Additional: Based on its dealings with advertisers, RadioTail is seeing CPMs from $15 to $25 typical, with some going up to $100.

Invitation-Only Networks

With many of the open networks, when advertisers come to the network to look for a show, they have a large list to choose from. This means you may become a number rather than a name. One of the areas of podcasting advertising that is very likely to boom is small, personal invite-only networks. Many of these networks will be started by companies that already have established relationships with advertisers, but now want to offer podcast advertising as another medium to their customers. Backbeat Media is one such company that had a long-time relationship with advertisers looking to advertise on Mac-centric websites (see Figure 18.8).

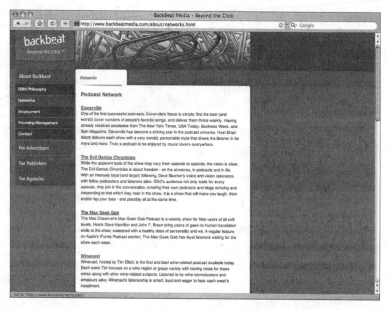

FIGURE 18.8

Backbeat Media podcasters network.

These smaller invite-only networks usually go after like-minded podcasts, thus making the pitch to advertisers simpler and offering the advertisers they know best the target audience they most desire. Because the networks are more focused and have fewer podcasts than a larger network, they should be able to negotiate a higher CPM for the podcasts.

The downside to the smaller networks is that they are not likely to have the same ability to bring more listeners to the shows that larger networks would (that is, if those larger networks choose to promote podcasting outside of their existing communities). Another downside is that smaller networks often have fewer advertisers looking to spend money when compared to the larger networks.

Here are two examples of notable invitation-only networks:

- **Backbeat Media (www.backbeatmedia.com)**

  Split: Typically 50% to the podcaster.

  Time commitment: Typically 1 year.

  Ad insertion: Manually by the podcaster.

  When ad plays: Agreed between the pocaster and advertiser.

  Stats: For MP3s the network hosts.

  Additional: By invite only (more of a boutique network). Podcasts in the Backbeat Media network in early 2006 include Coverville, The Evil Genius Chronicles, and Winecast.

- **TryPod Network (www.trypodnetwork.com)**

  Split: Podcasters "get the majority of the net revenue on a scale relevant to their downloads."

  Time commitment: 6 months.

  Ad insertion: Read and recorded by the host.

  When ad plays: One spot at the front, one at the end.

  Stats: The network provides stats to the podcaster.

  Additional: By invite only for "work-safe" shows. The network hosts your MP3s. Podcasts in the TryPod network in early 2006 include Jawbone Radio, Hometown Tales, and The Big Show.

Choosing a Network

Regardless of what type of network you think is best for you, we highly recommend talking to at least three different advertising networks before signing any contract. We also recommend getting a lawyer to review any contract, especially those that have any sort of time commitment with them. Additionally, talk to current members of those networks to see what they think.

One additional question you should ask the networks you are looking at is, *What are you going to do to help promote my show outside of the podcasting community?* If the answer is, "Well, we put you in our directory," then you need to realize that the responsibility for promoting your show will continue to rest entirely on your shoulders. An advertiser network listing you in a directory on its site is *not* show promotion. The networks that wind up making the most money for podcasters (and for the network) are the ones that bring in the most new listeners from outside the podcasting community to their podcasts. Networks that shuffle current listeners of podcasts from one show to another inside their network are of limited value. The key point to remember is that the networks you talk with should be able to clearly explain their strategy for bringing in new listeners from the outside world.

Automatic Ad Insertion Versus Podcaster-Inserted Ads

There are three basic ways for getting an advertisement on your show, and each method has it advantages and disadvantages:

- You as the podcaster can read the ad during your show.

  Advantages: This is the least intrusive method for your listeners. You read the ad (someone the listeners trust or at least know). It is also harder for the listener to tell when the ad starts and ends because it is in your voice, so the listener is less likely to try and scan forward to find the end of the advertisement.

  Disadvantages: That ad will be in the show forever. So if you and the advertiser have a falling out, you will either be forced to edit your old shows or will have to put up with old shows still promoting that advertiser. This can get really dicey if your new advertiser is a competitor to the old advertiser.

- You can edit/copy in a prerecorded advertisement supplied to you from the advertiser.

  Advantage: The ad usually is professionally produced and delivers exactly the message and tone that the advertiser is looking for.

  Disadvantages: The advertisement will likely be out of place with the rest of the show, both in sound and tone, and does not offer a good listener experience. Plus, that ad will be in the show forever. So if you and the advertiser have a falling out, you will either be forced to edit your old shows or will have to put up with old shows still promoting that advertiser.

- You can use a service that automatically (dynamically) adds in an advertisement when your show is downloaded.

  Advantages: You can have time- and location-specific advertisements added into your show at the point of download. This allows advertisements to be added to all your shows on your feed when they are downloaded. Thus, if a new subscriber really likes your show and decides to go back and listen to the last 20 shows, you get credit for 20 additional downloads. This is really nice for people with a large show catalog and whose shows are not time sensitive.

Disadvantages: The advertisement will likely be louder or softer than the rest of the audio in your show. So the listener may have to adjust the volume during the transition to and from the ad. While the listener is adjusting the volume, this may give him or her an excuse to switch off to another podcast. Technically, this method means you will need to host your podcasts on a specific site or will need to have your feed taken over. Be very careful when looking at this type of service to ask what you need to do technically to make it work. If the network insists on you hosting your podcast on its site, find out if there are additional costs and what happens to your shows if you leave that network.

When looking at an ad network, think about what method of ad insertion will be acceptable, not only for yourself but also for your listeners. Be upfront with your listeners; let them know you are looking at bringing in advertisers and ask them their thoughts on this subject. Six months is a really long time to lock into a method that alienates your listeners, especially considering how much time and effort it takes to build up that listener base.

Determining a Fair Price

What is a good CPM? This is the toughest question in podcasting, because several variables must be considered. If you have a very generic show (tech, comedy, music), you are going to be at the bottom of the CPM barrel. However, if you have a podcast that addresses a very specific niche (WhiteRoof Radio—MINI Cooper owners, SwineCast – Professional Swine Producers), you should expect the CPM to increase greatly. Imagine what someone would pay for a podcast whose audience is CEOs of Fortune 500 companies. You could easily have a bidding war between PING Golf Clubs, ExecuJet, and a major law firm that specializes in tax evasion.

"Sadly, I think we are going to see the CPM settle in lower than those of us in the business of doing this would like. It is similar to what we saw in the Mac [website] market years and years ago... where podcasting is its own little niche, which is great. It is a great community and I think it is fantastic to see it growing like this. However, it is full of a lot of hobbyists similar to the way the Mac web market was and still is to some degree. Six, seven, eight, nine, ten years ago we saw a lot of people out there, kids running their websites from home, and

*they were happy to be out there on the Web charging a dollar CPM.
And some of those kids actually had a good command of a decent-size
readership. So that drove the price of ads down in the Mac web market years and years ago, and it was a tough fight to get it back up.
My concern is that we are going to see the same thing happen in the
podcast market."*

—Dave Hamilton, President and COO of Backbeat Media

On Feb 9th of 2006, Rocketboom concluded an eBay auction in which bidders competed
for just 1 week of advertising on Rocketboom's Video Podcast (see Figure 18.9). The winning bid was $40,000. Based on the numbers Rocketboom was giving for estimated
downloads for that week, the CPM worked out to $40. However, it should be pointed out
that the $40,000 did include production time from Rocketboom to produce the commer-
cials. That said, Rocketboom still feels the $40 CPM is what it expects the show to pull
in on an on-going basis.

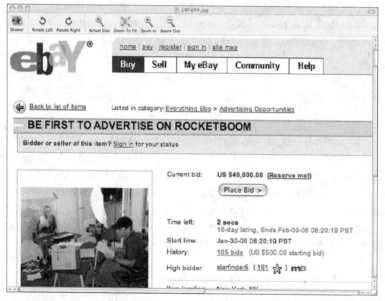

FIGURE 18.9

Rocketboom auction on eBay.

Jonathan Cobb at Kiptronic suggests you start by asking for $50 CPM when you are
negotiating with potential advertisers. Again, depending on the type of show and your
target audience, you may need to adjust that number up or down.

If you have a regional show, you should look at your local market to see what radio advertising is going for. If your potential advertiser is the local used-car lot, then take some time and go and meet with them. Bring in your media kit and your MP3 player to let them hear your show. If you have a regional show, it does put you at an advantage over global shows in that you can meet face to face with potential advertisers. However, what might be a good CPM in LA or New York City will probably be much tougher to command in Boise or Dayton.

The last factor in calculating a fair rate is, What is it worth to you? At what price are you willing to sell your listeners to a stranger? Make no mistake, that is what advertising is all about—aggregating your listeners so you can sell a piece of their life to a stranger holding a bag of money. So the question you need to ask is, how big a bag does it need to be?

We are not trying to talk you out of putting in advertisements; we just want to make sure you ask yourself why it is you are going to put in advertisements. Is it because you have to so you can afford to continue podcasting? Are you doing so because you would just like the extra money? Or are you doing it because everyone else is doing it? Once you know why you are putting in advertising, the question of "How much?" becomes a little easier to answer.

NOTE At this point in time there is no real data on what a good or bad CPM is or will be. We talked to all the major advertising networks trying to get that information. They all said the same thing: It depends quite a bit on the focus of the show and the demographics of the listener base. Even within genres there will be large differences in CPM. Take the food genre, a podcast about the best barbeque will have a much lower CPM than a podcast about fine wines. Finally, don't be afraid to ask other podcasters in your same subniche what they are getting for a CPM.

Using eBay

The best publicly known advertising deal in podcasting by early 2006 was not brokered by one of the advertising networks. It was brokered on eBay. The auction of 1 week of advertising on Rocketboom sold for $40,000. This means after eBay's roughly 1.6% cut (http://pages.ebay.com/help/sell/fees.html), Rocketboom took home 98.4% of the $40,000. This is a much better split than any ad network is offering. Granted, Rocketboom was in a unique situation where it had over 150,000 subscribers. But it does reinforce the statement earlier that sponsors and advertisers are attracted to audiences.

Rocketboom was not the first podcast to use eBay to auction off advertising, but it was the first to get a multiple-thousand–dollar sale. In early 2005, a couple of podcasts tried auctioning off advertising. One of the first podcasts to sell advertising on eBay was

Hometown Tales (www.hometowntales.com). Its first sale was for $80 for 1 month's worth of advertising. At the time, Hometown Tales had four shows a month with about 1,000 downloads per show. So the CPM was about $20.

However, for the most part eBay auctions of sponsorships and advertising spots have resulted in less than stellar CPMs, with some being downright ugly. Chances are, unless you have well over 10,000 subscribers to your show, you are going to find it difficult to get anyone excited about bidding for a chance to advertise on it.

The success of the Rocketboom auction is clearly helping drive more podcasters to eBay to try and sell advertising space. However, it is not clear yet whether it has helped drive potential advertisers to eBay to place bids on those auctions.

Joining Affiliate Programs

Up until now, we have been focusing on sponsorships and advertising as ways to generate revenue for your podcast. The rest of this chapter is focused on the other ways podcasters are generating revenue to support their addiction (no Dan, we are not talking about you).

One method used by many podcasters is affiliate links, where you, the podcaster, put up a special link on your site for a product you may have talked about on your show. This link is to a site where the listener can then purchase the product you mentioned, and you receive a cut of the action. The most popular of these is the Amazon Associates program (www.amazon.com; click Join Associates at the bottom of the screen).

With Amazon, you can receive "up to 10%" in referral fees on all "qualifying" purchases. The reality is you will likely receive about 7.5% to 8.5% on purchases, which is still a nice amount for just adding a link.

Joining the Amazon Associates program is free and requires that you simply fill out an online application. Then you are notified in 1 to 3 days on whether you were accepted. Pretty much as long as you have a website and you fill out the form correctly you should be accepted.

You then find the items in Amazon that you mentioned on your show and you want to have links to on your site. You copy over the HTML code for these items and place it in your site. You will need a site that you can edit at the HTML level and/or add in HTML code.

Here are two examples of podcasts that use this service:

- Burning 20 (www.burning20.com), a fitness and weight-loss podcast. The host, Adam Tinkoff, lists on his site the Tanita scale he uses to weigh himself on his show. This has led to quite a few purchases from his listeners.

■ The M Show (www.themshow.com) is a podcast in which host John Wall reviews different books and DVDs (see Figure 18.10). This is the perfect use of associate links. If you have a podcast where you are reviewing a product, by offering up the link you are actually providing an added value to your listeners. It keeps them from having to find the product you reviewed. You offer them a simple click and purchase of something you convinced them to buy during your review.

There are other affiliate programs beyond Amazon. If you have a poker podcast or talk about poker on your show, why not set up an affiliate link with one of the poker networks. One example is PokerAffiliate.com (www.pokeraffiliate.com), which represents a few different poker rooms.

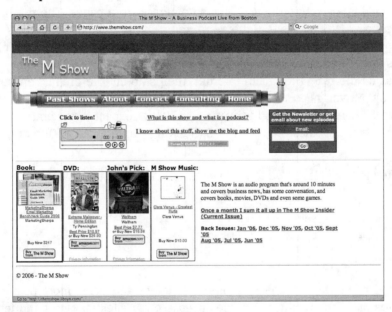

FIGURE 18.10
The M Show with Amazon Associate links.

Selling Swag

Selling swag (promotional merchandise) is a time-honored way for independent bands to make a little money while also spreading the word about their band. This practice was picked up early in the podcasting world with many podcasts signing up for accounts at the different t-shirt and merchandising sites.

If you have the time and energy, you can find a place online to print up your shirts for a low price. Then you can sell them directly from your site. The problem is you have to put up the initial money to fund the purchase of the t-shirts. You also have to handle the transactions, collect the money, and ship out the t-shirts. Most people do not have the time or the desire to handle this end of the business. Luckily, there are online sites that will do everything mentioned here and more.

CafePress and Other Services

One of the main online sites podcasters use to sell their swag is CafePress (www. cafepress.com). Both of us—Mur at www.cafepress.com/geekfu_ag and /isbw and Rob at www.cafepress.com/podcast411—have CafePress store pages. The reasons so many people choose CafePress is that there are no up-front costs, and CafePress has a wide variety of items beyond t-shirts. You simply upload the image(s) you want printed on a t-shirt, sweatshirt, coffee mug, or even a light switch cover (no joke), and the folks at CafePress do the rest. They build to order, then ship out the product and even collect the money. All you need to do is let your listeners know about the page where your items are for sale. We do need to warn you, do not expect to generate lots of income from these types of sales. In all of 2005, Rob only made about $50 from his CafePress store.

Other sites offer similar services to CafePress, including the following:

- www.zazzle.com
- www.spreadshirt.com
- www.99dogs.com
- www.printmojo.com

We should point out that CafePress is by far larger and much more popular than the other sites mentioned, which may mean those other sites may be hungrier and more willing to offer a different customer service experience or at least a slightly better cut.

CDs of Old Shows and Other Items

Another method podcasters use to generate revenue is to sell old episodes. You might ask who would be interested in buying old episodes of a podcast that you initially gave away for free. That was the same question people asked when Apple included a few TV shows on iTunes. But everyone quickly learned that people would purchase these older shows. Not all your listeners have been listening from day one. By offering up the old episodes, you are giving them a way to catch up on your show.

You have a few different options for selling your CDs. Chances are any PC you can use to create a podcast also has a rewritable CD (CD-RW) drive. If so, you can buy some empty jewel cases ($9.99 for 80), blank recordable CD-Rs ($7.99 for 50), and a CD-labeling kit ($9.99 for 40) from the local CompUSA. This will run you about $0.54 per finished CD, plus your time. As with the t-shirts, you will also have to handle the issue of collecting the funds and shipping out the CDs.

If you do not want to deal with this issue, you can create a master CD and send it off to CafePress.

The base cost from CafePress for the data CD is $8.99. So for that extra $8.45, CafePress will handle the production, distribution, and then collection of funds. If your main goal is more about promotion of your show and you want to offer the CD at the lowest cost, you are best off producing it yourself.

CAUTION

If your show is a music podcast, where you are featuring independent music, you will not be able to resell that music. Most of the licenses give you the right to rebroadcast the music, but not to sell it. If you fall in this group, skip to the next section in this chapter. You can only sell what you own the rights to. If you try to sell music owned by someone else, you *will* have legal trouble.

TIP

Make sure you choose the "Data CD" option and add your shows in MP3 format and not Audio format. This will allow you to put on at least 700 minutes of audio versus only 80 minutes for an audio CD. However, a "data CD" will not play in a standard CD player, only in those that can handle MP3 files and the CD players in computers.

Another avenue for selling CDs of your shows that will also give you access to many avenues of distribution is CD Baby (www.CDBaby.com). This is a service that both Dan from the Bitterest Pill (http://cdbaby.com/cd/danklass) and Grant from The Radio Adventures of Dr. Floyd (http://cdbaby.com/cd/drfloyd) have used, along with a number of other podcasters. Using CD Baby, you can also back door into iTunes to sell your CD, but not your individual podcasts. If you want to sell individual shows, you should go to Audible.com (see the "Premium Feeds" section later in this chapter).

We talked with the folks at Apple and they stated that they do have a relationship with CD Baby where they refer independent artists to CD Baby so that the artists can get their music in the iTunes store. That said, they were very emphatic about the point that this does not allow someone to charge for their podcast. It simply lets them sell their album (collection of past shows) in the music store. They also said 100% of podcasts on iTunes are free and there are no pay-for podcasts.

CD Baby also will place your CD collection of older shows on Napster, Rhapsody, MSN Music, and many other online sites, along with the iTunes music store. However, you need to sign up at CD Baby, and there are some small upfront fees to pay. The following are the steps you need to take to sign up:

1. Create a master CD of your shows in the CD-Digital Audio (CD-DA) format (the same format as a music CD that you'd play in your car). The fact that you must record to a conventional audio CD format means your podcast cannot be longer than 80 minutes. We did talk to the folks at CD Baby and asked them if they were willing to accept CDs with MP3s (which would allow for over 700 minutes of audio). Their answer was a resounding *no!* They stated they were in the business of selling audio CDs. So if you have a show that is a half hour or more, you might want to put together a "best of" CD.

2. Make five copies of the CD that you will send to CD Baby. If you don't want to deal with this minimal hassle, you can find different online companies that will produce the CD for you. DiskFaktory (www.diskfaktory.com) is one such company. With DiskFaktory, it will cost you about $3 per CD if you order 100 CDs. Obviously, it is best to produce the first five CDs on your own and then judge by the response if you need to go to an outside service to get this done in bulk.

3. Go to www.cdbaby.com, click Sell Your CD, and fill out the submission form. There is a "one-time-ever" charge of $35 to set up your CD in the store. You also need to register for a UPC barcode if you want to take advantage of having your CD listed in iTunes. This has a fee of $20.

4. Once you get the UPC barcode, include it with the CD and send off five copies to CD Baby. Not only does this make the CD available at CD Baby, it also makes it available at other online retailers, such as Tower Records.

5. You should sign up for the Digital Distribution option. This is free to any CD Baby member, but you need to have the UPC barcode. This is how you will get your album listed in iTunes, Rhapsody, Napster, MSN Music, and many other online music sites. You should note this option is exclusive in that you give CD Baby exclusive rights to distribute your album to the different online music services. This does **not** take away your right to distribute your shows via RSS, however.

The podcasters we talked with who are using this service did not report large sales—usually just a few sales a month, which is barely enough to cover the costs of doing this. They actually talked more about this as a way to increase awareness of their shows than as an actual moneymaker. There are many more people out there who know nothing about podcasting than there are that do. So this makes your show available to those people. Plus, you never know, your show might be that one show that takes off on CD Baby or in the iTunes music store. We would guess short comedy skit–type shows would do best in this medium and offer the best value to the listener.

The reality is that most podcasts that are over 20 minutes long will find it hard to sell a CD of just three or four shows for $10. That is why selling a CD with 700 minutes worth of MP3s on your site or through CafePress makes more sense and offers better value to the listener than going with CD Baby. CD Baby's real advantage is that your CD gets listed in iTunes and on other online music sites. If you are looking for someone other than CafePress, one good alternative is Lulu (www.lulu.com), which offers a storefront-type service for print-on-demand media with a base price of $5.50 (which compares favorably to Cafe Press's $8.99).

Tip Jar

One way to get money for your show is to just ask for it from your listeners. Simply putting a PayPal tip jar on your site and mentioning it in your show can generate revenue. Steve from Escape Pod was generating enough income from donations that not only was he able to purchase stories to be read on his show, he actually was cash-flow positive.

TWiT has taken the donation model one step further and offers up a forum with access only to those who donate to the show. With well over 100,000 listeners (some estimates put the audience at over 200,000), it is easy to see how a donation model could generate a significant amount of income for TWiT. So by offering up a members-only forum, TWiT is enticing its listeners to donate to the show.

Welcome to our new forums!

This is a place for TWiT donors to discuss our shows. You must have made a donation to TWiT to apply for membership.

If you would like to participate you'll need to complete the membership form. Make sure to supply your TWiT membership number (as returned to you from PayPal) or your PayPal email address. If you do not supply that information you will not be approved.

—From the TWiT website

If you are going to have a tip jar or a Donate Now button, your show should be commercial free. If you are going to subject your listeners to commercials, you should not expect them to also donate money to the show. That would be like Donald Trump coming on at the end of *The Apprentice* and asking you, the viewer, to send him more money.

Premium Feeds

Another method used to generate revenue is the creation of a premium feed, where each subscriber has to pay a certain amount to have access to your show. Think of this as pay-per-view for podcasting. The way this works best is for you to have a free feed that you use to create a large audience base and then you either transition over to a premium feed completely or create a second feed that is the premium feed. In February of 2006, Ricky Gervais announced that he would be switching over to a premium feed hosted through Audible.com, which allows the podcaster to create a premium feed using a service called Wordcast Pro (see Figure 18.11). We talked with John Federico from Audible.com about its services.

FIGURE 18.11

Wordcast Pro from Audible.com.

TotPM: *What is required for a listener to subscribe to a premium feed?*

John Federico: *Think about Wordcast as eBay for audio. Anyone can consume and anyone can produce, but like eBay you need an ID to make those transactions happen. If you already have an [Audible.com] ID, it is simple: you just put it in and you are subscribed. It is one click. If you are not [an Audible.com member], you create a username and* *password, put in your billing information, and then at the end of that process you are automatically presented with a feed for the premium show. When someone subscribes to your premium podcast in Wordcast Pro, they receive an RSS feed that is unique for both the show and for them.*

TotPM: *Who are the Audible.com services best suited for?*

John Federico: *We are positioned in the market as being a service for serious podcasters. So that means you are going to attempt to generate revenue directly from your content—either you are going to sell it or you are going to aggregate an audience and sell the media value to an advertiser. Or as a serious podcaster, you might be interested in things like circulation control or the ability to have accurate measurements, even though it might be for marketing purposes. You want to build a direct relationship with your subscribers so you may ask them to just provide a username and password in order to get the content. So it might support some other function within a corporation.*

The pricing for Audible's Wordcast Pro starts with a one-time activation fee of $50. Then there is a $0.02-per-download cost, and you also have a 20% transaction fee for paid content. So if you offered your podcast at $0.10 per show, Audible would get $0.02 for the transaction fee and $0.02 for the download, leaving you with $0.06, or $60 per 1,000. If your podcast has a large and very loyal following, maybe you could get $0.50 per show. In this case, Audible would get $0.12 and you would get $0.38, or $380 per 1,000 downloads net. (This is roughly what Ricky Gervais is charging if you get the whole series. On a per-show basis, he is asking for $1.95.) For podcasters looking to sell their shows on a premium basis (where the subscriber pays to play) Audible offers the best overall solution.

However, for most indie podcasters looking for a service to add advertising (aggregate an audience and sell the media value), Audible may not make much sense. Its download cost is $0.02 per download or a $20 CPM. If you received $40 for the CPM, half would go to Audible. And if you used its ad-insertion system, another $3.33 per thousand would also go to Audible. You would need to get at least a CPM of $90 from an advertiser to make Audible an equal value to many of the advertising networks mentioned previously in this chapter. However, if you have a niche show and you find that you can get a CPM of over $100, then Audible is a great solution. But if you are in the long tail of podcasting, you will find it very difficult to get a CPM above $50.

Another interesting service from Audible is the ability to provide a preapproved list of subscribers. Let's say you have a membership program, where for some amount per year your members get access to your site and private members-only content, and now you want to add access to your members-only

podcast. Rather than Audible forcing your members to go through another transaction to access your podcast, you can send in a list of email addresses to Audible and have those members preapproved to subscribe to that podcast. You can have a private podcast only available to the members you supply to Audible. This could be used by a corporation that wants to make training podcasts available to an external sales/rep force, as an example.

Unique and Interesting Methods

In the podcasting community, the level of creativity that has driven some of the best shows has also been used to come up with unique ways to generate revenue for those shows. One of the most creative ways to generate revenue for a show has to be when Tim Henson (from the Distorted View) sold the naming rights to his different body parts. The sale resulted in well over $500 in revenue. But this was not Tim's first attempt to make money for his show; early in 2005 Tim also auctioned off a stale Kaiser roll on eBay, which his listeners helped bid the price up to $30.

Another unique idea for generating revenue came from a podcast whose format can only be explained as "Huh?": the Counting Numbers Podcast (www.countingthenumbers.com). In this podcast, yup, you guessed it, the host counts numbers. In the first show, he counted from 1 to 500; in the second show, he counted from 501 to 1,000, and so on. He then turned this format into a way to generate money. He created a grid of numbers and sold off numbers on the grid. When someone buys a number, a link is added to that number, and by clicking on it you are directed to a page for that buyer. Also, if you purchase a number and he reads that number, he stops and lets the listeners know who the number is brought to them by. This is a unique spin on the Million Dollar Homepage (www.milliondollarhomepage.com). If you are not familiar with this site, it was started by a student in the U.K. to raise some money to buy a car and pay for college. He created a grid of 1,000×1,000 pixels and sold each pixel at $1 each. He did sell out the grid, and in doing so made one million dollars.

Speaking of the Million Dollar Homepage, Andy from Space Ship Radio created a service for podcasters called Click Grid (www.clickgrid.com) that allows podcasters to add in a smaller version of the million-dollar home page right on their website (see Figure 18.12). You can customize the shape of the grid to match your site and also the amount you charge per box. Prices typically range from $15 to $25, and grids have 300 to 1,000 boxes. If you are able to fill up your grid, you can generate from $5,000 to $25,000 per year on your grid.

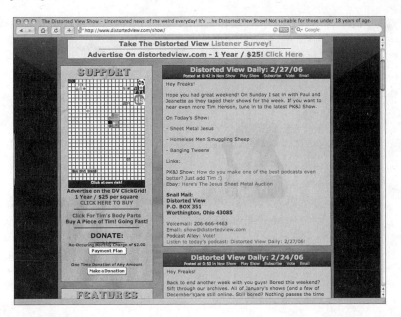

FIGURE 18.12

Click Grid on the Distorted View website.

Those who have made money podcasting have done so through the hard work of building up their audience and then picking a method to monetize their audience that they felt was the least likely to drive their listeners away. As a podcast producer, you have many different options available to you to help generate revenue from your podcast. You should look at your show and your audience and decide which methods will work the best, and make sure any potential advertiser has something that would be of interest to your audience. Then be ready to make a change if you guessed wrong.

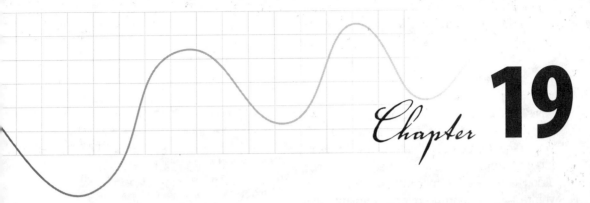

Chapter **19**

PODCASTING AS A MARKETING TOOL

"Partially we're doing it because it's cool. We have the ability to do it, and it's a good community tool. It's also another facet of the marketing strategy—right now everyone who listens is already part of the Lulu community, but we hope that we can soon reach potential interested creators and users of Lulu. And who knows? Maybe we'll be able to get people in the Lulu community to do their own podcast.... One of the things that Lulu is always working on is improving our community, and [podcasting has] been an asset to the growth of our company. It can tie marketing and the community together."

—Jason Adams, Lulu Radio

We've talked mostly about approaching podcasting from an individual's standpoint—how to make your hobby better and even how to generate some revenue. But it is no secret that podcasting can be a valuable tool for businesses. The ability to reach people is vital to any business or service, and podcasting gives you a new way to do that.

When the Internet gained popularity, companies needed to rethink how they reached audiences. They no longer had to think in terms of 30 seconds of audio or video, a magazine spread, or billboards. Suddenly they could leisurely explain who they were and what they could offer the public. Those that did a good job of entertaining people as well were the ones that received the most traffic.

The same can be said for podcasting. When you use a podcast as a marketing tool, at its basis it is simply an ad. As any non-football fan who watches the Super Bowl can tell you, a lot can be done with an ad. Podcasting can announce new products, give news associated with a product or service (if you're with a sporting goods company, you can include sports scores or commentary, for example), and act as a supplement to the information on your website.

> **TIP**
>
> Consider this: Podcasts can get your information to visually impaired customers who might not be able to access your website otherwise. Powerful screen readers are available, but some of the more "clever" website designs can confound them, making surfing the site frustrating for the user. If you get your message out in podcast form along with your site, vision-impaired users will appreciate it.

In some cases, the podcast can actually enhance your product. We'll talk more about this later, so read on!

Business in General

Jason Adams of Lulu Radio says his company's podcast serves as a supplement to its newsletter first, but he hopes its role will grow as it matures.

Lulu.com, a company that gives print-on-demand technology to book authors, musicians, calendar designers, and comic book artists, has so many clients it's hard for Lulu.com to acknowledge them all in its newsletter. As Lulu makes a strong presence at science fiction and comic book conventions (cons) throughout the year, it intends to use these trips to podcast on the road and give attention to its comic book authors and book authors who attend the cons.

The company also uses its podcast to give the customers a look inside at its people. At a recent company retreat, Lulu.com podcasted its yearly poetry slam, allowing the listeners to catch the poems voted best by the employees about their company. This human look at a company can do wonders for public opinion. Instead of presenting your business as a faceless corporation, you can use podcasting to bring out the human side of the company.

Traditional publishers are also getting into the podcasting game. The most popular thing for publishers to podcast is interviews with their authors, although the possibilities are endless. They could send someone along on a book tour to record readings or signings. Podiobooks.com has already shown the popularity of podcasting books—or even book excerpts.

The limits of podcasting really lie only with the limits of a marketing team's imagination.

One thing a podcast can do is establish the podcaster as an expert. Confidently speaking about a subject, whether it is politics or sports, catches people's ears and makes them listen. When your company creates a podcast on a wider topic instead of just making the podcast an ad for the company, it can do much to establish credibility.

In particular, this can do a lot for smaller businesses or freelancers trying to attract new clients because it allows them to show off their expertise. If someone is a freelance editor, for example, she could do a podcast about grammar, humorous typos, or news of the publishing world. A person who does home parties for a living (Tupperware, Pampered Chef, and so on) can host a podcast about cooking, organizing, or any tangential topic that relates to his product.

For an example of a podcast illustrating a company's strengths rather than serving as an advertisement, let's look at MWS Media (http://www.mwsmedia.com/). Run by Matthew Wayne Selznick, this is described as "a family of websites and other media [that] is dedicated to presenting the finest DIY, independent creative endeavors from all over the world, and supporting the DIY ethic through services and advocacy."

His DIY (do-it-yourself) ethic is something he strongly believes in, and something he epitomizes through his podiobook, *Brave Men Run* (www.bravemenrun.com; see Figure 19.1).

FIGURE 19.1

The **Brave Men Run** *site prominently displays links to MWS Studios and other DIY links.*

"BMR is an object lesson in DIY creativity, and I use it to promote that approach.... Since I've been preaching on DIY my entire adult creative life, it would have been hypocrisy—and a huge missed opportunity—to release BMR any other way... going the DIY route means being ready to think about things in a nontraditional manner, and being ready to step up when it comes to all those non-writerly things: promotion, communication, and so on.

"I believe in developing a relationship with the audience. It continues to astound me that people would trade their money to put my book on their bookshelves. So I answer every email, reply to every forum post, and engage in every chat. It's been terribly rewarding, gratifying, and energizing... and speaking pragmatically, I'm building a loyal audience who doesn't see me as some 'artiste' beyond their reach."

—Matthew Wayne Selznick, MWS Media

And here is his advice to people who consider focusing on podcasting for their business:

"I would recommend to creative people interested in podcasting: find a way to make your podcast work for your passion. If you're a writer, a podcast novel is a no-brainer marketing tool. Artists, share the creative process involved in your latest work. Actors, turn a recorder on during a read-through, or a rehearsal, or the whole darn process from writing the play to opening night.

"Podcasting is a tool... one that encourages a direct, one-on-one relationship with your potential audience. Find out how that tool can best be utilized to serve your vision. The audience is out there, waiting for you to press Record."

Movies, TV, and Radio

The first commercial podcasts were hit and miss, as you might expect. Some radio and TV companies thought that repackaging only snippets of their shows would suffice. Some morning radio talk shows had their ads stripped out and released in podcast form. NPR (National Public Radio) offered some of the earliest mainstream media podcasts. These shows became instant hits on iTunes, with a few shows in the top 20.

Still, the podcasts that really made a splash were the ones that *added* to the existing medium, not simply repackaged it. We've mentioned SciFi Channel's *Battlestar Galactica* before, but it bears repeating. When Ron Moore came out with the companion commentary to *BSG*, the fans of the show were entranced. This was a brilliant move on the SciFi Channel's part because not only was it offering something special to the fans, but it also virtually guaranteed that the audience would watch the episode twice, once for the dialogue and once for the commentary (see Figure 19.2). That's two chances the advertisers had to reach the viewers.

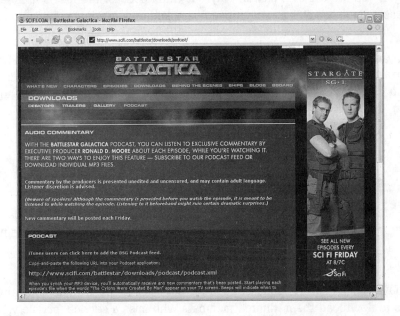

FIGURE 19.2

Battlestar Galactica remains one of the best TV-related podcasts originating from the source.

Re-releasing radio shows is becoming popular, as shown by NPR and some local stations, but because radio is already audio, they can offer bonus material that the listener can only get from the podcast. Both radio and TV shows can release podcasts of full interviews, for example, as they would have had to cut the interviews for time to fit on their time slots. Anything that can't fit into the normal time slot, actually, can be put on a podcast. An editorial from the station manager, late sports scores, and anything else that you want to squeeze in.

For movies or TV shows, fans are always hungry for behind-the-scenes material, bloopers, or even celebrity gossip. Interviews with stars, technical information from the crew, and even a commentary from the director are useful. Extra material is cut all the time from shows, DVDs, and movies because of time or space requirements, but podcasting holds none of these limitations. Anything that can't fit anywhere else can be placed in a podcast.

In the future, networks may well attempt to provide a new pilot through video podcasts to gauge interest. Movie studios could release scenes before a movie comes out. They could even release nonrated versions of shows—the versions the censors saw before editing. If you are a movie studio, why not video podcast the first 5 minutes of every movie as it is released? You can get people hooked on a movie, thus driving them to the theater to see the rest of it.

The key thing to remember is the majority of the shackles placed on TV, radio, and movies are removed when you move to the podcasting medium. No time limits, no censors, no FCC, no space limitations. There are only two questions you need to ask:

- What can I do with audio/video?
- How much information should I release at once?

Churches and Nonprofits

When Mur's Grandma Lafferty was in her final years, her health stopped her from attending church on a regular basis. She watched a service on TV from the nearest big city, 3 hours away, but she always regretted not being able to attend her local church again.

Nowadays, churches are podcasting their services to be available to anyone who wishes to download them. Church members who miss a service, people who want to remember a particularly powerful sermon, or prospective members would all be interested in a backlog of sermons available online.

Most churches notoriously have little money for "extravagancies" like websites or other newer methods of speaking to their members, but the fact that podcasting is cheap means that there is little in a church's way to getting a podcast. With an investment of maybe $200 for equipment, the church can have a professional-sounding podcast.

Because many places of worship have more than simply a weekly service, the opportunities for podcasts abound. Any meetings can be recorded. There could be a podcast to accompany a monthly newsletter or announcement bulletin. If a person goes on a church-related trip or retreat, she can podcast from her trip and share her experience with the members of the church.

Churches often do outreach to the community. A special podcast feed can be dedicated to a sick member, where church members can upload messages to him. Podcasting can hold supplemental information or material for a talk or demonstration the members are going to do.

Lastly, people on humanitarian trips or missions can report back to the people in the church and let them know how things are going.

For the religious community, podcasting serves as a powerful supplementary tool, supporting the messages and work, both inside and outside the church, that the members attempt to create.

Education

Back in our day, if you missed a class, you hoped you could borrow a cute classmate's notes. Sometimes you missed class for the sole reason of borrowing a cute classmate's notes. However, the kids of today must turn to different ways of flirting that aren't so clumsy because many professors are beginning to podcast their lectures.

The Internet has changed college life as we know it. Ten years ago, if you needed to hear a lecture, you'd need to be in class. To catch a schedule change or announcement, you'd have to be in class or catch your professor outside of class. But with podcasting, all that changes.

Podcasting allows professors to get their lectures out to all students, not just those who miss class (see Figure 19.3). Some might think that this causes students to be lazy and miss more classes; however, they can still get the information, not to mention they won't have the excuse of missing a lecture—it was right there in their podcatcher, so they have no excuse.

The saved lectures also allow students to listen again to confusing parts of lectures or parts they may have missed due to tuning out. (Admit it. You've done it.)

The university can podcast more than lectures, however. Places of education can host visiting lecturers and events, and not everyone who wants to attend is able. Perhaps the event is at full capacity; perhaps the person who wants to attend has a scheduling conflict. Podcasting can change all that. Quinnipiac University podcasts its special events, which helps the school get its money's worth by spreading the lecture to as many students/professors as possible.

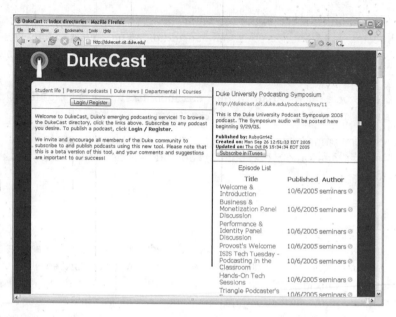

FIGURE 19.3

Duke University's podcasting service, linking everything from personal student podcasts to classroom-related lectures.

Mansfield University also takes a unique angle to podcasting. It interviews freshmen when they arrive at school and throughout the year, showing how they cope with school life. The intended audience is not the university, but high school kids and their parents. The university feels that this gives kids a clearer, more honest view of what college life is like than most universities.

"It's not a sales piece for Mansfield University, but rather something that will help people in the process of finding a college and being better prepared for it. I also do regular interviews with admissions directors on how to find the college right for you and the financial aid director on how to get the most out of financial aid."

—Dennis Miller, Mansfield University Director of Public Relations

Some schools, such as Duke University and Henrico County Public Schools in Virginia, enhance education by actually requiring their students to podcast. The students at Henrico County Public Schools podcast their art history assignments (www.art2know. com) to convey a passion for the subject and make what is otherwise dry and boring to teenagers interesting. They also podcast debates by students regarding art topics and have a question-and-answer session.

Other schools are podcasting their lectures and even reading assignments to allow more time in class for discussion or lab work. Some may say that the professors' amount of work increases a great deal at this stage, but more and more people are considering podcasting such a valuable tool that it is worth the extra time to benefit the classes.

Duke University embraced podcasting early on, and currently the university uses the tool in many of the previously mentioned ways. Duke also uses podcasting in language classes.

"Some classes are podcasting language practice sessions, music listening assignments, artwork samples for art history classes, and a variety of other audio materials for class assignments—for instance, PRI [Public Radio International] has given us access to many of their recorded programs."

—Richard Lucic, Duke University Associate Chair of the Department of Computer Science

Duke is not stopping there, however. In the future the university is working on the development of its own podcasting management tools. It is also making extensive moves to encourage podcasting in its students, according to Lucic:

"Duke is complementing its efforts in podcasting by giving students in selected classes iPods for their use in the course. Passing the course successfully allows you to keep the iPod permanently. Extensive podcasting training sessions for faculty are under development. Over 42 classes this semester are using iPods and/or podcasting. We held a Podcasting Symposium on campus last fall [2005] and are beginning to discuss a follow-up event for the coming fall."

—Richard Lucic, Duke University

Nongovernmental Organizations

Another group that could benefit from podcasting is nongovernmental organizations (NGOs). Most NGOs focus on activities in developing countries, operating at the local level in cities and towns and targeting low-income groups for their development.

Education is one of the biggest goals of NGOs. They typically approach education on two levels: one being the education of their members to better inform and aid them in their work, and the second being the education of prospective members.

An NGO could use podcasts to distribute lectures or workshops. The members could also distribute daily or weekly news items pertaining to the NGO.

A handful of NGOs have embraced podcasting. Disciples with Microphones, the podcast for the Catholic NGO Voice, is a tool to deliver interviews and reports from assemblies and conferences (see Figure 19.4). The Catholic NGO Voice describes the NGO as "an outreach dedicated to supporting authentic Catholic social teaching on human dignity and human rights issues." Considering that podcasting is a form of outreach by definition, this makes for a perfect fit.

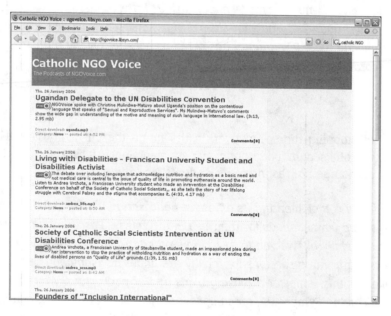

FIGURE 19.4

The Catholic NGO podcast reports on worldwide issues of interest to Catholics.

One frequent problem that charities and NGOs face is a lack of funding. Podcasting is a way that they can supplement their pledge drives, releasing interviews or special content as a treat to entice their listeners to donate to their cause. Pledge drives are done more frequently over radio and television because of their live, immediate feeling, but they would work well over a podcast also. With daily reports to let listeners know that their money is counting, along with the regular daily content, we believe podcasting would be a good pledge tool for charities and NGOs.

With a cheap mobile recording setup (Mur uses her iRiver 790 and a Sony plug-in microphone), NGO members can podcast from the field. If people want to know what the situation is really like where the NGO is doing work, or what services the NGO provides for the communities, there is no better way to show them. Relief workers at the scene of a disaster can do a soundseeing tour (or "soundscape") to describe to listeners what they're seeing, smelling, experiencing, or they can interview the people they are helping. Many times these stories are swept under the rug for a variety of reasons, and podcasting can make these voices heard.

All this, of course, also lets donators know how their money is being spent, and perhaps will entice them to spend more.

Lastly, NGOs are usually looking for more members and volunteers. Many podcasters will often run a bumper or promo for you out of the kindness of their hearts—or very likely for little money. An NGO could use the new medium of podcasting to get the word out via other podcasts to build their member base.

Government Agencies

Government agencies can use podcasting in much the same way that NGOs can. Many governmental organizations and agencies exist to educate the population—podcasting is just another way of getting that done.

Although the time-sensitive information the government puts out over radio and TV may not fit podcasting (Amber alerts or severe weather alerts), there are plenty of other announcement-type uses for podcasting. Many states are already doing a weekly podcast from the governor's office, putting his or her radio address into podcast form (see Figure 19.5). This not only gets the word out to more people (especially given that podcast listeners tend to shy away from radio), but also gives the government administration an air of being technologically savvy in an age when people may believe government agencies are behind the times.

> **NOTE**
> A couple of years ago, Mur sent an email to Jesse Helms (then-senator of North Carolina). His response started with how he was a down-to-earth man and didn't really understand these new technologies such as email. This did not instill a great sense of faith in Mur—she knew more about a simple thing like email than a powerful Washington political figure!

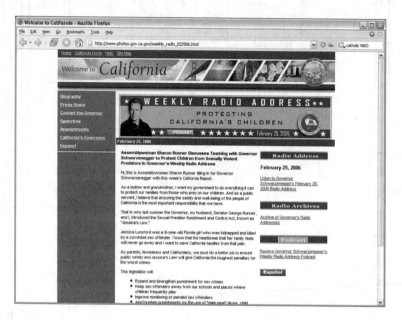

FIGURE 19.5

Podcasting is now mainstream; Governor Schwarzenegger is doing it.

Podcasting can help the government in little ways, such as reminding people to vote or volunteer or a notice that the currency is going to change physical appearance (again), or in large ways, such as giving the politicians direct access to the people's ears and allowing the people to know more about what's going on in the seats of power.

Where to Go from Here

As you have probably learned from spending time on the Internet, there's always something new to learn. Once you've finished this book, play around with your podcasts. Try some new things, explore your interests, take some chances. Keep up with the community because you'll continue to learn as long as you have contact with other podcasters.

We learned quite a bit from each other while doing this book. You don't podcast in a vacuum—if you try to, you'll stagnate. It's a fascinating and fun culture, and we encourage anyone who's interested to give it a try. We want to leave you with the following sage advice:

"It doesn't matter what equipment you have at all. You can throw 10 pounds [$17] at your equipment setup, you can throw 10,000 pounds ($17,000) at your setup. I think it is all about what your content is, really. What we do is all on a bit of paper. As long as you spend time writing stuff down, I think that is the most important thing. The most important piece of equipment in a podcasting setup is a pen and a bit of paper."

—Rob, Top of the Pods (www.topofthepods.com)

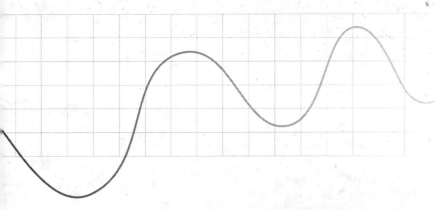

APPENDICES

Appendix A

MICROPHONE AND VOICE TIPS

Regardless of whether you've spent $20 or $1,000 on your podcasting rig, the way you record can make or break you.

Many people are addicted to instant gratification (Mur certainly is). So once they learn about podcasting, get their blog set up, buy their rig, they're rarin' to go. However, it does behoove them to slow down and take a moment to think about their recording practice.

In this appendix, we offer a few simple no-nonsense tips that can help improve the audible quality of your podcast.

Get to Know Your Microphone

Once you set up your mic, test it out with many tries before recording for good. Test different distances from your mouth (if you're wearing a headset, your mic should still be flexible enough to find a good spot), test what happens if you turn your head, and find a place where there will be the least amount of "noise" from your mouth (popping *p*'s, sibilant *s*'s, and so on).

Situate Yourself Comfortably

If you're leaning over your desk to talk into the mic, your back is going to start hurting, and this will reflect in your voice and your mood, which will come through loud and clear on your podcast. Find a place for the mic, even if you have to prop it up on books or take it from its stand and just hold it. You need to be comfortable for your voice to sound the best.

CAUTION

Many a beginning podcaster has been horrified to hear herself spiking her levels as she says *p*'s and *s*'s. The hiss of sibilant *s*'s has actually caused us to stop listening to some podcasts, as it can be literally painful to hear. To avoid this, try these tips:

- Speak over the top of the mic, not directly into it.
- Buy a pop filter (or if you're on a budget, make one from a pair of pantyhose, a cross stitch ring, and a coat hanger).
- Back off from the mic just a bit to where your voice still comes through but the forceful air that causes these vocal gaffes is dispersed.
- And for goodness sake, test out the mic before you start recording!

Some people believe the best way to record is to stand. Standing increases your energy levels, and you may feel more comfortable if you can pace. Mur has had comments from listeners that her tone was completely different on the podcasts where she stood and recorded with her handheld mic and iRiver than those where she sat down with her computer and mixer. Some mics will not allow standing, however, so you may want to keep that in mind before you buy. If you do stand or walk around, think of investing in a wireless headset. Whatever you end up doing, test the sound of the mic while moving, making sure it doesn't pick up any background noise of your movement, whether it be your walking or the mic brushing against something.

Whom Are You Talking To?

Even though you may be thinking, "I'm podcasting!" when you're recording, you will get the best conversational sound from imagining that you're *talking to someone* instead of *doing something*. Picture your audience (see Figure A.1). Who is it you are talking to? Presumably people like yourself who share the same passion you're trying to bring across in your podcast. If it makes you feel more comfortable, imagine a friend or loved one as your audience. How would you speak to them? Even if you have 10,000 listeners, think of yourself podcasting to just one person who shares your passion utterly instead of a massive audience.

So who are you podcasting to? (Photo by Lorri Auer—protected under a Creative Commons Attribution 2.0 License.)

Don't Be Afraid to Start Over

If you're recording and you just realized it sounds like, well, crap, start over. No one says that you have to put up that podcast. Along the same lines, no one says that a flub up in your early podcasts means the practice of podcasting is closed to you forever. Every veteran podcaster had a first podcast, and many of them were pretty bad. (Both of us are guilty.) But they plugged on, either starting over the bad stuff or just plowing ahead and knowing they would get better. Don't get discouraged.

Watch Those Levels

We mentioned earlier in the book that learning audio compression is one of the best things you can do to make yourself sound better. Compression brings your peaks a little lower to even out the sound. Still, while recording, make sure your levels aren't going through the roof. Compression can only do so much.

The one problem with this comes when you are reading your podcast from a script, a website, a news story, a book, or whatever pulls your eyes away from your audio program. In that case, do a good bit of practice to learn where you should be in regard to your microphone (as we mentioned earlier) and get comfortable with your mic and how your voice sounds. Recording with headphones should also help you keep track of your levels. If you hurt your own ears, it's likely your listeners will suffer as well.

If Editing, Mark Your File When You Mess Up

If you stumble or flub (or perhaps swear when you're trying to have a nonexplicit rated podcast), you could write down the time stamp to edit later if you happen to have a pen and paper ready. Or you could just make a sharp noise—rap your knuckles on the desk or clap your hands. This will cause a spike in the levels that will be easily identifiable as a place to edit when it comes time. The only caveat is that you must remove these spikes before you run your compression effect; otherwise, the sharp peaks will throw everything else off. An extended pause can also do the job of marking where you need to edit (which may not work if you have a tendency to pause frequently while recording).

Join Toastmasters

The best way to make yourself speak in a more confident and relaxed manner is to get practice. You can either pay for voice lessons, or join a group such as Toastmasters that aids people in public speaking, preparing speeches, and omitting the "ums" and pauses. Mur runs the podcasting rig for a friend of hers who is a member of Toastmasters (http://www.toastmasters.org/), and she had to do very little editing when the podcast was done. Her friend was only going from bullet points, but she spoke in a confident and relaxed tone and didn't once say "um." Frankly, it was amazing.

You can likely find more tips on the Internet, but those are the ones that have proved most valuable to us. You will find what works best for you, and you will also find that the most important tip is to gain experience. We all go through the early stumbling recordings. (And if you listen to someone's Episode 1 and they sound perfect, we'll bet cash money that person had previous training in either acting, Toastmasters, or radio. So remember, even they had their clumsy period, only not in podcasting.)

CREATIVE COMMONS EXPLAINED

"Here's the deal: I'm releasing this book under a license developed by the Creative Commons Project. This is a project that lets people like me roll our own license agreements for the distribution of our creative work under terms similar to those employed by the Free/Open Source Software movement.
It's a great project, and I'm proud to be a part of it."

Cory Doctorow, author of *Down and Out in the Magic Kingdom*, a novel available online under a Creative Commons Attribution-NonCommercial-NoDerivs License.

Quote from interview conducted at Creative Commons (www.creativecommons.org).

If you've listened to podcasts, it's likely you've heard the following: "This podcast is protected by a Creative Commons Attribution-NonCommercial-NoDerivs 2.5 License." Sometimes the podcaster will explain what this means, and other times he or she just assumes you already know. It's likely that if you've published your feed through Feedburner, you've encountered the question of whether you want to put a Creative Commons License on your podcast.

Creative Commons is an organization that makes licenses that protect your work. When you write a story, draw a picture, or record a podcast, you automatically hold the copyright to the material. This means that no one else has the right to print your story and hand it to a friend, or even burn your podcast to a CD, because that would be a violation of copyright. The other end of the spectrum is public domain, which means someone can take your story off the Web, make your heroic character into a criminal eater of puppies, and sell the story.

To many podcasters, neither of these scenarios are attractive. Most of us want people to entice others to listen to our podcasts, so burning the podcast to a CD and distributing it seems less like stealing and more like helping us with marketing. However, until Creative Commons came along, if we gave people permission to do that, we might be inadvertently allowing them to do anything they like with the work.

Creative Commons is the license that works in the Internet Age. You allow people to take your work and enjoy it, make copies, and distribute it. In effect, you get to choose the rules you put on the license, as follows:

- **Attribution**—When people reuse your work, are they required to say you created it?

- **Noncommercial**—Can people sell your work without your express permission?

- **Derivative Works**—Can people modify the work? Can they write fan fiction based on your story or change your photograph in Photoshop or splice your podcast words together to create different meanings than you'd originally stated?

- **Share Alike**—Once the person changes the work, he or she has to place an identical Creative Commons License on it when distributing the work.

Most podcasts are released under the Creative Commons Attribution-NonCommercial-NoDerivs 2.5 License. This means that you can download the podcast and distribute it, put it on your website, burn it to a CD, or whatever you like. But you must give attribution, telling people who originally created the podcast. You cannot sell it without permission from the podcaster. You cannot modify it in any way. This is the most restrictive Creative Commons License, but there are many others—11 possible licenses in total.

Creative Commons allows people to protect their work and still allow easy Internet distribution. It fits the podcasting world quite well.

One of the worst things about understanding copyright is that it's a legal term, with many-worded legal definitions going along with it that most of the population can't understand. The beauty of Creative Commons is that the site has a straight language (or as they call it, "human readable") definition of the rights and restrictions the various licenses give. There are two web comics designed to illustrate Creative Commons. The creators of the site understand that the "normal" populace needs to understand the legalities of these licenses, and the site does a fabulous job in explaining everything.

NOTE Author Cory Doctorow released an entire novel on the Internet with a Creative Commons License—at the same time the novel landed on the bookshelves through his publisher, Tor. No one had done this before, and Cory and his editor, Patrick Nielsen Hayden, thought it was a fabulous idea.

Since then, several podcasters have released short fiction and whole novels through podcasting using a Creative Commons License.

For more information, visit the Creative Commons home page at http://creativecommons.org (see Figure B.1).

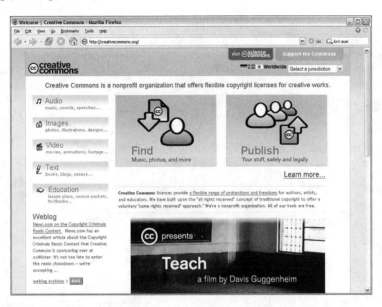

User-friendly site for Creative Commons.

It is important to understand that Creative Commons is not part of copyright law. It is sort of a handshake agreement stating that although your work is not in the public domain, you will allow certain uses of it.

"The Creative Commons Legal Code has been drafted with the intention that it will be enforceable in court. That said, we cannot account for every last nuance in the world's various copyright laws and/or the circumstances within which our licenses are applied and Creative Commons–licensed content is used. Please note, however, that our licenses contain "severability" clauses—meaning that, if a certain provision is found to be unenforceable in a certain place, that provision and only that provision drops out of the license, leaving the rest of the agreement intact."

—From Creativecommons.org

For more information regarding U.S. copyright law, check http://www.copyright.gov/circs/circ1.html#cr.

WEBSITES FOR MORE INFORMATION

Okay, so you've read the book and you're hungry for more. In case we missed something here, or you would like to study a certain topic in greater detail, we've compiled a list of sites for you to visit for more information.

Tutorials

Podcast411 Podcast Tutorials
http://www.podcast411.com/page5.html

Podfeed: Podwire: Podcasting Dos and Don'ts
http://www.podfeed.net/article.asp?id=105

Engadget Podcast 001
http://www.engadget.com/2004/10/05/engadget-podcast-001-10-05-2004-how-to-podcasting-get

Hugo Schotman: Audioblog Software Studio Setup—Technology Part 1
http://log.hugoschotman.com/hugo/2004/09/audio_blog_soft_1.html

Reel Reviews: Podcast About the Podcast
http://reelreviewsradio.com/archives/2004/12/27/podcast-about-the-podcast

Windley's Technometria: Understanding RSS
http://www.windley.com/outlines/rss.shtml

Zefhemel.com: Howto: Create Your Own Podcasting Show on Windows
http://www.zefhemel.com/archives/2004/10/11/how-to-create-your-own-podcasting-show

Webcrumbs: Recording Skype Calls
http://www.raggedcastle.com/webcrumbs/archives/003724.html

Digital Minds: Podcast How-To (Windows XP)
http://www.digitalminds.com.br/podcasts/howto

Podcasting News and Reviews

Podcheck Review

http://www.podcheck.com (see Figure C.1)

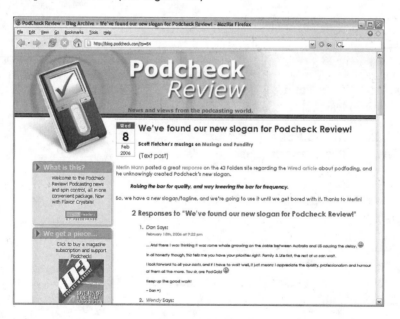

FIGURE C.1

Scott Fletcher's Podcheck is considered one of the best—and wittiest—commentaries on current podcasting events. Now if he would just podcast regularly....

Mobile Podcast
http://www.mobilepodcast.org

Podcast 411

http://www.podcast411.com

Behind the Scenes

http://www.btscast.com

Today in Podcasting

http://podcastpickle.com

Podcasting News

http://podcastingnews.com (see Figure C.2)

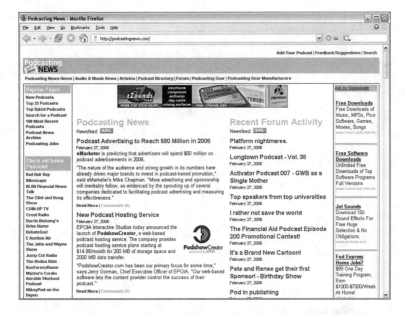

FIGURE C.2

Podcasting News presents one of the best sites for keeping up to date with the podosphere.

Index